THE BOOK OF
THE
BLACK BEAR

THE BOOK OF THE BLACK BEAR

Richard P. Smith

WINCHESTER PRESS
An Imprint of New Century Publishers, Inc.

Printing Code

11 12 13 14 14 15 16

Library of Congress Cataloging in Publication Data

Smith, Richard P., 1949–
   The book of the black bear.

   Bibliography: p.
   Includes index.
   1. Bear hunting. 2. Black bear. I. Title.
SK295.S65 1985   798.2′774446   85–6293
ISBN 0-8329-0370-1

*To black bears and the people
whose efforts and experience have led to a
better understanding of these animals.*

CONTENTS

PREFACE

Our American heritage abounds with tales of black bears. Unfortunately, this folklore is laden with half-truths, old wives' tales, and misinformation. By the time most of us were old enough to explore the great outdoors, we had been brainwashed by countless tales of horror in newspapers, books, magazines, television shows, and movies about bears. Unusual occurrences of a sensational nature are brought to the public's attention more frequently than typical events, with the result that our society too often characterizes the rare and unusual as the normal. Black bear maulings are classic examples.

Several factors have contributed to the rather meager factual foundation (until very recently) of our understanding of black bears. Early settlers were more interested in getting rid of bears than in learning how bears live. That is understandable, since the bears were considered a nuisance and constituted a significant threat to their food resources—particularly to their livestock, poultry, honey, and corn. In addition, the very secretive and elusive nature of black bears made them difficult to study.

Major breakthroughs in the past few decades have contributed to many advances in our understanding of black bears and how they live. The recent development of various techniques and technology, most notably radio-telemetry, made it possible for researchers to follow bears without influencing their behavior. In addition, public attitudes became much more "pro-bear," partly because these animals have gained esteem as big-game trophies and partly because they have been recognized as an integral and desired part of our ecosystem.

Currently, black bears are being studied by scientists more extensively and intensively throughout their range than at any point in history. Large quantities of new information is now being compiled by research teams throughout North America, but most of the literature reporting results of studies is rather technical and largely unavailable to the general public. Accordingly, I think one of the greatest values of this book is that Richard Smith was able to incorporate many of the latest advances and thoughts in bear research into this popular, comprehensive, and up-to-date book on black bears.

Gary L. Alt
Bear Biologist
Pennsylvania Game Commission

ACKNOWLEDGMENTS

I've got a lot of people to thank for their help, indirectly or directly, in gathering material for this book by sharing their experiences, knowledge and hunts with me, plus assisting with photos. It won't be possible to list them all, and please forgive me if I forget some that I should mention.

Thanks to Wisconsin's Art LaHa for passing along information about baiting black bears, whose help led to bagging my first bruins on my own. The list of houndmen who let me tag along and helped me better understand dogging bears includes the crew from Munising: Dan Flynn, El Harger (a bear biologist, too, who also answered my first questions on black bear biology), Jim Corriveau, Bill St. Martin, Paul Anderson, Kip, Bo, Larry, all of their families and more; Andy Tingstad, Ed Vander Zanden (who gave me my first bear hound), Lawrence Edwards, Russ Nelson, John and Donna Saxton and D. DeMoss. Two more dogmen and guides who provided helpful interviews are Leo Dollins and Wayne Bosowicz.

Colorado guide Jim Jarvis put me onto my first brown black bear and provided helpful information, along with his wife Pat. Hunter and trapper Jerry Weigold took time out from a busy schedule for an interview, and thanks also to Bill Niemi, Dave Pietro, Phin Walsh, Melvin Myllyla, Rene Meyskens, and Chuck Godfrey for their bear stories and help with photos.

Wildlife biologists across North America and other fish and game employees were tremendously helpful in providing biological information, plus hunting season and harvest information. Many of them are mentioned somewhere in the pages that follow. A special thanks is due Gary Alt for the time he spent with me and the information he provided. A specialist in black bear biology, Gary serves with the Pennsylvania Game Commission. If anyone knows the subject, he does, and he has been kind enough to write the preface to this book. A special word of thanks is also deserved by Gary's assistants, Pat Carr and Janice Gruttadauria.

Also, friends and family members who were always ready to help. At the top of the list are my mother and father, wife Lucy and sisters Kathy and Linda. Brother Bruce has always been a part of my bear hunts and Brother-in-law Bruce Dupras and Uncle George have willingly helped trail or drag bears. Beryl Jensen helped me drag one of my first bruins. Thanks also to friends Dave Raikko, Jim Haveman, Gene Ballew, Mike Hogan, Gary Lohman, Mike Holmes, Mike Pollard, Duaine Wenzel, Richard Robinson, Ray Juetten, Buck LeVasseur, George Gardner, Bob Eastman, Ted Nugent, Linda Judson, Phil Grable, and Tom Huggler who have played a part in my black bear experiences.

INTRODUCTION

This book is not just about hunting black bears.

Although much of it is devoted to hunting these animals with gun, bow, and camera, there is also much information about the animal's life history, biology, behavior, and present-day management.

The facts and figures contained on the pages that follow will prove valuable to outdoor enthusiasts who want to learn more about bruins and increase their chances of seeing them.

It's been more than 20 years since I became interested in black bears, first and always as a hunter, but also as a photographer and biologist. I've learned a lot about the animals over those years through personal experience, those of other hunters, and from wildlife biologists who have had the most intimate relationship of all with North America's most abundant species of bear.

I saw the need for a book that would put all of this information together for the reference of others, and here it is. I've gone to extremes to make sure all of the information in this book is as accurate as possible. There is already too much inaccurate, if not downright false, material about these animals in print. Black bears are clearly misunderstood and misrepresented far too often. I tried my best to set the record straight.

Richard P. Smith

CHAPTER
1

Black Bear Basics

Black bears are one of the most misunderstood big game animals in North America. It's easy to understand why. There is simply a lot of misinformation circulating about these animals. And it has been fashionable for too long to categorize black bears as dangerous beasts that must be feared, or perpetual pests that are worthless to have around.

Fortunately, the attitudes of some people toward black bears and their knowledge about them is beginning to change. There has always been a group of people who have been attracted to and interested in these animals. Although small at first, their ranks have grown to a significant level. This increasing interest in North America's most abundant member of the bear family, which has taken the shape of concern for their welfare in some areas, has led to more scientific studies about them. These studies have uncovered amazing new information.

Most black bears are easy to identify. As their name implies, many of them are predominantly black with brown muzzles. The amount of brown on snouts varies, as does the shade of brown. I've seen some bruins with very little brown on their muzzles, being almost totally black, and others with brown being more prominent than normal.

The amount of brown on the muzzle is not an indication of sex, as at least one hunter thought. He felt males have darker muzzles than females. I've seen both males and females with little brown on snouts in the same general area and males with just as much brown, if not more, than females in other areas. Tips on differentiating between the sexes will be mentioned later.

In addition to brown muzzles, some black bears have white markings on their chests. These markings are little more than spots on some animals and

American black bear with brown snout and otherwise black in color.

are prominent, V-shaped designs on others. I've seen both males and females with white on their chests, but it's been my experience that bears that have these markings are in the minority.

Not all black bears are black. Some are described as blue and others white, while the most common coat color other than black is various shades of brown. They can be blonde or cinnamon, dark brown, reddish brown and any shade in between.

In roughly the eastern half of the U.S. and Canada, better than 99 percent of black bears are black, with color variations being rare. Brown phase black bears occur more often in western Ontario and Minnesota, with an estimated six percent of the bear population in Minnesota being brown. On one occasion I saw a black sow with three brown cubs in Minnesota. Brown black bears become even more common in parts of the western U.S. and Canada.

In southwestern Colorado, for example, more than 80 percent of the population is dark brown or chocolate, with another five to eight percent the lighter blonde color phase. Black coated bruins are obviously in the minority there. Other Western states such as Wyoming and Montana have more of an even split between black and brown color phases, but there may be local variations.

The regional distribution of color phases in Washington is an example of how much variability there can be in one state. All bears were found to be black on the Olympic Peninsula and the northeast Willapa Hills during the course of studies there. Bears inhabiting the southeast Willapa Hills were found to be 78 percent black and 22 percent brown. The black phase accounted for 88 percent of the population along the Skookumchuck and Newaukum rivers and 82 percent along the Toutle, Green, and Coweeman rivers. As many as 30 percent of the bears along the Kalama and Lewis rivers were brown and 50 percent along the upper Cowlitz River. One particular bruin reported in Washington that must have been an unusual sight, was both black and brown. The upper half of its body was brown and the lower half black.

Brown-coated black bears are better adapted for living in open country like that found in parts of the West where there is more exposure to direct sunlight, than the black color phase. One test showed that black-coated animals in direct sunlight increase in temperature by a degree every 15 minutes while there was little change in body temperature of bears with brown hair. The test was halted to prevent overheating of the black animal. A study of the distribution of brown and black color phases on a mountain range in southern Arizona showed that light brown bears were most common on arid south slopes and darker animals were dominant on north slopes where it was more shaded, cooler, and wetter.

Not all black bears remain the same color all of their lives. Some animals that are brown as cubs become black. Older bears can change coat color, too. One biologist I spoke with in Colorado said a radio-collared bear that was found to be black in its den had been a chocolate color earlier in the year. He said bears that are dark brown during spring may be blonde through bleaching from the sun by fall. The blonde bears I've seen in Colorado actually exhibited two shades of brown. Their bodies were blonde with legs being dark brown.

True albino black bears are rare, but a number of them have been reported. One was captured and photographed in Clearfield County, Pennsylvania in 1969 by District Game Protectors Lynn Keller and Gerald Zeidler. The most recent record of an albino black bear is an animal bagged by bowhunter Brad Borden from Kalispell, Montana during May of 1983. It was a two-year-old female estimated between 110 and 130 pounds. A couple of off-white to yellowish-coated bears have been tagged by hunters in Michigan, but they didn't have the pink eyes, nose, and skin of a true albino. White-coated black bears in British Columbia, called Kermode bears, are not albinos either.

Kermode bears, which are found along the coast of British Columbia in the center of the province, have been considered as a separate race or subspecies of black bear in the past, but more recently are considered by biologists to simply be a different color phase. A photograph obtained from the British Columbia Government of a female Kermode with two black cubs in a tree is

Brad Borden from Kalispell, Montana, with albino black bear he bagged. (*Photo by JoAnn Speelman*)

evidence of this. Nonetheless, they are protected in the province. They were legal to hunt for about a year during the fall of 1964 and spring of 1965, but then were protected again because of concern for their welfare. Little was known about the animals and they are considered to be rare.

Michigan hunter Art Hutchings bagged a male Kermode on Princess Royal Island estimated at 400 pounds during the brief period these animals could be hunted. The bear was described as white on its sides and rump, with face, shoulders, and feet a bright yellowish-orange. The nose and tongue were gray, unlike most other black bears.

Some people have also described Kermode bears as having a very light brown coloration. One representative with this coloration was at the Stanley Park Zoo in Vancouver, British Columbia. Arthur Popham obtained a special permit to collect a Kermode bear before Hutchings shot his, and a mount of the animal he eventually bagged is in the Kansas City Museum in Missouri, according to one report. Hutchings' Kermode bearskin is in the Fred Bear Museum in Gainesville, Florida.

The blue color phase of black bear, referred to as Glacier bears, has also been classified as a separate subspecies. Their distribution is limited to southeast Alaska into northern British Columbia, and they are thought to be more common than Kermodes, but still not easy to find. Glacier bears can be hunted in Alaska, but are protected in British Columbia. The only Glacier bear known to be in captivity is in the San Diego Zoo in California. There is a full-mount Glacier bear in the Fred Bear Museum.

There are 16 subspecies of black bears that have been recognized besides the Kermode and Glacier varieties, although veteran bear biologist Charles

A female Kermode black bear with her two black cubs in British Columbia. (*Photo by Government of British Columbia*)

Jonkel said there isn't total agreement on exactly how many subspecies of the animal exist. Other than coat color, minor features such as characteristics of the skull and teeth are used to separate black bears into individual races. Differences in coat color are the only features that would be readily apparent to anyone seeing a bear in the wild.

The most common and widespread subspecies of black bear is *Ursus americanus americanus*. This scientific classification of black bears in Latin refers to their genus, species, and subspecies, in that order. They are in the same Class as other mammals (Mammalia), the same Order with other carnivores (Carnivora) and in the same Family (Ursidae) with other bears. Distribution of the most common subspecies of black bears covers most of Canada and Alaska, plus much of the U.S. where these animals are now found.

One commonly held belief about black bears is they are related to pigs. This is not true. As carnivores, they are more closely related to wolves, dogs, and raccoons. Despite the lack of relationship of black bears with swine, male bears are usually referred to as boars and females as sows.

In areas where the range of brown black bears and grizzly bears overlap, it is usually possible to distinguish one from the other. Grizzlies normally have distinct humps on their backs above the shoulders, while the backs of black bears offer a straight line profile. The heads of black bears, from forehead to nose, also slope downward in a straight line when viewed from the side. Faces of grizzlies are indented or dished.

Black bears have five claws on each foot. The claws are short and curved, well designed for climbing trees. The animals also use their claws for ripping stumps and logs apart, plus digging for roots and hornets' nests. Claws on the front feet are longer than those on the rear, since those in front are used for digging and securing prey.

The eyes of black bears are brown. I can verify their eye color with plenty of photos taken with telephoto lenses. The black bear's eyes are small in proportion to head size and in comparison with other big game animals, making eyesight one of Blackie's weakest senses. However, bruins see movement very well and it has been determined that they can distinguish colors.

Black bears have rounded ears, between four-and-a-half and five-and-a-half inches long, which enable them to hear well. Their sense of smell is also well-developed. Black tipped noses enable bears to locate food supplies and help them avoid danger.

Black bears have tails, but they are easy to overlook. The animals keep them clamped down against their rumps most of the time. Tails are roughly three to five inches long.

Most black bears are between four and six feet long, although a few big males will be longer. When on all four feet these animals don't stand very high off the ground, averaging between two and three feet at the shoulders. Ferns and other vegetation sometimes make it difficult for black bears to see any distance. To overcome this handicap they stand on their hind legs or climb stumps and fallen tree trunks.

Despite their short legs, black bears can run fast when they want to, at least for short distances. One bruin in Wisconsin estimated at 200 pounds was clocked at 33 miles an hour. Other bears reached speeds of 30 miles an hour, which is faster than any human can run. Black bears are also good swimmers and they enjoy spending time in water, especially during hot weather.

These animals seldom run if they don't have to, but they do a lot of walking, often traveling many miles during the course of a year. Males usually do more traveling than females, consequently they have larger home ranges or territories than females. In Pennsylvania, males have home ranges

Black bears are good swimmers and routinely go into water to cool off when the weather is hot.

that vary from 60-to-75 square miles, with their territory measuring five to 15 miles across at the widest point, according to biologist Gary Alt. He said females there have home ranges encompassing 12-to-15 square miles that are three-to-five miles across.

The size of areas traveled by bears in Pennsylvania are a good representation of the upper limits of home-range size in North America. The smallest home ranges for black bears were found on Long Island, which is part of southwest Washington's Willapa National Wildlife Refuge, and in Great Smokey Mountains National Park. On Long Island, males had average home ranges of two square miles and females .8 square miles.

In the Smokeys, males covered 4.2 square miles and females 2.6 square miles. Home ranges of bruins in other geographic regions can be anywhere in between those found in Pennsylvania and the Smokeys. The type, quality and extent of the habitat bears occupy generally determines how large a home range they will have. Bruins obviously have to travel farther to find enough food in poor habitat than in habitat where food is abundant. Bear densities may also have an impact on the size of home ranges.

Male black bears are most active during the breeding season which usually begins during late May, peaks during June and July, and continues into August in some cases. They cover a lot of ground looking for breeding females. The home range of adult males normally overlaps the home ranges of a number of mature females.

When on the move, state lines and the borders of different countries have no meaning to black bears. Males commonly cross from one state into another or from the U.S. into Canada and vice versa. A male that was ear-tagged in Minnesota, for example, was bagged near Lake Nipigon in Ontario.

Karen Noyce, with the Minnesota DNR, said the male was three years old at the time it was tagged and released on July 7, 1979 about seven miles north of Hovland, which is near the Canadian border. However, it is roughly 100 miles from the border to Lake Nipigon, and the animal probably did a lot of rambling before reaching the point where it was shot. Ohio bowhunter Randall Collins bagged that bear on May 11, 1982 while hunting with guide Wayne Bosowicz. It weighed 260 pounds then and 122 pounds when tagged in 1979.

Activity of breeding females also peaks during June and July, but they don't cover the territory that males do. Travel of females with newborn cubs is restricted during spring and summer months due to the youngsters, but increases toward fall, peaking during September, as cubs become more mobile.

Biologists know that black bears have the ability to navigate over long distances, but they haven't figured out how the animals do it. The homing ability of black bears is amazing. Nuisance bears that have been live-trapped and moved long distances, far enough to be out of their home ranges, have returned to the point of capture numerous times. A few bruins have found their way home after being moved 140 to 150 miles, with homing trips under 100 miles more common.

Mature males and breeding females can be on the move at virtually every hour of the day during June and July. During fall months old males have a tendency to be more nocturnal than other bears, with most activity concentrated early and late in the day. When actively feeding, however, and especially when food is scarce or scattered, bears can be on the move at any hour.

Weights of black bears, like home ranges, vary considerably from one part of the continent to another. The heaviest individuals are always males. Females average smaller than males to begin with, and once sows start having cubs, the drain of raising a family keeps their weight down. A live weight of approximately 350 pounds is close to the maximum attainable by females. Some of the largest males have reached weights of 700-to-800 pounds.

The heaviest black bear on record with a verified weight, according to Leonard Lee Rue III in his book *Furbearing Animals of North America*, tipped the scales at 802½ pounds live weight. The bruin was shot in the vicinity of Stevens Point, Wisconsin in 1885. Pennsylvania hunter Orwin Srock shot a big black bear in that state in 1981 that weighed an even 700 pounds. Another heavyweight from Newfoundland weighed 687 pounds, according to bear biologist Shane Mahoney.

Only dressed weights are available for most other big black bears bagged by hunters, so live weights can only be estimated. A New York bear bagged in 1975 by Sam Ball had a dressed weight of 660 pounds. In Wisconsin, a black bear weighing 652 pounds was tagged by Otto Hedbany in 1963 and Dean Kerscher collected one that field dressed at 643 pounds in 1968. Michigan's biggest bear on record weighed 613 pounds and was taken by bowhunter Hawley Rhew in 1974.

One method commonly used for estimating the live weight from dressed weights of black bears is to add 15 percent of the dressed weight (L (live weight) = D (dressed weight) + .15 x D). While this may apply to average size black bears, I think it overestimates the live weight of big bears. Ten percent is a more accurate representation of weight loss for big bears, according to a couple of examples.

A bruin bagged in Michigan's Upper Peninsula weighed 417 pounds live weight and 379 pounds dressed, losing 10 percent of its dressed weight. A Pennsylvania bear weighed 632 pounds live weight and 572 pounds after viscera was removed, losing 10.5 percent of its dressed weight. Another smaller Pennsylvania bear had a live weight of 165 pounds and weighed 137 pounds when dressed, having lost 20 percent of its dressed weight. So the bigger the bear, the less weight it loses in terms of a percentage of the dressed weight, when field dressed.

With this information in mind, the New York bear weighing 660 pounds dressed probably weighed around 726 pounds when alive. The two slightly smaller bruins from Wisconsin would have also been over 700 pounds and Michigan's heaviest black bear probably weighed around 675 pounds when shot.

Keep in mind that these weights represent the upper limit attainable by black bears. Most bears of this species are much lighter, with dressed weights of average animals ranging between 120 and 200 pounds. Most people have a tendency to overestimate the size of bruins for a number of reasons. One major reason why many black bears look bigger than they are during spring and fall months is because the hairs on their coats are long. A table showing average weights of male and female black bears in various states is included in this chapter.

There are tremendous seasonal variations in weights of black bears in addition to variations from one part of the continent to another. The largest weight gains are usually recorded during late summer and fall when fruits and nuts are abundant. Information gathered in Pennsylvania shows that cubs averaged a weight gain of half-a-pound a day under these circumstances, while subadults and adult females gained an average of one pound a day and adult males put on as much as two pounds a day. One male gained 128 pounds in 60 days, starting at 348 pounds on July 19 and reaching 476 pounds on September 19. Another male in Wisconsin put on 130 pounds in two months time between mid-August and mid-October.

In some areas, long-legged, lanky bears are referred to as "dog bears" and those that appear to have short legs with bellies hanging close to the ground are called "hog bears." What most people who use these terms fail to realize is that both designations will apply to the same animal at different times of the year. For example: one big male that Gary Alt caught during mid-summer when it was at its lightest weight of the year was referred to as a "dog bear" by an onlooker. Later that fall when it was captured again and had gained over 100 pounds, a bystander referred to the animal as a "hog bear." Young black bears are usually lean and lanky, but fill out as they age.

Weight increases aren't as dramatic during years that food availability is limited. In years when there is a total failure of berry and mast crops, the survival of young black bears may be threatened. West Virginia bear biologist Joe Rieffenberger reported eight incidents of starvation in the fall of 1982 due to mast failure. Lynn Rogers from Minnesota also reported starvation deaths of five yearling black bears after drought and frost reduced natural food supplies several years in a row. Losses of yearlings to malnutrition has also been recorded in Alaska and Colorado.

Predation accounts for other black bear deaths, with young animals accounting for most of the losses. Adult male black bears are known to be cannibalistic. Grizzly bears and wolves also prey on black bears when they get the chance. There is one record of a big boar black bear killing a sow and her yearling cubs in a den in Michigan's Upper Peninsula. In Minnesota, a sow and her newborn cubs were killed in their den by a pack of wolves. Bears are also killed by vehicles as they try to cross the highways. In Pennsylvania, an average of 130 bruins a year die that way.

I also have records of three black bears that were electrocuted, one in Texas and two in Michigan. All three climbed poles holding power lines, apparently attracted by the buzzing of electricity through the lines. The bears may have thought bees were responsible for the noise. The two bears that were electrocuted in Michigan were killed at the same site at different times.

Black bears have the potential of living much longer than most people may realize. Individuals that reach 20 and 30 years of age have been recorded, both in the wild and in captivity. However, the record belongs to a male shot in New York in 1974. It was 41¾ years old. Another bruin from the same state was 34¾ years old when shot. Bears over 30 years old have been aged in other states.

An old, gray-muzzled sow that Terry Frint shot in Ontario one spring was probably in her 20s, if not over 30, but we'll never know for sure. Her teeth were well worn from years of use and Terry sent some of the teeth through the mail to have her age determined, but they fell out of the envelope and were lost.

Black bears are aged by looking at a cross section of a tooth under a microscope. Small premolar teeth are used most often for the determination. The inside of teeth have rings, or annuli, representing each year of a bear's life. Premolars are located directly behind canine teeth on the upper and lower jaws. They can be removed by cutting the gum with a knife in front of and behind the tooth, then extracting it with a pair of pliers.

Although classified as carnivores, black bears are actually omnivores, meaning they have a varied diet including both plant and animal matter, and their teeth are well suited for this purpose. They do eat meat when they can, but also graze on grass and other vegetation, dig up roots, plus consume a wide variety of berries, fruits, nuts, and insects. The bulk of the diets of most black bears consists of items other than meat. These animals are absolute geniuses when it comes to filling their stomachs.

Stomach analysis of black bears in Washington found that an average of 86 percent of the contents was composed of vegetation, and similar results have been recorded in other states. Insects comprised another nine percent of the contents and the final five percent was of mammals, birds, and fish. Specific items eaten that proved to be important foods, at least during certain times of the year, were wood fiber, skunk cabbage, huckleberry, fungus, salal,

Premolar teeth are used most often to determine ages of black bears by examining a cross section under a microscope and counting the rings or annuli. Here, a knife is being used to loosen a premolar behind a canine tooth.

cascara, devil's club, grasses, blackberry, apple, evergreen needles, insects, and meat.

Wood fiber or sapwood was eaten most frequently during April, May, and June. The bark of evergreen trees is peeled by bears to get at the inner sapwood, sometimes resulting in injury or death to trees. The Washington Forest Protection Association hired bear hunters and trappers for years in an effort to reduce this type of damage to trees. Now sport hunters do most of the bear population control in problem areas. This type of feeding activity is basically restricted to the northwest U.S. and adjoining portions of Canada.

Skunk cabbage, huckleberry, fungus, grasses, evergreen needles, and meat were consumed in varying amounts practically every month that black

Morel mushrooms like these are eaten by black bears during the spring.

bears were active. Although evergreen needles occurred frequently in black bear stomachs, they were never present in large amounts. Leaves and blossoms of huckleberry plants were eaten before berries were ripe, with peak use during November. Fungus was most important during August and September. Meat consumption was highest during April.

Salal was eaten from June through October, but was most important during August and September. Cascara use peaked during September and October, with devil's club appearing most frequently during May through July. Blackberries were consumed with regularity during July and August, and November was when Washington black bears fed on apples most heavily. Insects were eaten from April through September, but were most important in July and August.

In Minnesota, black bears depend on grass and other green plants, buds, catkins, leaves, mushrooms, insects, and what meat they can find during spring months. Buds, catkins, and leaves of aspen trees are eaten regularly by black bears, but they will also feed on the same items from other types of trees. Fruits and berries are summer staples, along with insects.

Wild strawberries are usually ripe first, followed by blueberries, raspberries, service berries (also called June berries or sugar plums) and blackberries. When blueberries are abundant, bruins will concentrate much of their feeding time on them. Important foods eaten during late summer into fall are dogwood berries, hazel nuts, and wild cherries. Mountain ash berries and apples are consumed during fall, along with the all-time favorites—acorns, beech nuts and hickory nuts. Black bears will also eat acorns and beech nuts during the spring, following years of good production when some of the mast crop remains on the ground.

Black bear foods are similar to those in Minnesota throughout the eastern half of their range. Squawroot was also found to be important in the spring and summer diets of bears in Great Smokey Mountains National Park. I've also seen evidence of black bears feeding on these parasitic plants in Michigan.

In areas where fruits and nuts may not be available during the fall or when there has been a failure of the mast crop, black bears turn to vegetation

Wild strawberries are among the first berries to ripen during the summer, and bears love them.

and meat for sustenance. The major nut producing trees in the western portion of the black bear's range are white bark pines which are found in the Rocky and Sierra Nevada Mountains. Red squirrels store quantities of these pine nuts in various locations, which black bears frequently seek out and consume. This reduces the amount of effort western bears have to spend to obtain a meal. Pine nuts are eaten during both spring and fall months when available.

Pinyon pine nuts are also eaten by black bears in Utah, and the seeds of limber pines are utilized as food in Montana. Some other black bear foods unique to the western part of their range are manzanita berries (bearberry), the fruit of prickly pear cactus in desert areas like those found in Arizona, coffeeberry, salmonberry, bitterberry, elderberry, snowberry, and buffalo-berry. Pears were reported eaten along with apples where these fruit trees were

Two berry pickers, both looking for wild strawberries.

available in California. Cranberries are an important spring and fall black bear food in Alaska, and are eaten in other states where they are found.

As far as consumption of animal matter goes, black bears are opportunists. They will catch and eat whatever they can. They eat fish such as suckers, salmon, and trout when they are abundant and easily caught during spring and fall spawning runs. Suckers discarded on riverbanks by fishermen are also consumed. Frogs are sometimes eaten. A Michigan bear that was hit by a car as it entered a roadway from a streambed disgorged a large quantity of frogs it had apparently just eaten.

Birds and birds' eggs are consumed when the opportunity presents itself. So are small to medium-size mammals. Michigan trapper Greg Ledy told me about finding the carcasses of three beavers that a black bear had caught and killed one spring, then covered them with vegetation for a later meal. He said it looked like the bear laid at the base of a beaver dam at night and grabbed the beavers with a forepaw as they swam by, then bit them behind the head.

Black bears will also eat deer fawns plus elk, moose, and caribou calves. Most bruins simply stumble across these young animals and take advantage of the opportunity for a meal. At least three yearling black bears got lucky when they gained access to a square-mile enclosure used for whitetail deer research at the Cusino Wildlife Experiment Station in Michigan's Upper Peninsula during different years when fawns were being born. All three bears caught and ate a number of fawns in the enclosure. The bears probably got in the area by climbing the fence.

Opportunistic predation on fawns and calves by black bears has been recorded in other areas, but in situations where healthy population of deer, elk, moose, and caribou are involved, losses to bears are not significant in regard to overall population levels. The loss of moose calves to black bears was studied on the Kenai National Wildlife Refuge in Alaska over four years (1978–82), for example, and during that time bears were only seen on seven calf kills. Different bears were involved in each case and they represented various age classes. Three of the bears were adult males, two were adult females and two were juveniles (one male and one female).

Bears were observed chasing moose calves whenever they were encountered, but the bruins were unsuccessful in all but one attempt. In most cases, a cow and calf either outran the bear, a cow defended her calf, or the bear gave up pursuit. The calf kill that was observed involved a cow with two calves. They were walking along the shoreline of a lake with one calf in front of the cow and one behind. A sow with two cubs was in mature timber nearby and ran out, catching and killing the trailing calf before its mother had a chance to react. In response to the attack, the cow and remaining calf started swimming across the lake. However, the surviving calf only made it halfway across when it weakened and eventually drowned.

Black bears seldom prey on adult deer and moose, unless the animals are handicapped in some way. A whitetail deer, for instance, was being watched at night with the aid of a spotlight in Cades Cove of Great Smokey Mountains National Park. The deer's visibility was hampered by the light, and a black bear took advantage of the opportunity to attack and kill the whitetail. Bruins also feed on deer and other game injured or killed by hunters and vehicles. In many cases when hunter kills are involved, bears simply feed on entrails remaining at the kill site. In the spring, black bears frequently scavenge the carcasses of animals that died as a result of harsh winter weather. They also eat beaver carcasses discarded by trappers after pelts are removed.

One location that appears to be an exception as far as black bear predation on big game is Newfoundland. Bear biologist Shane Mahoney said these bears prey on adult moose and caribou on the island, in addition to calves. Bears have actually been observed killing adult caribou and have been found on freshly killed adult moose a number of times.

Mahoney said black bears there operate from an ambush situation. Since they take their prey by surprise and "are much quicker off the mark," bears stand a good chance of catching what they are after. When an animal is caught, Mahoney said bears grab both of the animal's flanks with front paws and pull it down, then tear into the head, killing it. He added that black bears neatly skin their prey, whether calf or adult, before beginning to eat.

Why are Newfoundland's black bears more active predators than elsewhere? Mahoney said he feels the circumstances there have resulted from a "combination of big, strong bears and a limited food supply." Newfoundland has a low density of black bears, but many of those that inhabit the island are large, according to the biologist.

Black bears occasionally prey on livestock and poultry such as cattle, calves, horses, sheep, goats, pigs, and chickens. When natural foods are scarce, Blackie turns to any alternative food source that is available. Free roaming livestock in black bear habitat is readily accessible to hungry bears and some losses can be expected. However, as scavengers, bears are sometimes wrongfully accused of killing livestock that may have died of natural causes or was killed by another predator.

When it comes to wrecking bee hives though, black bears usually stand alone in the amount of damage they do. Honey, and the insects that make it, are high on the black bear's list of preferred foods. Owners of bee yards in bear country can best protect their investment by enclosing it with an electric fence using three strands of barbed wire 10 inches apart, with the first strand 10 inches off the ground, according to Gary Alt. He said barbless wire is less likely to administer a shock to bears because of the length and density of their hair. Beef suet should be wrapped around wires to attract the attention of any black bears that are interested in honey, according to Alt, so they are sure to get a shock when trying to secure the suet.

An alternative to protecting bee hives with an electric fence is elevating them on a platform that is about 10 feet high. Metal poles that can't be climbed by bruins should be used to hold up platforms.

Some of man's crops such as corn and oats are also appealing to black bears, and they do their share of damage in fields that are readily accessible to them, along with raccoons and deer. Like livestock placed in black bear habitat, there's bound to be some damage to crops grown in bear country, especially where fields extend to the edge of habitat frequented by the animals. Due to the size of most corn and oat fields, they can't be protected from bears as effectively as bee yards can.

Not all food black bears obtain directly or indirectly from man is given up unwillingly. Where hunting black bears over bait is legal, the animals' natural food supply is supplemented by handouts during a portion of the year that may range from a few weeks to a number of months. Some non-hunting individuals also feed bears, along with other wildlife, at or near their homes on a regular basis because they like to see the animals. In areas where black bears have access to open pit dumps and dumpsites where bear-proof containers aren't in use, the animals feed and grow fat on discarded "people food."

Available evidence shows that bruins that supplement their diet with food from man, whether provided directly at feeders or indirectly at dumps, are generally healthier and more productive of young than bears subsisting solely on a natural diet. Information gathered about black bears while they've been observed at these feeding sites is also valuable.

Penis visible just forward of hind legs of this black bear identifies it as a male. It can be difficult to differentiate between the sexes during the fall. Even during spring and summer, a close look at the animals is necessary to sex them.

However, there are circumstances under which black bears shouldn't be fed. This rule applies to national parks and other public areas where black bears and people frequently come in close contact.

Back at the beginning of this chapter I promised to provide tips on differentiating between male and female black bears. Here are some examples.

Black bears can be difficult to sex when viewed in the wild, especially during the fall. An animal with cubs, whether during spring or fall, is obviously a sow. However, immature females and those that have either lost or separated from cubs will be harder to sex.

Males are easiest to distinguish from lone females during spring and summer months. Their testicles are usually prominent then, visible between hind legs. A long tuft of pointed hair that hangs down from the belly marks the location of the penis.

By late fall testicles are no longer visible, having been drawn up into the abdomen, and scrotums are obscured by hair. Bears seen at this time of year without cubs, and in a position where a penis isn't visible, could be either a male or female. Body size can be a clue though. Males are generally bigger than females, with larger heads and longer bodies. However, this isn't foolproof either because an adult female may be larger than a young male. Belly hairs of sows are normally long during the fall and can be mistaken for a penis.

If two adult-size animals are seen together during June and July, the larger of the two will often be a male, especially if it is following the other animal. Male bears will grunt when following a female in heat.

Average Live Weights of Black Bears In Pounds

State	Males	Females
Arizona	275	150
California	223	138
Florida	305	189
Michigan	287	183
Montana	211	125
New Hampshire	263	183
New York	237	150
North Carolina	368	197
Pennsylvania	402	203
Vermont	238	109
Washington	195	116.5

Province		
Quebec	141 (June & July)	112 (June & July)

Estimating Black Bear Weight From Chest Girth

Chest Girth (inches)	Estimated Live Weight (pounds)	Estimated Dressed Weight
25	65	55
26	73	62
27	81	69
28	89	76
29	98	83
30	108	92
31	117	99
32	128	109
33	138	117
34	149	127
35	161	137
36	173	147
37	185	157
38	198	168
39	211	179
40	225	191
41	239	203
42	253	215
43	268	228
44	284	241
45	300	255
46	316	269
47	332	282
48	350	297
49	367	312
50	385	327
51	403	343
52	422	359
53	442	375
54	461	392
55	481	409
56	502	427
57	522	444
58	544	462
59	566	480
60	588	500

CHAPTER 2

Black Bear Biology

The life cycle of black bears is a world apart from other popular big game animals. Many bruins spend approximately three to seven months out of the year, during winter, in a dormant state. They seek shelter from the cold winter weather and generally slumber so they don't have to worry about feeding themselves during the leanest months of the year. Yet, this is when their young are born in a weak and helpless state after developing for a mere six weeks in their mothers' womb, even though she was bred seven months earlier.

As mentioned earlier, the breeding season for black bears begins during late May and extends into August, with most matings taking place during June and July. Although mature males generally participate in reproductive activities on an annual basis, few females do. In the best of habitat, some sows successfully mate when they are 2½ years old. Most of them become mothers-to-be at 3½ and 4½ years of age. Females in poor habitat may not conceive until they are 6½ or 7½ years old.

Most mature females that are nursing young cubs during the breeding season do not breed. The production of milk normally prevents them from becoming fertile (going into estrus). However, there are a couple of cases on record, one in North Carolina and one in Pennsylvania, where nursing sows have been bred. Roger Powell with North Carolina State University suggested that estrus may not be blocked in sows that are in food-rich areas and in good condition, enabling them to raise cubs every year rather than skipping a year. There is also a possibility that those sows may have been separated from their cubs for a short time. An interruption of lactation for as short a time as two days can initiate estrus.

Pair of cubs curled up in the nest. Their mother has peeled bark from the tree to line the nest.

Circumstances under which sows are normally known to breed during consecutive years is when they lose their cubs prior to or during the summer breeding season, which halts lactation. Since large males are known to prey on cubs, that raises an interesting question. Is cannibalism among males directed toward producing another estrus cycle in females as well as securing a source of protein to nourish their bodies? An answer may never be known, but it's something to speculate about.

Although most mature sows produce cubs every other year, some may skip two or more years between litters, especially during years when natural food production is poor. Lynn Rogers has done some research in Minnesota that indicates there is a minimum weight sows must attain before denning, for the final stage of development of cubs to be initiated. Mature sows generally weighing less than 150-to-160 pounds when they entered dens did not produce cubs.

Once mature females go into estrus, they remain in a breeding condition until bred, according to Gary Alt. Although one male will stay with a breeding female for two or three days, some females will mate with more than one male. At a location where black bears are fed and observed in Pennsylvania, three different males mated with the same female one evening. Where more than one male is involved in breeding, such as in this case, not all cubs in the same litter will necessarily be sired by the same male.

Male black bears are polygamous, more so than females. They reach sexual maturity when 2½ years old, in some cases, but maturation is delayed until 3½ through 5½ years old in many areas. Males that cross the path of a female in estrus will trail her much the same way a whitetail buck will follow a doe in heat. Two males competing for the same female sometimes fight.

One June in Montana's Glacier National Park, my wife and I encountered a male and female together. The smaller female departed first, then was followed by the male. We remained where we were for a few minutes and saw another larger male come along that was following the same female. The second male was obviously irritated. As he walked through the timber he swatted a number of dead trees, knocking them to the ground with loud crashes.

We stayed around a while longer, listening for sounds of a fight, but didn't hear anything. When there is an obvious difference in size between males, the smaller animal usually retreats. Fights are most common between males similar in size.

Most mature male black bears still have plenty of fat reserves when they leave dens during the spring. They continue using these energy reserves through the breeding season, losing weight in the process. For this reason, breeding males usually reach their lightest weight of the year during July, but quickly start regaining what they've lost during late summer.

Once a female is bred and eggs are fertilized, development of the eggs begins, but they only reach what is called the blastocyst stage when development stops. Round blastocysts are so small they are difficult to see without a microscope. Rather than becoming connected to the wall of the uterus like developing eggs of most mammals, blastocysts remain suspended in fluid within the uterus. Blastocysts eventually implant on the uterus wall about the time a female enters a den for the winter and develop rapidly during six to eight weeks. Cubs are born at the end of that time while in a den. Gary Alt said that in Pennsylvania, the final stage of development of black bear cubs begins around December 1.

This reproductive process is called delayed implantation. Although female black bears are actually pregnant for seven months, cubs develop in a fraction of that time. Due to the fact that cub development doesn't usually begin until denning, it can be difficult to determine if sows bagged during fall hunting seasons are pregnant.

By the time cubs leave dens with their mothers, youngsters from small litters will average larger in size than those from big litters. Cubs weigh an average of 12 ounces at birth and may weigh between five and nine pounds by late March.

Cubs weigh 12 ounces at birth, on the average, according to Gary Alt. Thirty-three newborn cubs he weighed ranged between 10.2 and 16 ounces. By the time they leave the den, cubs from small litters will average larger in size than cubs from large litters. There's obviously less milk to go around when four or five cubs must be fed versus one or two. In Pennsylvania, single cubs

Black bears utilize a variety of sites for dens. One bruin spent the winter in a hole it dug under this stump.

averaged 9.5 pounds by late March compared to 6.8 pounds for twins and 5.3 pounds for three and four-cub litters.

Black bear cubs have little, if any, hair at birth and their eyes are closed. However, hair grows quickly and covers the small animals' bodies. Their eyes generally open when six weeks old.

Litter size varies from one through five. Average litter size in the western portion of the black bear's range is between one and two. In the East, it's between two and three. Pennsylvania bears are among the most productive. Alt said over half of the sows there give birth to three cubs and litters of four are as common as twins. He added that litters of five are as common as single cubs. Sows with four cubs have been reported in Maine, Michigan, and Minnesota. I have record of a Michigan sow with five cubs.

Sows giving birth for the first time generally have one or two cubs. The largest litters are produced by experienced mothers that are in good physical condition. The record for the most cub production by a wild black bear is probably held by a radio-collared female Alt monitored from 1974 through 1984. She raised 26 cubs during that time, giving birth to a minimum of four cubs at a time.

The sex ratio of cubs usually favors males slightly. Alt said he found an average of 57 males and 43 females for every 100 cubs. There is normally a higher rate of mortality among the male segment of most black bear populations than females, which might account for more males than females produced.

Most cubs are born during January and February, but some are born during late December and some during early March. Melvin Myllyla discovered a sow with cubs in upper Michigan on December 27. Jerry Weigold reported he and his brother found a sow with cubs that were pink and appeared hairless, indicating they weren't born long before, on March 1. The average birth date of 20 litters in Pennsylvania was January 14, with a range from January 1-25.

Black bear dens are probably not as large as most people think they are. Based on measurements of 400 dens, Alt says the average den entrance is 17 inches wide and 18 inches high. They average 5½ feet from front to back and are 32 inches wide by 23 inches high. As far as volume, dens average 19 cubic feet, according to Alt.

Bruins use a variety of sites for dens. Females usually select more sheltered locations than males, but not always. Black bears may den in rock caves, hollow trees or logs, old beaver houses or culverts; under uprooted trees, stumps, brushpiles or manmade structures; and some simply build a nest on top of the snow or curl up in a convenient location such as on the top of a muskrat house. Basically, anything that suits a bear can be used for a den. Their thick coats usually protect them from the cold when curled up.

In some areas such as the Smokeys, females show a preference for denning in tree cavities off the ground. Most of the females in the park are thought to den in trees, with cavities being as much as 80 feet above ground level. Reports of black bears using elevated dens have also come from Georgia, Arkansas, and Michigan. Disturbance of animals in these locations is minimal, which is a major reason why they use them.

When using a nest, black bears will simply curl up in a thick patch of cover and break off branches or twigs to use as a base, then add grass, leaves, and tree bark as bedding. Males make nests most often, but I photographed a sow with cubs in a nest one time. Bears that den in more protected locations will rake bedding into them, too.

The timing of when denning begins among black bears varies from year to year in the same region, with greater variations from one region to another. Females den earlier than males in most cases. Length of time spent in dens gradually decreases from north to south, as would be expected. Bruins in the southern part of their range such as in Florida may not den at all. A

This Michigan black bear, a young male, remained awake all winter, taking advantage of food it was given on a regular basis. The animal denned in a barrel filled with straw provided by Frank Pollard.

young male in Virginia that was monitored did not den either and similar records are available from other southern states.

There's even a case of a young male in Michigan's Upper Peninsula, where winters are typically long and cold, that did not go into a normal winter sleep. There was human interference in this situation though. The animal showed up at a rural residence sometime during December and human disturbance forced it up a tree. Concerned about the animal's welfare because of cold weather, Frank Pollard put an empty barrel filled with straw at the base of the tree. The bruin accepted the manmade shelter as its home, but left it daily to eat food the Pollard family put outside the "den."

Food availability, the presence or lack of it, plays a role in when black bears enter dens for the winter. They are generally active longer when food is available and will den earlier when quality food is scarce. Decreasing day length (photoperiod) during the fall also plays a role as to when bears enter dens, probably more so than prevailing weather conditions. One year during early November, Richard Robinson stumbled across a sow and a cub sleeping soundly under a fallen tree when temperatures were in the 70s.

I returned to the den with Robinson. As we approached the location, the cub left the den and climbed a nearby tree. The sow remained under the fallen tree. We stood within a matter of feet from her and talked in normal tones. She struggled to raise her head a couple of times in recognition of the fact we were there, but could never keep it up for long, which was an indication of how drowsy she was.

Those bears didn't remain there for the winter though. I checked on them about a week later and they were gone. A heavy rain had fallen in the meantime, and I'm sure they got wet because the location offered little protection. Ken Lowe reported another bear in upper Michigan that was temporarily denned on October 1 when temperatures were in the 80s, then moved following thundershowers.

The transition from normal activity to total dormancy is probably a gradual process in most cases. Bruins may fast and sleep for days at a time in temporary dens like those used in the two examples above, before finally settling into a permanent location that will be occupied throughout the winter. Black bears in permanent winter quarters may even change locations, if sufficiently disturbed by dogs or people. Females with cubs that are chased from dens sometimes abandon their cubs.

The ease with which bears awaken from winter sleep varies considerably. Some animals may leave dens at the mere approach of people, while others can actually be touched and moved without waking up. That sow and newborn cubs that Jerry and Terry Weigold found on March 1 were located while the pair were hunting snowshoe hares. Fresh tracks of a hare led into a hollow log occupied by the bears. Unaware that the bears were there, and without looking, Terry jabbed a long stick into the log in an effort to chase the snowshoe out. In the process, he poked the sleeping sow. The animal barely moved in response to the disturbance. Jerry said they couldn't see the hare, and he's convinced it hopped over the bear and was hiding behind her.

Another time during winter, Jerry jumped on top of a brushpile and fell through, dumping snow and other debris on a sleeping black bear. He said the animal rolled around, groaning and growling while he struggled to get out of there. Weigold eventually got out of the brushpile, making a lot of noise in the process, but the bear stayed put. The Weigolds watched that bear throughout the winter and they were able to tell it was an old one. Its teeth were noted when the bear yawned and they were badly worn.

Winter or spring thaws sometimes flood dens or cause them to collapse,

Cubs as young as five months, weighing as little as 18 pounds, can survive on their own if orphaned, according to a Michigan study.

usually resulting in departure of the residents. Some cubs are lost under these circumstances, according to Alt.

Sows with newborn cubs probably get less sleep than other bears during the winter. Cubs are often noisy, making contented buzzing sounds while nursing and squalling or bawling when upset or hungry. When sows with cubs are discovered in dens, it's sometimes the noises that cubs make that lead people to them. I've attempted to photograph a number of sows with cubs in dens and most of the females were very much awake.

Denned black bears can be observed and photographed under most circumstances without creating any problems. Biologists do it on a routine basis. However, disturbance should be kept to a minimum, especially when sows with cubs are involved. Too much noise or continued disturbance may force a sow to abandon her cubs. If a sow with cubs appears upset or runs off, leave

Young black bears frequently play and wrestle with each other. A female (left) and male were caught during a bout here, at a point where it looks like they are hugging.

the area immediately to increase the chances of her returning. The location of cubs that are abandoned for good should be reported to appropriate state and provincial wildlife officials such as biologists and conservation officers.

The black bear's normal body temperature is slightly higher than for humans—between 100 and 101 degrees Fahrenheit. When in dens, their temperature may drop to as low as 88 degrees, but can be as high as 98. Heart rate may slow to about 10 beats per minute when asleep and breathing slows to one breath every 45 seconds in some animals.

Due to slowed body functions and the lack of food intake, black bears don't have to eliminate waste from their bodies like they normally would. Although these animals may not urinate while denned, they do occasionally defecate, especially bears that are in dens for six to seven months. I've seen droppings deposited by denned bears between visits to den sites on a number of occasions.

Black bears do not form fecal plugs before denning or while denned. Feces form in the lower digestive tract of bruins from dead cells while denned and may contain hair from a bear licking itself, plus debris from the den that may be ingested. Although denned black bears don't eat, females with cubs will consume waste from their cubs. Bears commonly eliminate large quantities of waste products from their bodies after they leave dens.

Hardened outer layers of foot pads are shed by black bears while in dens. Consequently, bruins may lick the bottoms of their feet after pads are shed, and their feet may be tender for this reason when they leave dens. As with the beginning of denning, black bears slowly become active again during spring, sometimes remaining near dens for a while after they leave them. Sows with cubs are usually the last to leave dens, and when they do, they commonly remain nearby for weeks. Males generally emerge from dens before females, whether or not sows have cubs.

The timing of den emergence varies from north to south, with the weather having an impact on when this happens. A table in this chapter contains average dates for the beginning and end of black bear denning in areas where this information is available. Keep in mind that denning dates usually vary from year-to-year and the timing listed represents averages.

Sows that are nursing cubs will normally lose 30 to 35 percent of their weight while in dens, and sometimes more. Other black bears lose an average of 20 percent of their peak fall weight during the denning period. A pregnant sow that weighs 300 pounds when she enters her den, for example, will lose an average of 90 to 105 pounds by the time she leaves the den with her cubs. A male with the same fall weight may only lose 60 to 75 pounds. Both sexes keep losing weight until their caloric intake substantially increases, which is usually sometime during the summer.

Cubs will continue nursing until August, but will start eating solids before then. Mother and cubs remain together throughout the year and normally occupy the same den during the cubs' first winter. Cubs that lose their mothers will instinctively seek out a den on their own, provided they are weaned when orphaned. A study conducted in Michigan by Al Erickson showed that orphaned cubs as young as five months old and weighing as little as 18 pounds can survive on their own. However, the mortality of orphaned cubs is probably higher than those that remain under their mother's care.

Dens that females enter with youngsters that are almost a year old are seldom the same ones they occupied the previous winter. In fact, den re-use by black bears is very low in areas where an abundance of den sites are available. The opposite may be true in locations where suitable den sites are limited. In Pennsylvania, Gary Alt has documented re-use of dens in 27 cases, only 4.8 percent of the time den re-use was possible. Eighteen dens were re-used once, three were reoccupied twice and only one den was re-used three times. About half of the time dens were re-used, the same adult female or one of her daughters was involved.

When black bears are about a year old, canine teeth will replace the milk teeth that formerly occupied those positions. After their second winter, young black bears are referred to as yearlings. Families split up at this time, with yearling males dispersing as far as 80 to 100 miles and females often settling down in a portion of their mother's home range. Long-distance dispersal of young males prevents inbreeding. However, yearling dispersal takes place whether or not the animals' mother is alive. Alt said when males disperse, they usually head out in one particular direction and keep going at that heading until they settle into a new home range. These bears are often the ones that show up in towns and cities as they travel cross-country.

Two males test each other. Males sometimes fight during the breeding season when competing for a sow.

Once yearlings are on their own, females go into another estrus cycle. Mature sows normally only have cubs every other year because of the long time they spend with their young. Other than the association of sows with cubs, and females with males during the breeding season, black bears are basically solitary animals. However, concentrations of food, whether natural or provided by man, in small areas will bring the animals together, and their social interactions can be interesting to watch.

A hierarchy of dominant and subordinate animals usually develops at most feeding sites that attract a number of black bears. The biggest males, plus sows with cubs, generally command the most respect, and yearlings are at the bottom of the pecking order. Subordinate animals usually move out of the way of dominant bears, but if they don't they may be chased away. Young bears are usually tolerant of each other.

Threat displays are occasionally exhibited between two bruins when choice feeding sites are being contested or one animal gets too close to another. A sound frequently heard from one bear warning another is referred to as "huffing" by biologist Steve Herrero from Alberta. When making this noise, bruins inhale and exhale loudly a number of times in quick succession. This warning sound is also called "woofing." Black bears also snort by loudly expelling air through their nose and mouth.

When two bears are close together facing each other in a challenging position with heads down and backs arched, they sometimes make a "gurgling" sound. This is an odd rumbling sound that goes up and down in volume and is hard to describe. A person who heard it for the first time said it sounded like the bear that made it was crying.

"Jawing" is a rapid opening and closing of the mouth with a distinct clicking sound resulting from teeth coming together. Some people refer to this warning as bears "popping their teeth," and that's exactly what it sounds like. A "paw swat" or "false charge" sometimes accompanies a vocal warning. When using the paw swat a bear usually strikes the ground or a tree. During a false charge bears will move quickly toward the bear being warned, but stop after going a short distance, only a step or two in some cases.

Black bears will use the same threat and warning signals toward people who get in their way as they do with other bears.

As far as submissive behavior goes, one hunter who was feeding bears in Michigan said he watched a subordinate animal roll on its back with its legs in the air, a submissive posture often exhibited by dogs, in the presence of a dominant male, allowing the male to thoroughly sniff its body. He didn't say if the subordinate animal was a male or female, and perhaps wasn't able to tell. The same hunter said he saw a dominant male urinate on subordinates.

Yearling and sub-adult black bears frequently wrestle and play with each other, and this behavior is sometimes observed. I've seen pairs of young males engage in wrestling matches, plus males and females. When females are involved in bouts they often playfully run off for short distances periodically, then pounce on males when they follow. Gary Alt's father, Floyd, once observed a group of seven young males playing in a field from his airplane. He said six of the animals were paired off as if they were dancing.

Average Denning Dates

State or Province	Entry	Emergence
Alaska	early to mid-October	late April/early May
Alberta	early November	late March
Arizona	late November	late March/early April
California	mid-December	mid-March
Colorado	late Oct./early Nov.	late March/early April

Idaho	late Oct./early Nov.	mid-April
Maine	late Nov./early Dec.	early April
Michigan	mid-November	mid-April
Minnesota	early November	early April
Montana	early November	mid-May
New York	late Nov./early Dec.	early April
North Carolina	late December	late March
Ontario	late Oct./Nov.	late April/May
Virginia	late Dec./early Jan.	late March
Coastal Washington	early December	early March

CHAPTER
3

Black Bear Sign

There are three basic types of sign left by black bears—tracks, droppings, and indications of feeding activity. Other indications that bears are or have been in an area are "bear trees." The full significance of bear trees is not yet fully understood, but they appear to be territorial markers or signposts primarily used by adult male black bears.

Boars reportedly stand on hind legs with their backs against marker trees, rubbing and scratching themselves on the trunk, while reaching around with their mouth and biting the bark or treetop. In some cases, claws may also be used to mark tree trunks. Various sizes and types of trees are marked by black bears in this fashion. Oak and hemlock trees marked by bruins can be seen in Pennsylvania. A variety of hardwoods and softwoods are marked by bears in Great Smokey Mountains National Park. In midwestern states and Ontario I've seen young evergreen trees from about five feet in height on up to 10 or 12, marked.

Some trees have been marked by bears for years. On large trees, pieces of bark are chewed or clawed away, revealing the inner wood, with gouges left in the wood. Large scars develop on trees used over a long period of time. Young evergreen trees that I've seen marked by black bears characteristically exhibit broken tops that may or may not remain attached to the tree trunk. Clumps of bear hair are usually visible on stubs of broken limbs where a bear has rubbed.

The height of bite marks generally corresponds to the height of the bear that made them. The bear's scent is also left on the tree as a result of rubbing. There appears to be a connection between tree-marking behavior among mature boars and the breeding season because most marking occurs before

I examine a bear tree, which in this case is a young evergreen.
The top has been broken off and hair is rubbed off on the trunk.

and during the peak mating activity — May through July. Tree marking by male bears may serve the same function as scrapes made by whitetail bucks —calling cards advertising their availability to receptive females.

In addition to living trees, bears mark signs, poles, and buildings. Most markers are along bear trails and are readily visible.

Tree tops or limbs that have been broken recently will exhibit light-colored wood at the break. Syrup-like sap that hasn't yet hardened should also be in evidence. Inner wood of damaged limbs and tree trunks darken and become dry over a period of time after exposure to the air.

Another place to look for black bear hair is on the undersides of fallen trees that are suspended between two and three feet above the ground. When traveling through heavy cover, bruins often go under these windfalls and hair rubs off in the process, especially on stubs of limbs that project downward. Hairs may also be left on low-hanging tree branches.

Claw marks left on the side of a shack by a black bear. Bruins will mark signs, buildings and other manmade objects in their territory.

Sign of black bear feeding activity can also be found on trees. Bruins are often destructive when feeding on trees and the evidence of their presence is easy to distinguish. As an example, the bark of coniferous trees such as Douglas fir, spruce, and redwoods is stripped by hungry bears that are after the inner sapwood. Sometimes bark is removed in a band all the way around the trunk, which is called girdling and results in the death of the tree. Loss of trees to girdling by black bears is a well-known problem in Washington. I saw my first evidence of black bears stripping the bark of white cedar trees in Michigan's northern Lower Peninsula recently. Blackie does this type of feeding in the spring when there is a scarcity of other types of food.

Foraging bruins can be just as destructive to fruit trees such as wild cherry, serviceberry, and apple. I've seen numerous cherry and berry trees completely broken down by feeding bears. Some trees that have sturdy enough trunks to resist breakage end up with many of their limbs broken after a bear feeding spree, which limits the trees' chances of survival. Future fruit-producing potential is limited on trees that survive this damage.

All feeding activity on trees does not result in glaring nor long-lasting damage however. The only evidence that a bruin has visited some fruit trees are claw marks in the bark and the breakage of a few small limbs. Some limbs are broken by feeding black bears in nut-bearing trees such as oak and beech, but the most frequent sign of their visits to these trees are claw-scarred trunks. The bark turns black where claws have scarred it. The same sign can be seen on the trunks of aspen trees, which black bears climb in the spring to feed on buds and catkins.

Fall is the time to check fruit and nut trees for signs of feeding activity. Recently broken limbs should have fresh green leaves still attached. Leaves will die and turn brown after limbs have been broken a while. Wood visible inside fresh claw marks will not yet have darkened. Count on Blackie returning to a tree that still bears a food supply. If signs of feeding activity are a year or more old and the tree has a supply of fruit or nuts again, a bruin will probably stop by for his share once they ripen.

Some black bears spend most of their time foraging on nuts that have fallen to the ground rather than climb trees to get them. For this reason, the absence of claw marks on the trunks of mast-producing trees does not mean there are no bears in the area. Other signs such as tracks and droppings should be sought to determine if bears are using groves of nut trees.

Black bears are also fond of insects in addition to fruits and nuts. To get at ants, hornets, and bees, bears often roll rocks and logs, rip stumps and logs apart, and dig holes. Claw marks can usually be found on logs and stumps that Blackie has visited. Scratches from claws are sometimes visible on displaced rocks. Remnants of a hornet or bees' nest at the bottom of a hole in the ground or in a ripped stump or tree is a sure sign a black bear was responsible. Large areas of soil may also be excavated by bears in search of plant tubers and bulbs.

Black bear droppings are distinctive and are not likely to be mistaken for those left by any other game animal in North America, except possibly in locations where the range of black and grizzly bears overlap. Dung is usually deposited in large piles. Numerous piles of droppings will be evident in favored feeding areas. Bear dung is normally white, brown, or black, depending upon what the animals are feeding on at the time. Evidence of the type of food bruins have been dining on most recently can be determined by examining droppings.

Black bear scats seldom appear fresh for more than a few days, unless the weather is cold. Piles of dung usually dry out and start to break down quickly.

The size of droppings may indicate, to some extent, the size of the animal that deposited them. Presence of bear scat of average size in the same area

Pile of black bear droppings during spring. Blades of grass are
visible in dung, indicating that the animal has been doing a lot of
grazing. The quantity and size of droppings can be an indication
of the bear's size.

with small, raccoon-size dung may indicate the presence of a sow with one or
more cubs, for example. As a general rule, the larger the droppings the larger
the bear. Black bear scat averages 1¼ to 1½ inches in diameter, but may
measure as much as two inches. After looking at black bear droppings over a
period of time hunters will get a feel for what larger-than-average droppings
look like without measuring them. The same holds true for tracks.

Tracks left by black bears can be a lot harder to find than many novice
hunters realize. Despite the black bear's bulk, the animals have to walk over
soft ground such as sand or mud to leave distinct impressions of their feet. The
best places to look for bear tracks are along sand or gravel roads, muddy

woods roads, in patches of sand or mud near feeding areas, and along banks of rivers and streams. However, many gravel roads in bear country are too hard to show much, if any, sign of a bear's passing. It takes an experienced eye to pick out the shallow imprints or scuff marks left by a bruin's large, flat feet on these roads.

The most efficient way to check gravel or sand roads for tracks is on foot. If gravel roads are checked from a vehicle, they should be driven at a snail's pace, preferably with a spotter on a front fender. Rain usually washes out tracks on woods roads, so if one is located shortly after a rain it is bound to be fresh. Some bear hunters who use hounds "drag" woods roads on a daily basis by pulling a tree branch, log or old bedspring behind their vehicles to ensure that any tracks seen the next morning are less than 24 hours old. A bear that walks across a road that has been dragged is more likely to leave tracks that are easy to see than on a road that hasn't been.

Bear tracks usually consist of imprints of foot pads and toes, with five toes per foot. A track left by a black bear's hind foot is similar in appearance to a print left by a barefoot person. The pad is longer than it is wide. Rear pads are widest just behind the toes and taper down to a narrow, rounded heel. Front pads are at least twice as wide as the distance from front to back.

Black bears have short claws compared to grizzlies and impressions from claws don't usually show in front of toe marks, unless the prints are made in soft sand or mud or the animal that made them was running. When claw marks are present in black bear tracks, the small indentations they leave are often close to toes. Claw marks are more prominent in tracks made by grizzly bears.

It is usually possible to get a general idea how big a bear is by the size of its tracks. The front pad of an average black bear will measure from 3½-to-four inches across. Rear pads on an average black will be from five-to-six inches in length. This measurement only takes the pad into account, not the toes.

My definition of an average black bear is one that has a dressed weight of 120 to 200 pounds. Heavier bruins are better than average in my book, and will generally, but not always, have larger pad measurements than those listed above. Boars have larger feet than sows.

Hunters who find tracks with front pad marks that measure five-to-six inches across and rear pads that span about eight inches, are looking at the prints of a trophy-class black bear. I measured the pads on a Michigan bear that had a dressed weight of 520 pounds. The front pad was six inches in width and the pad on a hind foot measured 8½ inches from front to back.

Front foot measurements of male and female black bears in New York illustrate the difference in track size made by each. The average width of front feet of sows from yearlings (1½ years old) on up to animals 10½ years old was 3.12 to 3.76 inches. Average measurements for males in the same age classes were 3.79 to five inches. Males 7½ years of age and older seldom had front foot measurements less than 4.5 inches. Most significant, however, is the fact that yearling males had wider front feet, although not by much, than all of the sows measured, meaning there is very little, if any, overlap in front foot size

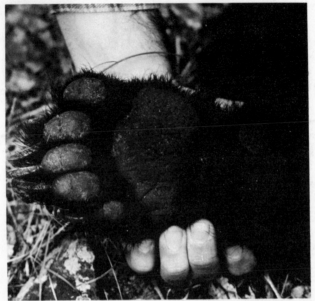

Front foot of a black bear with main pad wider than it is deep. Big males have front foot pads that are at least five inches wide.

Hind foot of a black bear. Notice that claws are shorter than on the front foot.

between the sexes. Any print of a front foot that is at least four inches across should have been made by a boar.

Measurements of hind feet of black bears in Washington came up with similar results. The length and width of pads on hind feet were combined to report the results there. Those measurements for adult females were greater than or equal to 8.4 inches, but less than 10 inches. Width and length of rear pads of the majority of adult males were greater or equal to 10 inches.

Regular trails will be packed down in areas frequented by black bears. All vegetation is usually flattened along these trails and may even be worn down to bare soil from extended heavy use, such as at a bait site or garbage dump. Bear trails sometimes tunnel through thickets at a height of about three feet. Trails used by a heavy bear will develop depressions every place the animal puts its feet because the animals have a tendency to step in the same spots each time they walk the same route.

Footprints without claw marks visible. Print of the hind foot is in front of track from the front foot. Impression of a front foot has also been left on top of print from the hind foot.

Black bear beds are similar in size to those made by deer, but more rounded, appearing circular. Deer beds tend to be made in more of an oblong or oval shape. Bruins may bed down in grass, but often lay at the base of large trees. It isn't unusual to see bear beds at or near bait sites. The animals frequently lay down to feed.

Wallows are commonly used by black bears to keep cool during hot summer months. Gary Alt showed me several wallows in a swamp. They consisted of circular pools of spring water. A well-worn bear trail was evident at the wallows. Bears leaving wallows sometimes shake mud and water on nearby trees and vegetation.

Smart black bear hunters will spend as much time as possible scouting for bear signs before hunting seasons begin so they can make the best use of valuable hunting time. Preseason or prehunt scouting is especially important for hunters who intend to use bait or hunt natural feeding areas, but will also work to the advantage of houndmen. Black bears are simply not as abundant as other big game such as deer, and range farther. Consequently, it often takes a lot of time and effort to locate Blackie's favored haunts.

Once prime bear country has been pinpointed, hunters are well on their way to success. It has been my experience that 60-to-70 percent of the time devoted to black bears is spent looking for a place to hunt and 30-to-40 percent hunting. Sometimes looking for a place to hunt requires an even larger share of the total time spent on a bear hunt.

When I'm scouting an area for bear activity, I usually look for prime sources of food first. If any bruins are around, signs of their presence should be in the vicinity. Black bears usually do a good job of looking after their stomachs.

CHAPTER
4

Are They Dangerous?

Black bears can be dangerous, but as a rule they aren't. The few exceptions are most often bears that simply have not learned to fear man. This is the case with park bears, and it can also be true of bears in remote wilderness settings where they have little contact with man.

The vast majority of incidents where people have been injured or killed by black bears have been in remote areas or parks. From 1948 through 1980 there were 16 people killed by black bears, according to verified reports in the book *Killer Bears* by Mike Cramond. In one case a single bear killed three people, and in another two people were killed by the same bruin, so 13 different bears were involved. All but three of them were in Canada, Alaska, or parks.

Of the 69 listings of people being attacked and injured by black bears in the book, 42 of those were in parks. Among the remaining 27, all but six were in Canada or Alaska.

The purpose of pointing this out is not to discourage people from venturing into national parks or remote areas of Canada and Alaska. Even though black bears can be considered potentially more dangerous in these locations than elsewhere, the odds of encountering an aggressive bruin are still slim. Over that 32-year period there had to have been countless times when black bears and people came in contact with one another, although in many of the cases the people probably didn't know it.

I believe that some cases involving black bears and people are blown out of proportion by the media. Black bear attacks are rare enough that the media make the most out of them when they do occur. Confrontations between black bears and people may also be on the increase as man continues pushing farther into remote locations, developing tracts of land that once were the

Although it may look as if this black bear has his paw raised threateningly, the animal is simply taking a step. Bears like this one are not normally dangerous.

This young black bear is not stalking the person
in the background; it's simply curious. Both the
person and bear were picking wild strawberries.

home of black bears. Visitation rates at national parks are also on the increase, bringing millions of people into black bear habitat.

If black bears weren't the easy-going, stay-out-of-man's-way animals that
they most often are, there would be many more unpleasant accounts of bear
attacks recorded than there are now. Anyone who willingly enters black bear
habitat should accept the responsibility of trying to avoid trouble with bears
as well as the risks involved, slight as they are, of being among bears. More
often than not, people are responsible for bear attacks, if for no other reason
than simply being on the black bear's turf. It seems as though black bears are
often blamed for causing personal injury when the animals were only doing
what may have been natural for them under the circumstances.

Black bears and people can be compatible. Hikers, campers, photographers, and hunters are probably at greater risk from falls resulting in
broken bones while afield than attacks from black bears, even from wounded
animals. Wounded bears and those cornered by hounds are certainly potentially dangerous because the animals can be expected to try to defend themselves, but again, black bears that fit in this category aren't as dangerous as
many people may realize. Hunters are most likely to encounter black bears
that are wounded or cornered and they are usually carrying guns in preparation for what may happen.

I know of some hunters who have received minor injuries from bruins
while hunting, but the hunters have always gotten the upper hand. Injured
black bears will run rather than fight more often than not, and the facts

support this. Not one listing of people injured or killed by black bears in *Killer Bears* involved a hunter. In a single case, a previously wounded bruin attacked a man in British Columbia and he managed to kill the animal.

If black bears were as dangerous as many people believe, most of the prominent researchers in the U.S. and Canada would have been killed or maimed long ago, and the number of people willing to study these interesting animals would be declining rather than increasing.

These men and women handle hundreds, if not thousands, of black bears annually, routinely entering dens, actively chasing sows with cubs in an effort to tree them, and working with agitated animals caught in snares and live traps. A handful of these people have received minor injuries from black bears, but nothing of major consequence. Pat Carr from Pennsylvania is one of the researchers who received minor injuries from a bear. Pat has worked with bruins under Gary Alt in Pennsylvania and in Great Smokey Mountains National Park.

The incident happened on Pat's first experience with a snared black bear. He was with Gary and two game protectors when they approached a huge male weighing over 500 pounds in a snare. The bear charged them when they got close and the cable, which was kinked and weakened, snapped. Gary jumped in the air when the cable broke and the bear went right under one of his legs. That left Pat in the bear's path and he took off running with the bear right behind him.

Pat made an abrupt change in course at one point, turning sharply to one side. Most black bears would have broken off pursuit there, continuing in the direction they were headed, but this one didn't. It turned with Pat and swatted him on the shoulder, knocking him down into the ground hard. The bear then walked over Pat, stepping on the ground rather than on him, and left the scene.

Because Pat was wearing heavy clothes, only a couple of minor scratches resulted from being hit by the bear. However, his ribs were bruised from hitting the ground so hard. That experience heightened Pat's interest in black bears rather than souring it because he knew only too well that bear could have easily killed him, but it didn't. In most cases, black bears will go out of their way to avoid trouble. The bruin that hit Pat was agitated enough to instinctively strike out, but obviously wasn't the cold-blooded killer that these animals are sometimes made out to be.

There also has been confusion between black bears and their relative the grizzly. They are two totally different animals and seldom behave the same. Female black bears are seldom as protective of their cubs, for example, as grizzlies with young. Black bear biologists such as Alt routinely chase sows and cubs in an effort to tree the cubs so they can be captured and tagged. While spending a week with Gary during June we chased and treed a sow with cubs on two consecutive days without experiencing any problems, and we weren't using hounds either.

Gary said that some sows will put on a good show, bluff charging and woofing, but most of them will send cubs up a tree and leave or climb a tree with them. Sows that behave in an unusually aggressive manner are either tranquilized before handling the cubs or are left alone. As forest dwellers, young black bears are often safe in trees and don't need their mother's protection, unless caught in the open or actually captured on the ground by a predator.

This does not mean that outdoor people don't have to be cautious in the presence of a sow and cubs. It's always a good idea to avoid getting between a sow with cubs or pursuing cubs. It does mean that there is no reason to panic when in the presence of sows and cubs. Simply keep a cool head and back out of the way as quickly as possible, facing the sow if she's visible. Sows sometimes bluff charge, advancing a short distance toward an intruder, then stopping. Try not to turn and run, which can trigger an attack. Sometimes talking to an aroused bear as you back up helps keep you calm, even if it has no effect on the bear.

Of the cases listed in *Killer Bears* in which the sex of the offending animal was known, males were responsible for more attacks than females, eleven versus eight. The sex of attacking black bears was unknown in most situations. If this information were known I suspect the percentage of males would easily outnumber females. As a rule, males are simply more aggressive than females. Interestingly enough, of all of the black bears responsible for actually killing people on which the sex was known, every one proved to be males.

The fact that many people tend to fear the unknown or what they don't understand, applies only too well to black bears. For this reason, behavior that may be simply a warning such as a bluff charge, or actions based on curiosity such as a bear approaching or following a person, are often misinterpreted as aggression because the animal involved is a bear. Bears are sometimes curious just like deer can be, but most people respond totally differently to the two. If a deer approaches a person, he usually gets excited and hopes the animal comes closer. Many individuals approached by a black bear normally become scared and respond accordingly.

Last summer, for instance, I was watching three black bears at a dump in northern Minnesota. A couple from Illinois was also observing the bears. All three bears were males, which are most commonly seen at dumps, with one being an adult and the other two probably yearlings. A herring gull was caught on something among the garbage and it flapped its wings in a vain attempt to fly when bears came close to it, but both animals ignored the bird.

After the adult left and the two smaller animals were on the opposite side of the garbage pile from the gull, about 30 to 40 yards, I decided to free the gull. Upon reaching the bird it struggled to get away as it had when the bears came close. Monofilament fishing line was wrapped around one of the gull's legs, so I grabbed the line and pulled the bird toward me to hold it still while I cut the line as close to its foot as possible.

Meanwhile, the man from Illinois said, "Hey pard, one of those bears is getting close, you'd better watch out," with obvious concern in his voice.

When I looked around, one of the yearlings was watching me, but was still about 25 yards away, no real reason for alarm as far as I could see. I figured the commotion probably aroused the bear's curiosity. The line wasn't cut yet, so I quickly did that and tossed the gull into the air toward the bear, expecting that to catch the animal's attention. However, at that point I noticed that the bear was looking directly at me and its gaze never shifted when the gull flew, as it advanced toward me.

Its ears were up in a normal position and the hair on its neck was down, so I was sure the animal was still curious, but I wasn't positive of its intentions. It was getting close enough to make me uncomfortable, so I said something to it in a normal tone, but that had no effect. It kept coming.

Then I raised my voice and hollered, "Back off now," at the same time I snapped my fingers. That stopped the animal, as if it understood what I said. It hesitated for a moment, then turned and walked away. The bear didn't understand the words, of course; it reacted to the volume of my voice.

By that time the man from Illinois was hyperventilating, genuinely concerned that he was about to see a person attacked by a black bear right before his eyes. He was impressed by the simple actions on my part that it took to stop the bear, too. My interpretation of what was happening was obviously different than his, and I think I was correct in my assessment of the situation. I suspect the bear either thought I was putting food for it where I stood or perhaps was going to feed it something by hand. When it realized that wasn't the case, it left.

Anyone can do what I did in that situation, but I don't recommend putting yourself in such a spot intentionally. I certainly didn't, having no idea that bear's curiosity would be aroused by freeing the gull. If I would have known what was going to happen I would have waited until the other two bears left before releasing the bird.

I've read countless times that black bears aren't predictable. I strongly disagree, convinced that these animals *are predictable* in many cases. The more a person watches black bears, the more they learn about the animals and the better they are able to predict how the animals will respond or react under a certain set of circumstances. This is true for any form of wildlife, not just black bears.

As a photographer, I've come to realize black bears will tolerate my presence as long as I don't crowd them and all of my movements are slow and deliberate. I also know when to back off, either as a result of clues given by an individual animal or when two of them get in an argument and one of them may suddenly turn and run. I've had bears run by me a matter of feet away, either to escape another animal or flee from an approaching motorcycle, but I try to give them plenty of room whenever possible.

How are black bears predictable? The vast majority of them will leave the area when encountering a human. Bears that people see first usually haven't seen, heard, or smelled them yet. A shout will normally take care of that. Individuals who don't want to alarm a bear can simply watch the animal until it goes out of sight. Hikers, campers and berry pickers who prefer not to see any bears should make noise such as whistling and carrying a radio or bells. Carrying on a conversation with companions works, too.

If a bear is encountered that refuses to leave, and even comes closer, holler some more in an effort to scare the animal away while also attracting the attention of other people who may be nearby. Groups of people are more intimidating to a black bear than a lone person. At the same time you are hollering, look for a sturdy stick or branch that can serve as a club.

Black bears frequently give clues to their disposition through positioning of ears and hair, plus their actions. Bruins that have ears laid back and the hair up on the back of necks are definitely in a bad mood. Animals that snort, woof, swat the air or vegetation and advance quickly toward a person aren't happy either. Bears that approach uncertainly with ears up could be curious, but they also may be trying to size up the prospects for a meal.

Always face a bold black bear. If it tries to circle behind you, move with it. Turning and running or climbing a tree are wasted effort under most circumstances. These bears can outrun and outclimb anybody. Here again, don't confuse black bears with grizzly bears. A tree may provide escape from a grizzly because their claws are not adapted for climbing like those of their smaller relatives.

A number of people attacked by black bears have been pulled out of trees by bruins. At least one person who died did so as a result of injuries sustained in a fall from a tree rather than damage done by the bear. That person may have survived if he hadn't climbed a tree.

Although climbing a tree is not a good way to escape a black bear, going into the water of a river or lake may be, provided the water is deep enough. People can certainly keep their heads above water in deeper water than black bears can. Black bears are good swimmers, too, but may be reluctant to follow a person into the water or carry out an attack in that element.

When, and if, a black bear does approach and a person has the time, dropping a pack, fishing creel or other item is a good thing to do. If there's food inside it may distract the animal long enough to allow a person to escape. Once the item is dropped, back away and keep going as far as possible until reaching safety.

In situations where a bear moves in close and a club is handy, it can be used to fan the air between the bruin and the person or to beat on trees while hollering. This tactic worked for Wayne Pangborn when he met an over-curious black while fishing for brook trout on a stream in Michigan's Upper Peninsula. When he first encountered the bear at close range he reacted by hollering at it, which temporarily scared it off.

To put some distance between himself and the bear, Pangborn crossed the stream he had been fishing, only to discover the bruin was following him. At that point he threw his creel, containing several trout, toward the bear, which distracted the animal briefly, but it quickly turned its attention back to the fisherman. The desperate angler then grabbed pieces of wood for clubs. He used the clubs to swing at the bear and beat on trees to fend the animal off for nearly a mile until he reached his car.

If a bear gets close enough to hit with a club, the end of the nose is a good target. This part of a black bear's anatomy is very sensitive.

Some black bear attacks come suddenly without warning, offering a person no opportunity to defend himself. When this happens, the recommended procedure is to assume a fetal position with bent legs protecting the stomach and hands clasped together around the back of the neck. The animal will often bite and claw its victim, but it is often best to try to play dead. Screams and struggling usually prolong the attack. An individual in this situation should wait until the bear is gone before attempting to get up. If a bruin is still in sight when movement resumes, it may renew the attack.

Although passive response is recommended when under immediate attack by black bears, and most people who have done this survived, others have survived by fighting, either using a knife or their fists. A lot depends on the victim's size, strength, inclination, and the circumstances. Some who tried to fight off a black bear apparently made the wrong choice, having been killed for their efforts. However, they may have been anyway.

The best way of all to handle confrontations with black bears is to avoid them in the first place. Most bruins favor this approach as well when it comes to dealing with people. When camping in bear country all food and sweet smelling items such as toothpaste and perfumes should be kept at least 60 feet from a tent.

Avoid cooking inside a tent in bear country because odors will linger, especially if things are spilled. Also try not to keep clothes inside tents containing odors that may attract black bears such as fish, blood from game, or food stains.

There is evidence that bears may be attracted to human menstrual odors, so women who are in bear country during their menstrual cycles should be extra careful about disposal of tampons and pads. A study using polar bears in Manitoba found that the animals were attracted to used tampons. Black bears in Ontario have shown a similar response.

While I maintain that black bears are generally not dangerous, there are exceptions, and outdoor enthusiasts in black bear habitat should be mindful of this, doing what they can to avoid confrontations with bears. The animals are certainly capable of being dangerous, using their speed and strength to catch and kill or injure people, if they choose to. Fortunately for us, black bears seldom react that way toward humans. They should be respected for the way they are, not feared.

CHAPTER
5

Photography

Black bears can be difficult photographic subjects for a number of reasons. Most importantly, they can be hard to see, period. It's tough to photograph what you can't see. Once Blackie is in sight, it can sometimes be a problem to keep him there long enough and get close enough to obtain good photographs.

By good photographs I mean clear and sharp images that are more than a dark speck in the landscape. Photos must also be properly exposed. That's where another problem comes in. Because of their color, black bears can be harder than many other wildlife subjects to expose properly.

There are ways around these problems, however. But before worrying about seeing a black bear to photograph, you should make sure you have the right equipment. The most widely used camera today, by both professionals and amateurs, is the 35mm. These cameras are light enough to carry almost anywhere and are extremely versatile due to the variety of films available and the interchangability of lenses.

There are two basic types of 35mm cameras—rangefinders and single lens reflex (SLR) models. Rangefinder cameras are not designed for interchanging lenses and when you look through the viewfinder you aren't looking through the lens. Both of these features limit such a camera's usefulness for photographing black bears, although some of the first black bear photos I took years ago were with a 35mm rangefinder camera. The exposures weren't as good as most of those I'm taking today, but some of them aren't bad, considering what I had to work with and the circumstances. The problem with rangefinder cameras for use on bears is that photographers using them have to be close to the animals for good results. Too close, in most cases.

Lenses for 35mm cameras that have 50mm focal lengths are considered

Here I'm using a wide-angle lens in an effort to photograph a black bear owned by Leo Dollins. (*Photo by Tom Huggler*)

"normal," meaning subjects look roughly the same in relationship to the photographer when viewed through this size lens as they do with his or her eyes (normal vision). Lenses greater than 50mm appear to bring subjects closer and make them look larger than normal lenses and are referred to as telephotos. Wide-angle lenses are less than 50mm, making subjects look smaller and farther away than normal lenses.

Most rangefinder cameras come equipped with wide-angle lenses, with focal lengths from 35 to 40mm most common. My rangefinder camera had a 40mm lens. The black bear I photographed with that camera was a sow with a

Judy and Tarzan took advantage of my position, making it impossible to photograph from that angle. (*Photo by Tom Huggler*)

cub that was coming into bait placed between two large trees. One evening I got in position on the lowest limb of one of the trees, being 10 to 15 feet above the spot where I expected the bears to be feeding later.

As it turned out, the sow came in alone and I started happily exposing film. I had a super 8mm movie camera with me in addition to the still camera. Even though both cameras made noise, the bear either didn't hear them or ignored them, concentrating on her meal. However, the sow did hear the sound of me ripping open a box containing a new roll of movie film and looked up at me.

She obviously didn't like what she saw because her ears went back and she stood up against the tree next to the one I was in, huffing and slapping the tree trunk threateningly with a forepaw. Then she climbed that tree to a point even with me and swatted the air between us as she made a swipe or two in my direction. Despite wobbly legs, I continued exposing film and tried to talk to the angry bear in a reassuring tone. That must have helped calm her down because after a couple of minutes of threats she slid back to the ground to resume her meal, ignoring me once again.

I now suspect the sow thought I was another bear when she saw me and may have been concerned for her cub's safety, which was probably waiting for

My wife Lucy demonstrates equipment I use to photograph wild black bears—300mm, f2.8 lens with Metz flash on a tripod.

her in the woods nearby. Once the she-bear realized I was simply a human, she relaxed. I didn't care what the reason was behind the bear's actions at the time. As soon as she finished eating and left I also vacated the premises in a hurry, and with a sigh of relief. I also made up my mind there-and-then to get a single lens reflex 35mm camera with a suitable telephoto lens for future black bear photography from a distance, and that's the combination I recommend for anyone serious about photographing bruins.

Wide-angle lenses like those on rangefinder, instamatic, and disc cameras are just not suitable for photographing black bears in most situations. One exception is when dealing with a tame bear that can be trusted. A situation such as that is one of the only times I've used a wide-angle lens to photograph a black bear since the episode mentioned above.

Leo Dollins has two tame bears, an old female named Judy and a young male named Tarzan. Leo has a permit from the Michigan Department of Natural Resources to keep the bears, both of which were obtained from game farms. The animals are pets, and he uses them to help train his bear dogs. On the day I interviewed Leo to gather information for this book, fellow photographers Tom Huggler, Al Stewart, and I spent about an hour photographing his two bears in his fenced backyard.

At one point I laid on the ground in front of Judy in an attempt to get some closeups of her from a low angle, using a wide-angle lens. It was a good idea in principle, but not in practice. Judy couldn't resist the opportunity to check me and my cameras out with her nose and Tarzan soon took advantage of my vulnerable position, too, wanting to play. The few exposures I took while I could turned out poorly.

Even in a situation when photographing tame bears and it's possible to get close to them, a telephoto lens often yields the best results. Most of the photos I took that day were with a 135mm lens, which is approximately equivalent to 2½-power magnification. With that lens I was able to stand away from the bears and they would still take up much of the frame. The telephoto also enabled me to compose pictures that would not include man-made features such as a fence or buildings, which would be distracting in photographs.

Tom and I also photographed Boo Boo, a bear owned by Chuck Godfrey. While Tom used a wide-angle lens for many of his photos, I relied on a normal lens and my 135.

A flash is usually better for low-light photos than high-speed film because the artificial light brings out more details (which is important on animals as dark as black bears) and gives a greater depth of field.

One other situation where I've used a wide-angle lens to photograph black bears was when trying to get an image of a sow and cubs that were in an enclosed den. I preset the distance from the den entrance to the bears, estimating it as best I could, then simply pointed the camera in the right direction and took a number of exposures. I used a flash to light up the dark interior of the den. The wide angle took in most of the den's interior, getting what I wanted without having to look through the lens, which would have been difficult under the circumstances.

SLR cameras offer more versatility. Photographers are able to look directly through lenses with these cameras. The image a photographer sees when the shutter is tripped will be what appears on the processed film. This enables photographers to accurately compose the photos they want by looking through the lens. Unlike rangefinder cameras, most SLRs are designed for quickly and easily changing lenses.

Most of the 35mm SLR cameras on the market are quality pieces of equipment, usually with a number of models offered by each manufacturer. Some of the more popular makes of 35mm SLRs are Canon, Nikon, Pentax, Yashica, Minolta, and Olympus. There are so many features available on today's cameras that each photographer should examine them thoroughly before making a choice. The selections range from cameras that are fully manual to fully automatic, with many variations in between. Keep in mind that each feature added beyond manual models also adds to the price, just like on automobiles, with manual cameras usually being cheapest.

One of the most important features a SLR camera should have is through-the-lens metering, meaning the lighting can be set while looking through the lens at the same time the photograph is being composed and the lens focused on the subject. This feature is important because time is often of the essence when capturing bears on film. The quicker a frame can be properly exposed, the better, on the chance a bruin doesn't linger. For this reason automatic cameras can be better than manuals in some cases.

Before buying a SLR camera, check on the variety of lenses it will accept. If the selection is limited for the brand you are interested in, it may be better to make another choice. You may only want or can afford one or two lenses at the time you make your initial purchase, but may want to add to your lens collection in the future. Keep this in mind. I know of some photographers who initially bought off-brand cameras, only to find out later the lenses they wanted weren't available. They then had to purchase a new camera, not making the best use of their initial investment.

Most SLRs come with normal lenses. However, if your main photographic interest is photographing black bears and other wildlife, arrange to get a telephoto or zoom lens with the camera body. It will probably cost more, but you'll be getting what you really want right off the bat. Zoom lenses can be adjusted for different focal lengths, in effect providing several lenses in one. However, it is the longest focal length or greatest magnification that will often prove the most useful for photographing bears.

Zoom lenses with maximum focal lengths ranging from 100 to 500mm are available, but those from 135 to 300mm are best suited for photographing black bears. The 100mm, although certainly better than a normal lens, doesn't provide the best combination of magnification and light-gathering ability and neither does the 500mm. The amount of light that passes through a lens to strike the film is controlled by the size opening of the diaphragm inside the lens. The settings for diaphragm apertures (openings) are referred to as f-stops, which are designated in numbers usually ranging from 1.8 to 32. The smallest f-stop numbers designate the largest apertures and the largest numbered f-stops, the smallest.

Since bruins are often photographed under low-light situations, telephoto lenses that offer the largest apertures possible will be the most useful. As a general rule, the greater the magnification a lens is, the smaller its largest lens opening will be. Zooms with 35-135mm focal lengths can be obtained with a maximum aperture or f stop of 3.5, for example. Zooms with more magnification, such as 100-300mm, have maximum apertures of 5.6.

Photographers who select zoom telephotos sacrifice some light gathering ability for the convenience of having a number of focal lengths in one lens. Fixed focal length lenses rank as the best choices for low-light wildlife photography, and these are the types of lenses I use for capturing images of black bears on film. Some of the best 135mm lenses can be obtained with a maximum aperture of f/2, 200mm with f/2.8 and 400mm with f/4.5. As would be expected, lenses with the best light-gathering ability will be more expensive than those of the same magnification, but having smaller maximum apertures.

Photographers have to weigh the cost of equipment along with its advantages to them and how much it will be used, before making purchases. I own a 300mm, f/2.8 lens that I do most of my black bear photography with, which

Some interesting photos are possible at dumps. In this one, a bear jumps from one dumpster to another. A fast shutter speed is required to stop the action—at least 1/500th of a second.

would be impractical for most amateur photographers to own due to its cost. However, as a professional photographer I consider the lens worth the money. Most of the bear photos in this book were either taken with 300mm (I used an f/5.6 model before obtaining the more expensive one) or 135mm lenses. The 135mm lens I now use is an f/2.5, which replaced an f/2.8.

Another factor that controls the amount of light that exposes film besides f stops is shutter speed. Controls for setting shutter speeds are on the camera body and generally range from one or two seconds up to one-thousandth of a second, or even faster on some cameras. Shutter speeds measure how fast the camera shutter is open during each exposure. Modern light meters are designed to weigh both the shutter speed and f stop to indicate settings for both that will permit just the right amount of light to strike each frame of film to produce the best exposures. In effect, a balance is reached between both settings to achieve proper lighting.

In situations where there is a lot of light, fast shutter speeds and small apertures may yield good exposures. However, as the light diminishes, either the lens will have to be opened or the shutter speed slowed so enough light reaches the film. Fast shutter speeds in the 1/500th to 1/1000th of a second range are desirable for photographing action such as a bear running or two animals fighting. Shutter speeds in this range should stop the action. Slower shutter speed (1/250th of a second) should stop a walking bear. Below that speed, satisfactory exposures may be obtained by swinging the camera with a moving bear.

This bear was so anxious to see what goodies were in this barrel about to be emptied at a dump, that it couldn't wait, digging in prematurely.

Something else to keep in mind when it comes to shutter speeds is camera movement. Fast shutter speeds will compensate for slight camera movements. When using slow speeds though (1/125th of a second or less), images will be blurred if the camera does not remain completely still during the exposure. To reduce or eliminate camera movement, steady it as much as possible by bracing arms against your body or on knees when sitting. For additional support, lean against a tree or other solid object. However, supporting a camera on a tripod is the best way of reducing camera movement.

When it comes to taking photos, press the shutter release smoothly with steady pressure. Don't punch it. If a camera is on a tripod, a short cable release can be used to trip the shutter, eliminating any movement. Cable releases are especially useful when using very slow shutter speeds.

Over the years I've learned that I can hand-hold my 135mm lens and obtain fairly consistent exposures at 1/250th of a second, and sometimes at 1/125th of a second. At slower speeds I have to find a rest or put the camera on a tripod. I feel confident shooting my 300mm lens at 1/250th of a second from a rest, but prefer a tripod for slower speeds. Some photographers are steadier than others, so each will have to determine his own limits.

The best way to determine if slides or negatives are fuzzy or blurred is to look at them with 8X or 10X loops available at most camera stores. Flaws on slides are not always readily apparent when projected, nor in average size prints made from negatives, although enlargements will bring them out. If you ever hope to have any of your photos published, keep in mind that slides are preferred in color and prints in black and white. Kodak's Kodachrome 64 slide film is preferred for reproduction because of its fine grain, and is most widely used by professionals. Most of the black and white photos in this book were taken with Tri-X film with an ASA rating of 400.

ASA numbers designate the light gathering ability of films, and SLR cameras have dials that must be set for the film to get proper exposures. The larger the ASA number, the greater the film's ability to gather light. Therefore, high ASA films are great for taking photographs under low-light conditions. Both print and slide films rated at 1000 ASA are available, and Kodak has a professional Ektachrome film that can be used as high as 3200 ASA.

An alternative to using fast film under low-light conditions is to attach a flash to a camera. It takes a good one to throw light far enough for photographing black bears in most situations though. Most won't give proper exposures beyond 20 to 30 feet with 64 ASA film, which isn't far enough under most circumstances. However, the Metz flash I'm presently using extends the range for 64 film to about 45 feet at f/2.8, and I've used it a number of times to photograph black bears as the available light faded or on overcast, rainy days. Some cameras, such as my Canons, have certain shutter speeds that must be used to synchronize with a flash.

Besides setting the lighting by way of f stops and shutter speeds, the only other camera adjustments that have to be made before taking photos is focusing. As a general rule, it is recommended to focus on a black bear's eyes for the best results. "Depth of field" will determine how much area in front of and behind the eyes will also be in focus. Maximum apertures produce the narrowest depths of field and the smallest lens openings (f/22 and f/32) yield the best depth of field.

When it comes to locating black bears to photograph, some of the same strategies used by hunters, which are outlined in other chapters, can be used to good advantage, especially baiting and hunting with hounds. The best time to obtain photographs of bears in front of hounds is during training or pursuit seasons. When relying on baits, best results can also be obtained before hunting seasons open. If you are both a photographer and hunter, as I am, try to take photos at different baits than those you hope to hunt, because once a bear has been photographed, it may not return or only feed at night.

Photographers also have opportunities to "shoot" bears where hunters can't, like within the boundaries of national parks and at garbage dumps. Steps have been taken in most national parks such as Yellowstone to keep black bears and people apart to avoid conflicts between the two. As a result, the chances of seeing black bears in most parks are not high. However, I know of two exceptions—Glacier National Park and Great Smokey Mountains National Park—and Yosemite may be good, too.

The Smokeys have a high density of bears, and the situation between bears and people there illustrates that it is possible to have a visible black bear population without the animals relying on handouts. Feeding bears was a problem at one time in the Smokeys, but it has been greatly reduced through strict enforcement of "don't feed the bears" regulations.

Garbage dumps may not be the most picturesque or appealing locations to photograph black bears, but they certainly are great places to see bruins, at least in some places. The animals are attracted to open pit dumps to rummage for scraps of food contained in household garbage, and they find plenty of food to keep them coming back for more. It is perhaps more enjoyable watching the animals and seeing how they react to one another and people than photographing them. However, I have spent many hours at dumps in Michigan, Minnesota, and Canada capturing images of black bears on film. Because dump bears usually get a lot of exposure to people, they will often tolerate photographers at closer distances and for longer periods of time than totally wild animals.

I spent most of one summer photographing bruins at a dump, and they got as used to me being around them as I was with them around me. At least one of the bears, a mature male with a white blaze on his chest, eventually became trusting enough to let me follow him into the woods when he left the dump. However, I had to keep my distance, and when I got too bothersome he would let me know. He usually did this by making a quick step or two in my direction while slapping a sapling or tree and snorting as if to say, "Alright, that's enough."

I always respected his wishes and left when he expressed irritation at my presence.

Whenever photographing black bears at dumps I frequently talk to them in normal, reassuring tones much the same as I would talk to a dog. If I want to move in close I do so slowly, a foot or two at a time. When the animal appears nervous or turns to leave, I know I've gotten too close and back off to give the animal room so it doesn't feel pressured. It doesn't take long to determine how close I can get without disturbing the bears.

I've had curious bears walk by me a matter of feet away while I spoke to them. If a bear appears too interested in me and gets too close, raising my voice usually stops and turns them. When it doesn't, I holler and slap my hands or stomp a foot, which has always worked for me.

When there is direct sunlight on a black bear, exposing the animal properly is usually possible by following a light meter. On cloudy days or when in the shade, open the lens at least one f stop beyond what most light meters say, for best exposures of black bears. If a bear's surroundings are light colored or there is strong lighting behind it, overexpose by two or three stops. This is easy to do with manual cameras and shouldn't be a problem on automatic cameras that can be switched to the manual mode.

As an example of how to properly expose a black bear in the shade, let's say the shutter speed is 1/125th of a second and the light meter indicates the f stop should be 5.6. Set the f stop at 4 instead, or 2.8 for two stops overexposure. What I try to do to ensure at least one or two frames will be properly exposed, if uncertain of the lighting, is bracket, meaning I take one or two exposures at the settings the light meter suggests, then open the lens one stop for a couple

This black bear resting on a bank at a dump looks like he had a rough night.

more and do the same at two stops over. If dealing with real bright light, I may close the lens one stop over what the light meter reads for a couple of exposures, just to make sure.

I enjoy photographing black bears as much, if not more, than any other form of wildlife. I've learned a lot about the animals while so involved, and even more while hunting them.

CHAPTER
6

Guns and Loads

Where a black bear is hit is often more important than what caliber rifle it is shot with. However, there are certain calibers of rifles and handguns that are better than others for bagging a black bear. The same is true for shotgun gauges.

A .22 magnum rifle, for example, will kill a black bear, but that choice certainly does not qualify as a bear gun. Under the right conditions and in the right hands, a .22 magnum will kill a bruin, but, as a rule, bullets from this small caliber don't have what it takes to do the job quickly, cleanly, and consistently. Guns and loads that produce clean kills most consistently are those that are recommended here.

There are so many popular calibers, at least in rifles, that meet these requirements, it doesn't make much sense for hunters who are serious about trying for this most common member of the bear family to use anything else. Basically, any centerfire rifle .30 caliber or larger is a good choice for bagging a black bear. This general rule can be broadened just a bit to include the .270, a versatile and widely used caliber for big game hunting. The 7mm magnum is also a good choice.

Most of the bears I've killed with a centerfire rifle have fallen to a .30-06. In my opinion, that caliber is among the best for collecting the makings for a rug. Wayne Bosowicz, who operates black bear hunting camps in Ontario and Maine, and whose hunters have tagged hundreds of bruins, agrees.

"There's no match for the .30-06, period," he said when I interviewed him.

Leo Dollins, another veteran bear hunter and guide, often uses rifles in .44 magnum and .444 calibers. D. DeMoss views the .358 Norma magnum as the

Dean Vick used a .30-06 bolt-action rifle to bag this black bear. This
is a popular and very effective rifle for black bear hunting.

best rifle for big black bears, although he has also used the .350 Remington
magnum and .45/70 with good results. Lawrence Edwards, another bear
guide, has shot plenty of bears with a .30-30. Additional centerfire rifle calibers
that are proven bear getters are the .300, .308, .300 magnum, 8mm magnum,
.32 and .35.

There are other lighter rifle calibers such as the .243 that have accounted
for black bears, and will probably continue to do so, but the light, fast bullets
available for that caliber and others like it are not best suited to consistently
penetrate layers of muscle, fat and bone to reach a black bear's vitals. A hit on
the shoulder blade of a bruin with a 100-grain .243 bullet, for example, may
break the shoulder, but stop short of the chest cavity. A 150-grain slug from a
.30-06, on the other hand, will break the near shoulder, take out the lungs, and
damage the opposite shoulder as well.

Is it possible to be overgunned for black bear? My answer is yes, if a
hunter goes to such a big caliber that he or she is afraid of the recoil, resulting
in flinching and poor or inconsistent accuracy. Bears are easy to kill if hit
properly. The caliber rifle used will not compensate for bad hits. A poor hit is a
poor hit whether made with a .458 or a .30-30. Hunters who wrongly believe
one of the magnums is required to anchor a black bear may be more likely to
make a bad hit with them than a rifle they can handle more easily such as a
.270 or .308.

Here's an example of how some hunters get the wrong impression about what it takes to kill a black bear. I talked with a bear hunter who was convinced that a .30-06 was not adequate for black bears after his first kill in Nova Scotia. He did bag an average-size bear on the hunt with an ought-six. However, the bruin went about 100 yards after the shot before dropping. He admitted the hit wasn't the best, missing lungs and heart, but for some reason felt it was the rifle's fault.

As a result, he returned the following year with a rifle in .460 caliber. Fortunately, he practiced with the rifle, becoming proficient with it. The man eventually got a shot at a bear, hitting it in the chest and dropped it on the spot. He was pleased with the performance of the big bore, of course, but failed to realize a .30-06 would have put that bruin down just as quickly with the same type of hit.

I've used both 180 and 150-grain soft-nose bullets in my .30-06 and have gotten the best results with 150s. The heavier bullets sometimes go completely through a bear, not having mushroomed completely and wasting some of their energy. The slightly faster 150s expand more and are often found just under the skin on the side opposite entry, expending all of their energy inside the carcass. Put another way, I've flattened more black bears in their tracks with 150-grain slugs than 180s, and would recommend their use in any caliber for which they are available.

In calibers that 150s or a similar weight bullet are not available, heavier bullets will have to do. Bullets for .44 magnums only come in 240-grain, for instance. However, there are two bullet styles available, soft point and semi-

Bullets in 150-grain weight, when available, are better than heavier bullets for bear hunting. These bullets in that weight performed well on bruins.

jacketed hollow point. Soft-points are the better choice because hollow point bullets sometimes mushroom too fast, not producing enough penetration.

There's more to rifle selection for black bear hunting than caliber. How much a rifle weighs, type of sights and action it has also enter into the picture. The primary hunting method you plan on using will dictate, to some extent, what choices you make. If you're hunting with hounds, for example, you want a light, fast-handling rifle that will be easy to carry. A sling makes carrying a rifle easier on these types of hunts and will leave your hands free to handle dogs, should the need arise.

Iron sights are adequate for most hound hunts, but telescopic sights are a good choice for stand hunting. Scopes are invaluable for their light-gathering ability early and late in the day, plus magnification and ease of aiming at medium-to-long ranges. Some shots at bruins feeding on grass during the spring in western states and Canada can be at hundreds of yards, while most shots when watching baited sites are 75 yards or less. Either fixed or low-power variable scopes such as 1½-5 are fine for stand hunting where shots are expected to be 100 yards or less, while the 2½-8 or 3-9 power variables are better suited for use in areas where shots can be longer.

Rifle weight isn't as important when stand or still-hunting and stalking

Dave Richey with a bruin he bagged with a .50 caliber muzzleloader using a maxi-ball. Front-loaders are effective black bear medicine in that caliber or larger.

as it is when chasing after hounds. Bolt action rifles are generally more accurate than other actions, and will be most beneficial when hunting openings. Beyond that, rifle actions are a matter of personal choice.

Black powder rifles in .50 caliber and larger are recommended for black bear hunting. Percussion cap models are better than flintlocks because it's easier to keep the powder dry, and when taking a shot the powder charge ignites instantly. With flintlocks there is a split second delay between hammerfall and discharge, during which time the rifle must be held on target to ensure accuracy.

Two bruins have fallen to my Thompson/Center .50 caliber Hawken. Fellow outdoor writer Dave Richey also killed a black bear with a similar musket while hunting with me. All three black powder bears were shot with 370 grain maxi-balls propelled by 80 to 100 grains of FFg powder. Two of the bruins ran 50 yards before piling up. The third dropped on the spot.

Although we used bullet-shaped maxi-balls to bag our bears, round balls

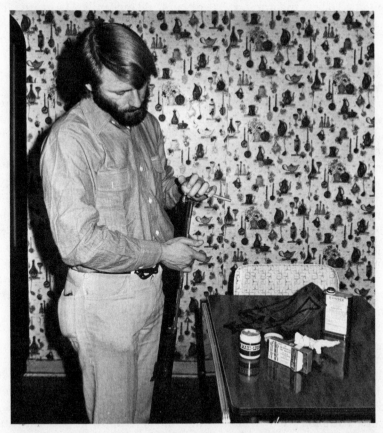

I preload a musket with a lubricated maxi-ball the evening before a bear hunt. Most muskets aren't considered loaded (percussion models, at least) until a cap is on the nipple.

should also do the job. Ballistically, round balls are faster and have more energy than maxis. We decided to use maxis due to their greater weight. Round balls for .50 caliber muskets weigh 175 grains.

Maxi-balls propelled by 100 grains of FFg black powder have a muzzle velocity of 1,418 feet per second and 1,652 foot pounds of energy, according to a Thompson/Center booklet. Round balls with the same powder charge leave the muzzle at 2,052 feet per second and have 1,739 foot pounds of energy. Maxi-balls out of a .50 caliber front loader with 100 grains of powder have ballistics comparable to the .45/70 and round balls come closest to the .44 magnum. There are also conical, hollow-based bullets available for use with muzzleloaders called mini-balls. The major difference between minis and maxis is that maxis have a flat base.

Most muzzleloaders come with owner's manuals that list the best loads to use in them for hunting. However, as a general rule, the amount of powder to use for big game hunting loads can be determined by multiplying the caliber by two (powder charge in grains = caliber $\times$ 2). For .50 calibers then, a good load would be 100 grains and for .54 calibers 108 (actually 110 grains for ease of measuring).

Be sure to test various loads in your rifle though, to determine which produces the best accuracy. Some .50 calibers will group more consistently with 80 or 90-grain loads than 100. Shoot various loads at different distances, too, to check their trajectory.

Residue from burned black powder builds up inside the barrels of muskets after several shots, making it increasingly difficult to load. For this reason, it is a good idea to bring a cleaning rod and patches to the range to swab the barrel between shots.

There are several types of black powder that vary in size of individual powder granules. Fg powder has the coarsest granules and is generally used in shotguns. FFFg has fine granules and is most often used to charge handguns and prime the pan of flintlocks. FFg powder is in between and is generally recommended for use in rifles.

No patch is required between powder and maxi-balls. Lubricant is added directly to these lead bullets and a ramrod is used to seat them on top of the powder. When using round balls, patches are required, either lubricated cloth patches or plastic cup-shaped patches made by Butler Creek Corporation in Jackson Hole, Wyoming. I've used both and have had more consistent groups with plastic patches, but test them yourself to determine which works best in your rifle.

It's necessary to carry plenty of accessories when hunting with a muzzleloader. Besides powder and maxi or lead balls and patches, you will need a powder measure, a starter to start round balls or maxis down the barrel, plus percussion caps or flints, depending on the type of musket used. If using a percussion cap model you will also want to carry a nipple wrench and an extra nipple. Leather pouches called possibles bags are often used to carry these accessories, but a couple of big pockets will also do.

To speed up reloading I generally carry two or three premeasured charges of powder with me. I used to put each charge in empty, plastic 35mm film containers and prelubricated maxi-balls in other containers. Now I use double-ended plastic tubes with caps on each end made by Butler Creek Corporation that serve the same purpose. The powder charge goes in one end and the maxi or lead ball and patch in the other.

What about shotguns for hunting black bears? A 12 gauge shooting slugs is okay, but if you have a choice between using a shotgun and a rifle of one of the calibers recommended earlier, use the rifle. Generally speaking, buckshot should not be used for black bear hunting. Buckshot does the job sometimes, usually at close range, and at others, fails. Because buckshot does not produce consistent results I can't recommend its use.

I was with a friend of mine who shot his first black bear with a 12 gauge shotgun. Jim had a slug in the chamber and 00 buckshot in the magazine for backup. A bruin gave him a perfect chest shot at 20 yards when it stood up on its hind legs to reach bait in a tree, and Jim made a good hit.

However, the bear dropped to all fours and ran rather than going down. Jim hit the bruin twice with buckshot as it ran. The bear only went 50 yards before piling up.

The slug had done the only damage, hitting the lungs. The buckshot that was recovered didn't make it through the bruin's heavy layer of fat. Buckshot loads have been improved since then, but I still think they are a poor choice for bear hunting. Hunters who decide to hunt black bears with a 12 gauge shotgun and slugs should use a slug barrel with iron sights or mounted with a scope that allow accurate aiming.

Hunters serious about bagging a black bear with a revolver have two proven choices—the .41 and .44 magnums. The .357 magnum will kill black bears, but it's not a bear gun, according to Leo Dollins, and I agree. There is a relatively new choice in six-shooters, the .357 maximum, that may prove its worth for black bear hunting. However, at the present time, only semi-jacketed hollow-point bullets in 158 and 180-grain weights are available commercially for this caliber.

Soft-point bullets are a better choice for black bear hunting than hollow points in all handgun calibers. Bullets in 210-grain can be used with .41 magnums and 240 grain loads for the .44 magnum. Revolvers selected for bear hunting should have barrels that are at least six inches in length.

Many hound hunters elect to carry revolvers instead of rifles for a number of reasons. Sidearms are lighter and easier to carry than long guns when following dogs. When holstered, a hunter's hands are free to handle hounds. Perhaps most important though, handguns can be easier to handle than rifles when in the middle of a bear and dog fight. At close quarters, which often exist in such a situation, a handgun can be more maneuverable than a rifle to put a bullet in a bear without endangering dogs.

The area of big game hunting with handguns was revolutionized with the advent of single-shot models such as Thompson/Center's Contender that could handle cartridges formerly reserved for rifles. Contenders are available with 10 and 14-inch, interchangeable barrels in a number of calibers suitable

One look at this black bear and you know the bullet will have to provide good penetration to ensure a clean kill, even at short range. This is an important consideration in choosing a load. With a .44 magnum handgun, for instance, the question is whether to use a 240-grain soft point or semi-jacketed hollow point—and the answer is the soft point. (Photo by Leonard Lee Rue III)

for black bear hunting. The .30-30 Winchester with 150 grain bullets is a prime example. Rick Powell shot a black bear with a Thompson/Center Contender in that caliber last fall. The bear was treed by Lawrence Edwards' hounds. Other calibers to choose from are the .35 Remington, .41 magnum and .44 magnum. Faster velocities and more energy are obtained with the same bullets from 14-inch barrels than 10-inch barrels.

One of the best calibers in single-shot handguns for black bear hunting is not available from Thompson/Center, but barrels can be custom-made by the man who came up with it—J. D. Jones from Bloomingdale, Ohio, who is with SSK Industries. The caliber is the .375 JDJ, named after Jones. Cartridges are hand loaded from .444 Marlin brass with 220 grain soft-nose bullets.

If you are considering using a .45 caliber handgun for black bear hunting, I would suggest forgetting it. A fellow hunting with some friends of mine tried to shoot a bruin their hounds had treed with a .45 and none of the slugs penetrated into the animal's body cavity. The bullets spent all of their energy plowing through hide and fat. That 200-pound boar was killed with a .44 magnum handgun when the .45 proved ineffective.

CHAPTER
7

Bows and Broadheads

Bows rated at 50-pound-pull are generally accepted as a minimum for black bear hunting. Women and youngsters who are serious about bear hunting, but who can't handle bows of that poundage, should try to get as close to 50 as they can.

What makes bow selection difficult today is the multitude of designs to choose from. When I started bowhunting, bow styles were still relatively simple, limited to recurves and long bows, with recurves being the most popular. Since then the compound bow was developed and has taken over in popularity, although there are still plenty of archers hunting with recurves, and there has been a resurgence in the use of long bows following the same trend as gun hunters turning to muskets from centerfire rifles.

Most compound bows have been fitted with two or four round pulleys or eccentric wheels, although this is beginning to change with the introduction of compounds equipped with cam-shaped pulleys in recent years. Another recent innovation on compounds are those modified for "overdraw" where the arrow rest is actually behind the sight window rather than in it.

Long bows represent the simplest and oldest form of bowhunting equipment, with long limbs that have a slight or gradual curve in them. These bows are appropriately named because they are usually more than 70 inches long with many in the 76 to 78-inch range. Bows of that length are required to propel hunting arrows at desirable speeds (170-185 feet per second).

The design and development of recurve bows resulted in slightly faster arrow speeds (up to 190 feet per second) from shorter limbs. Limbs of recurves bend inward at sharper angles than long bows, then curve outward near their tips. Recurve bows vary in length from around 50 inches to 68. Longer re-

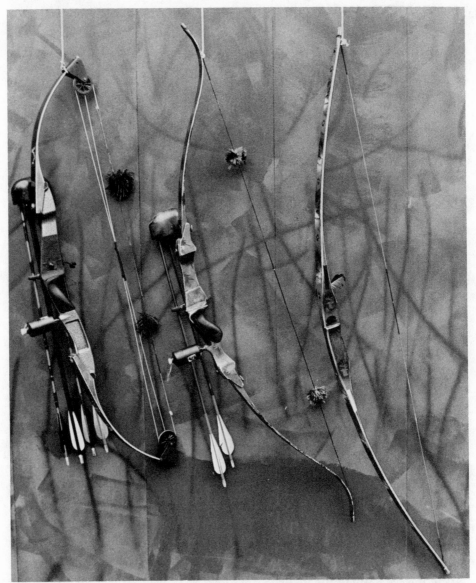

Compound bow, recurve bow and long bow (left to right) can all be used for black bears.

curves shoot faster arrows and are smoother drawing and releasing than the super shorties, making them more desirable for hunting. Sixty inches is a good average length for recurve bows used for hunting, with those a little longer probably being better choices than bows four or five inches shorter.

My favorite recurve, with which I shot my first bow-bagged black bears, measured 60 inches in length and has a 52-pound draw weight. The bow was

Dale Gray stillhunts with a long bow and a back quiver filled with arrows.

made by the American Archery Company in Oconto Falls, Wisconsin, which may or may not still be in business. I claimed three bears with that bow before switching to a compound.

Pulley-operated compound bows that combine cables with the string increase arrow speed, producing flatter arrow trajectories, another notch above recurves. And that isn't all. Compounds made it possible to shoot heavy draw weights while only holding a fraction of that weight (30 to 50 percent) at full draw. Long bows and recurves become progressively harder to pull back the farther they are drawn, with maximum force exerted on fingers at full draw. This makes it difficult to hold heavy hunting bows of those designs at full draw very long without getting shaky and making a sloppy release.

Compounds, on the other hand, are hardest to draw when the arrow is only partway back to your anchor point. When the string is pulled far enough so the pulleys "roll over," the holding weight drops off or relaxes a certain percentage, depending on the bow used and the number of pulleys it has. The difference between draw weight and holding weight of most two-wheel compounds is 50 percent, while four-wheelers usually drop off a lesser amount. Compound bows with less of a let-off often shoot slightly faster arrows.

Another advantage some compounds have over recurves and long bows is that they are available in adjustable draw weights, usually 10 to 15-pound increments. So bowhunters can purchase compounds with 50-to-60, 45-to-60 or 60-to-70 pound pull, for instance, and may elect to start shooting at the lighter draw weight for target practice, eventually working up to maximum poundage for hunting. Compounds average shorter in overall length than recurves, but are generally heavier, too, due to the materials used in their construction.

Cam and overdraw bows are simply modified compounds, with increased arrow speeds the primary reason for the modifications. Replace round pulleys with programmed cams and the result is a generally faster, more powerful bow. The only difference I can detect between bows with round versus cam pulleys, other than arrow speed and penetration power, is the latter are a little harder to draw. The string has to be pulled farther back before the bow "breaks" or relaxes in draw weight.

This is something that is easy to get used to with practice though. I've bear hunted with a PSE Vector, a cam bow, the past couple of years. When I first got the bow I had difficulty drawing it at 60 pounds, being used to a 50-pound round-wheel compound. However, after a couple of weeks of drawing the bow around the house several times a day, my muscles adjusted to the added strain.

Overdraw bows are compounds modified to shoot shorter, lighter arrows than normally used for hunting. Arrow rests are moved back behind the sight window to accommodate shorter arrows. Light arrows generally fly faster than heavy ones, producing flatter trajectories. However, due to the arrow's relationship to the bow behind the sight window, as well as arrow weight, smooth releases are a must. For this reason, most bowhunters who have overdraw bows use string releases.

The use of light arrows with overdraw bows has shown that arrow weight isn't necessarily as important in regard to penetration on big game as formerly thought. For years there has been emphasis on the use of heavy arrows to achieve maximum penetration on big game animals. Arrow penetration on big game with shafts released from overdraw bows has been terrific, proving that arrow weight alone isn't the only factor affecting penetration. Arrow speed is probably important, too, along with other factors.

There isn't much information on arrow speeds from overdraw bows at the present time because they are so new. However, Tom Nelson at Anderson Archery in Grand Ledge, Michigan said a friend of his consistently gets 254 feet-per-second with 25-inch arrows in 2013 size out of his overdraw bow. Tom said his friend's bow is set at around 70 pounds. Before modifying his bow for

I used a compound bow with power cams made by PSE to bag two black bears, with the arrow passing completely through both animals due to sharp heads and increased speed over round-wheel compounds of the same draw weight.

overdraw use the man was shooting 31-inch, 2219 shafts at 210 feet-per-second.

For comparison, Tom said that cam bows shoot arrows at 220-230 feet-per-second and round-wheel compounds average 200 feet-per-second. It should be understood, however, that arrow speed varies tremendously from one bow to the next among the same types, depending on draw weight and arrow weight. Remember that arrow speed does not kill a bear, arrow placement and sharp broadheads do. Fast arrows and flat trajectories are more important bow-hunting considerations when after mule deer, antelope, and caribou than black bear.

That basically covers the types of bows available today for bear hunters to choose from. To give a more complete picture of the selection though, there are a few more things to add. In regard to recurve bows, for instance, these are available in takedown as well as one-piece models. Takedown bows have distinct advantages over one-piece recurves or compounds if you intend to hunt with hounds. They can be strapped to a packframe, leaving hands free to fend off brush, climb slopes, or handle dogs before, during and after the hunt.

Long and recurve bows can and should be unstrung at the end of the day, plus for transport by airplane, in vehicles and on horseback, unless hunters intend on carrying the bow by hand when on horseback. Compound bows remain strung at all times, except perhaps when changing strings. Due to the mechanical nature of compounds it is easier for something to happen to them affecting the way they shoot. They must be properly tuned to achieve the best arrow flight.

The more simple design of recurve and long bows reduces the chances that something will go wrong with them, although limbs can be twisted if they aren't strung and unstrung properly. For this reason, a bow stringer should always be used for stringing and unstringing stick bows.

Most modern bows, with the exception of long bows, are designed to accommodate sights and other accessories such as stabilizers, string trackers and more. Nonetheless, if you plan on using these items, or others like them, be sure the bow you choose for bear hunting has places for them. If at all possible, obtain a bow for hunting that is camouflaged at the factory. Otherwise you will have to camouflage shiny limbs yourself. Camo tape or spray paint can be used. The job doesn't have to be fancy. The objective is simply to dull the bow's finish and reduce its visibility to game when in the woods.

I recommend round-wheel or cam compounds for most bowhunters interested in bagging a bear. Now that I've used a cam bow, taking two bruins with my PSE, it would be tough going back to a round-wheel compound. I like the extra speed and power, which I've learned to handle comfortably and accurately. In both cases when I connected with the cam bow, the arrow went completely through the bears, with energy to spare. I only had that happen on one other bow-bagged bear, which was arrowed with my recurve. I prefer complete arrow penetration on bears because the presence of entry and exit holes increases the chances of having a good blood trail to follow.

If you're a traditionalist and like to keep your equipment simple, long or recurve bows are good choices. Steer clear of stick bows with fiberglass limbs, selecting recurves and long bows made of layers of wood and glass, with glass as the outer layer. Long bows are suited for bowhunters with good instinctive shooting ability, although there's nothing that says you have to put a sight on a recurve or compound either. Recurves are slightly better for black bear hunting than long bows because they are shorter and easier to handle in thick cover and they throw a slightly faster arrow.

Hunters interested in more arrow speed than available from cam bows and willing to use a string release should try an overdraw bow. Both PSE and Martin have overdraw bows on the market, plus kits that can be used to convert conventional compounds to overdraw capability.

Hunters who get a compound and don't know how to tune it themselves should have someone knowledgeable do it for them. A compound that is out of tune is difficult to shoot properly. Have the draw weight checked to be sure it is accurate.

Hunters need to know their draw length to select the proper compound bow, plus arrows of the appropriate length. An easy way to determine draw length is to hold the end of a yardstick on the center of the chest so it parallels the ground and reach out toward the end of it as far as possible with both arms. The measurement at the tip of the fingers is the draw length.

It is important to shoot arrows matched to a bow, which is why hunters should know the actual draw weight. Fortunately, arrow manufacturers make it fairly easy to make the right arrow choices. Easton has an arrow selection chart for aluminum shafts that clearly shows what shaft sizes to choose for stick and compound bows in respect to draw weight. When selecting arrows for compound bows, it is important to know the holding weight at full draw as well as peak weight.

Both broadheads with presharpened blades and those that require sharpening by hand are adequate for black bear hunting; those in the latter category are usually cheaper than the former. The head at top is a Rocky Mountain and underneath it is a Zwickey head.

Draw weight of long and recurve bows is based on 28-inch draw length. Hunters who shoot arrows less than 28 inches should subtract three pounds draw weight for every inch less than 28. Add three pounds pull for every inch the bow is drawn beyond 28 inches.

Aluminum arrows are the choice of most serious bowhunters because they are light and strong, plus they are usually closely matched from one shaft to another in the same size. Arrows are also made of cedar, fiberglass, and some other materials. Wooden cedar arrows have a tendency to warp, but are still the preferred shaft material among some traditional bowhunters. Cedar arrows should not be used with compound bows.

Arrows can be fletched with plastic vanes or feathers. Vanes are waterproof and feathers aren't, although they can be waterproofed to some extent by spraying them with hairspray or a spray made specifically for the purpose. Feathers can be shot off arrow shelves and vanes can't, requiring the use of an arrow rest. Feathers are also more forgiving of a poor release than vanes, but are noisy if bumped or brushed against anything.

One material is as good as the other. The choice between the two is simply a matter of what you are used to or what you want. I've gone back to feathers after using vanes for years and am happy with their performance.

What goes on the other end of the arrow—the broadhead—is more important than the fletching. There are a lot of different broadheads to choose from, many of which should be adequate for bear hunting. The two basic types of broadheads available are those that require sharpening before use and those with presharpened, replaceable blades.

A number of good choices in the former category are Bear Razorheads, Pearson Switchblades, Zwickey Black Diamond Deltas and Eskimoes, plus Rothhaar Snuffers. Bear and Pearson heads are similar, with two main blades, and they are designed for the addition of razorblade inserts to give them four blades. The Zwickey Deltas and Eskimoes are available in either two or four-blade models, with the Deltas being the larger of the two. Snuffers are large, heavy three-bladed heads that should only be used with bows pulling 60 pounds or more due to their size.

Examples of broadheads with presharpened blades that have proven themselves on black bears are Rocky Mountains, Savoras, Brute Fours plus Razorback 4s and 5s. As the name implies, Razorbacks are available in either four or five-blade models, and Brute Fours have four blades. Rocky Mountains and Savoras come in three and four-blade models.

Small, two-bladed broadheads are required for use with overdraw bows. Tom Nelson said Zwickey Eskimoes and Satellites are used by some bowhunters with overdraw bows. The Hunter's Edge is another small head that works with overdraw bows.

Personally, I prefer the Bear Razorhead, having killed all of the bowbagged bears to my credit with this head. Even though the newer Bear heads are supposed to be ready to hunt with right from the package, I don't think they are sharp enough, requiring a touchup to make them razor-sharp. Hunters who aren't willing to take the time to sharpen heads like the Razorhead, Delta and Snuffer properly should use presharpened models.

There are a variety of sharpening tools available to aid in effectively sharpening broadheads. Most bowhunters use a file and/or whetstone to put smooth, sharp edges on their heads. The key to putting the best edge on broadheads is to maintain the same angle between sharpening tool and edge as it is being sharpened.

The importance of using sharp broadheads for bear hunting with bow and arrow cannot be overemphasized. If an arrow does not hit a bear in an ideal location, a sharp head should still produce a clean kill. At least there is a better chance of that being the result than if a dull or poorly sharpened head is used. A nonfatal hit with a sharp broadhead usually heals quickly.

Bow quivers are required for carrying broadheads afield. Be sure to use one that has a hood or case to cover broadheads and prevent accidental contact between cutting edges and your anatomy. Quivers that attach to bows, plus those worn on the back or on belts are available. I prefer bow quivers because extra arrows are readily available, should they be needed.

Bowhunters will need a glove, tab or release aid for holding the bowstring during the draw and release. I've always shot with a glove, but tabs may give smoother releases and release aids provide the most consistent, smooth releases. Try them all to determine what suits you best.

Don't forget to put a nocking point on your bowstring so arrows are nocked in the same place for every shot. Small metal rings with rubber cores that clamp on strings make great nocking points. These should go ⅛ to ½-inch above a point at a 90-degree angle to the arrow rest, on the string, and arrows should be positioned underneath them.

Other optional bowhunting accessories include armguards, sights, silencers, and string tracking devices. If you have a problem with your bowstring slapping your forearm or hitting loose clothing, an armguard is obviously a wise choice. You won't need a sight, consisting of one to several pins set for different yardages, if your arrows group consistently without one. However, if your accuracy is inconsistent without a sight I recommend using one, which should improve matters.

I tried instinctive sighting the first year or two I bowhunted, with terrible results. Then I tried a sight and my shooting improved tremendously. The aiming points made me pick a specific spot to aim at on game animals rather than aiming at the entire critter.

Silencers can be added to bowstrings to reduce noise. Rubber bands sometimes work as well as those available commercially.

I highly recommend the use of string trackers for black bear hunting because bruins simply don't bleed as freely as deer, and can be difficult to trail as a result. String trackers don't always work perfectly. When they do though, they can make the job of recovering a bear easier. I've had good luck with the Game Tracker. If you do use a string tracker, test it beforehand to see how arrows fly and to make sure the string pulls out freely.

CHAPTER
8

Aiming

There are several factors generally responsible for misses or bad hits on bears. One that can be controlled is familiarity with guns and bows, meaning you should know where bullets and broadheads hit at different distances. The second is shot placement, knowing *where* to put a bullet or broadhead to produce quick, clean kills, then doing it when the time is right.

Emotions are more difficult for hunters to control and account for their share of blown shots. Some hunters become excited upon seeing a black bear and lose track of what they are doing, either failing to aim when they shoot or not shooting at all.

Another emotion that grips some hunters is fear. Fear of what might happen if they hit the animal. Consequently, these hunters sometimes miss. Bear fever is the best way to label misses caused by emotions. It's similar to buck fever, but more complicated because of the potential danger.

There's no good excuse for not having a gun or bow sighted in. All guns and bows should be tested for accuracy before they are used on a black bear hunt. Hunters who hope to use a recently acquired gun or bow or one that hasn't been shot for a long time, will probably have to adjust the sights so it shoots where it is aimed with consistency.

To sight in an untested gun or bow, make the first shots at close range—10 to 15 yards—so that if sights are way out of line bullets and arrows should still hit the target. Hunters who don't have access to a target range should go to a location with a suitable backstop where it is legal to shoot. Gravel pits are good choices for testing firearms and clean sand banks free of rocks are great for stopping arrows.

It is important to sight in a bow with the type of heads you plan to hunt

All guns used for black bear hunting should be sighted in from as steady a position as possible before hunting.

with because arrows tipped with field points won't necessarily fly the same when broadheads are in place. Also, one type of broadhead may fly differently than another.

The same goes for sighting in guns. Use the same bullets and loads that you will be hunting with. In most cases, different weight bullets will have different points of impact. Even the same weight bullets made by different manufacturers don't usually group the same.

Blocks of Styrofoam make good target material for broadheads, although paper or cardboard targets serve the same purpose, as long as there is a good backstop directly behind them. I generally use large paper grocery bags as targets for handguns and rifles. A round bullseye is inked in the center of the bag, or a paper plate with a bullseye is stapled on, and the bag placed in front of a sandbank. A few rocks in the bottom of the bag will hold it in place. It's nothing fancy, but it serves the purpose, as will any number of other materials.

Before attempting to sight in a gun with telescopic sights make absolutely sure all screws are tight on mounts and the scope is secured solidly. If it's not secure you will be wasting your time because recoil from each shot will move the scope.

To properly sight in any gun it should be shot from as steady a position as possible, meaning from a rest. A benchrest is best, but lacking that, use a vehicle, tree, rock, post, or the ground (from a prone position) to steady guns so

When firing handguns or rifles on the range, some type of ear protection should be used. Dave Raikko is using ear plugs in this case.

sights aren't moving across the target during shots. Always use a pad of some sort between the rest and the rifle or shotgun. Sand bags, cushions, rolled up coats or gun cases are all satisfactory. Never rest a rifle directly on something hard. When shooting a handgun, a rest is generally used to steady hands and arms.

Gun hunters can make killing shots on bruins from just about any angle, but the classic broadside and head-on shots are preferred. The best way to put a black bear down quickly is to break one or both shoulders, and an animal that is broadside to the shooter is perfect for this type of shot. Aim for the center of the shoulder blade. A bruin hit in this location isn't going far, if anywhere. I've dropped numerous black bears in their tracks with this hit. The outline of the shoulder blade may be visible, but if it's not, aim for a point in the center of the body directly above a front leg.

Don't aim for the shoulder blade if shooting a light, fast bullet out of a .243 or similar caliber. This shot is only for guns and loads recommended in an earlier chapter. If using a rifle lighter than those mentioned, aim for a point behind the shoulder to ensure penetration into the chest cavity.

If a bear is facing the hunter on all four legs with its head up, or while sitting on its haunches, a bullet in the center of the chest will anchor the animal quickly. The same holds true on bears that stand on their hind legs for a better look around. Aim for the center of the chest. A frequent hunting partner of mine, Jim Haveman, shot a bruin in that position on a rainy day as

Classic broadside shot. The plus sign marks the preferred aiming point for gun hunters and X is where bowhunters should aim. However, they should wait for the bear to take a step before releasing an arrow. The near leg should be perpendicular to the body or forward of it to reduce the chance of the arrow hitting the shoulder blade. Gun hunters can shoot at any time.

it stood up to check for food in a tree. The bear ran after the hit, but barely covered 50 yards before dropping, leaving a steady trail of blood.

On bears that sit or stand with their backs to hunters, aim for the center of the back. A hit there will break the backbone and put the animal down on the spot. The same aiming point can be used when hunting black bears with a rifle from a tree stand, where legal, on bruins that are standing on all four legs and facing away from the hunter. Hold for the center of the back between the shoulders.

This bruin is angling away slightly, so both gun and bow hunters should aim behind the shoulder, in line with the opposite shoulder.

Shot placement will be slightly different on bears angling away or toward hunters than when broadside or head on. Forget about aiming at the near shoulder blade on bruins that are angling away. Aim for a point behind the near shoulder in line with the far shoulder on bears facing away at a gentle to moderate angle. When facing away at a sharp angle, aim for a point behind the ribs so the bullet will range forward into the chest cavity. Put a bullet in the right side of the chest on bears angling toward you from left to right and in the left side when moving toward you from right to left.

The head shot is an instant killer, but the kill zone isn't as large here as most hunters might think. Discounting the snout, jaws, muscle, and hide, the brain cavity of an average black bear is no bigger than a grapefruit. I measured the braincase on the skull of an average bear and it was approximately three by four inches. A hit around the edges is undesirable, so subtract an inch from each measurement and you end up with a two-by-three-inch target.

Such a shot doesn't leave much margin for error. An unsteady rifle, jerking the trigger or movement of the bear's head could result in a miss or poor hit. A hit in the head also ensures damage to a bear's skull, eliminating any opportunity it could be measured for record-book consideration. For these reasons, head shots are not generally the best type to take, except when hunting with hounds and an instant kill is required to save dogs from injury.

For all practical purposes, chest and shoulder shots are the ones to rely on most often when black bear hunting. There is a respectable margin for error with either one. Bullets that go a few inches high or low, left or right of center should still kill cleanly. Simply don't shoot at a bear if you aren't certain you can make a killing shot.

Another bit of advice that can reduce, if not eliminate, the chances of losing a bear once it is hit is to be ready to follow the first shot up immediately with a second and third, if needed. No matter how good you think a bruin is

Here's a good chest shot for gun hunters. A hit in either location will result in a clean kill.

hit, if it shows any sign of life, shoot it again. If the animal drops out of sight or runs, get after it right away. At least get to the spot where the animal was hit.

If the bear is no longer visible, listen for any sound that may indicate its whereabouts such as crashing brush or a death moan. It isn't unusual for a bear that is down for keeps to moan one to several times just before expiring. I've heard them do it numerous times. Mark the location of any sound carefully that might give away a hit bear's location, then proceed carefully to that point.

There's a whole different set of rules for bowhunters when it comes to shooting a black bear. Archers have to be much more selective about shot placement than gun hunters. The absolute best shot on a bear with a bow is when an animal is angling away so an arrow can be placed behind the shoulder blade and into the lungs, although a broadside shot is also acceptable.

The point of aim when a bruin is facing away at a slight angle should be directly behind the shoulder blade. If at a sharp angle, bowhunters should aim for a point behind the ribs where the arrow will enter and angle forward into the chest cavity. A broadhead that hits the ribs of a bear that is angling sharply away from a bowhunter has a tendency to ricochet along the ribs just under the skin rather than cutting through them, resulting in a nonfatal hit.

On broadside shots, arrows should hit behind the shoulder blade as close as possible to it. On a vertical axis, bowhunters occupying ground blinds should aim for the center of the body. Those in tree stands should try for entry in the upper half of the body, allowing for downward trajectory of the arrow.

This bear is moving away at a gentle angle, and
is in an excellent position for a shot from bow
or gun.

On bears that are angling away sharply, it is important to aim for a point far back on the body so
the bullet or broadhead will range forward into
the vitals. It is essential for bowhunters to put arrows behind the ribcage at such an angle. Otherwise, broadheads have a tendency to ricochet
along the ribs rather than cutting through them.

Bow shots at bears at all other angles should be avoided. The strike zone for chest shots is too small for most bowhunters to hit consistently, with lots of bone to deflect or stop arrows. There are even more bones to cause problems on bears directly below bowhunters in tree stands. It often takes patience to wait for a bear to move into the proper position for a bow shot, but the wait is generally worthwhile. If a bear is nervous, it sometimes helps to wait for the animal to relax before taking a shot, too. A relaxed bear seldom travels as far as one that was uptight when shot.

It's an entirely different problem when the bear is relaxed and the hunter is uptight, struck with a case of bear fever. I'm not totally immune to the malady myself, but I happen to be the type of person who usually gets excited and shaky after the shot rather than before.

If your contact with bears is limited and you think you may have a problem with bear fever, hiring a guide who will be with you when you shoot may be the route to go. A friend to hunt with you for moral support and act as a backup can be a help. Bear fever is less likely to be a problem the more secure and confident a hunter feels about facing a bear in a hunting situation. Bear hunters who have sighted in their guns or bows, plus know where to place their shots, have every reason to feel confident about making a kill, should the opportunity for a shot present itself.

CHAPTER
9

Baiting

Baiting is perhaps the most effective way for a lone hunter to connect on a black bear.

It's so effective that it is not legal in all states and provinces that permit black bear hunting. The technique would result in too high a harvest in some states with limited black bear populations and/or large numbers of bear hunters. In some cases in the western U.S. and Canada, baiting is prohibited or restricted because grizzly bears would be attracted to baits as readily, and more readily in some cases, than black bears, which is an undesirable situation. In the future, baiting may be restricted or eliminated in areas where it was formerly permitted due to declining bear populations or a desire on the part of bear biologists to reduce the bear harvest.

Bait can be put on the ground, hung from trees in a variety of ways, put in barrels, or placed in holes. Some states such as Wisconsin require that bait be placed in a hole no larger than two feet square, while others have no restrictions on the placing of bait. Be sure to become familiar with the regulations pertaining to baiting in the state or province where you intend to hunt to avoid problems.

What hunters bait with is generally not as important as where it's put. A good bait location would be a spot black bears already use in the vicinity of a natural food supply as well as in or near security cover where bears will feel at ease during legal shooting hours. It should have a suitable place for a ground blind or tree stand in a position where incoming bears aren't likely to detect a hunter. In addition, bait hunters should select a site where they feel there will be little or no competition from other hunters. If several people are baiting in the same vicinity, a hunter's chances of success are diminished because bears

A black bear looks up from bait placed on the ground to check out a sound it heard.

Large barrels are popular for holding bear bait, where legal, but smaller garbage cans like this one are easier to carry to bait sites away from roads. Logs are put over the top to keep ravens and small animals out. Bait barrels should have holes in the bottom to allow water to drain out.

become less active as human activity increases. Bruins are thus more likely to feed after dark than during daylight. Also, the same bear feeding at your spot might be visiting a competitor's bait, and if he sees the animal first, you may be out of luck.

If baiting where hunting with hounds is also permitted, select bait sites in areas that aren't appealing to hunters using dogs.

Houndmen usually prefer to hunt locations with a network of woods or logging roads to increase their chances of keeping contact with the dogs and intercepting a bear ahead of the hounds. Locations with a number of paved roads that receive a lot of vehicular traffic are usually avoided, because dogs could be killed by cars if they chase a bear across a heavily traveled road.

Hunters who will be hunting on private land won't have to be as concerned about competition as those on public property, but locating a spot that meets the other criteria is just as important. Look for bear sign to determine where the animals are or have been. It is sometimes easier to look for or locate a good source of natural food than make a concerted search for bear sign in that area. In the spring, black bears do a lot of grazing on greens such as grass and clover. They also feed on roots, insects, spawning fish such as suckers, and scavenge on carcasses of deer, elk, moose, cows, and horses.

Water is important to black bears in the spring. Their systems need water after leaving dens and they drink from creeks, rivers, and lakes, as well as utilizing the heavy cover often associated with water for daytime resting areas. River valleys or drainages are also natural travel routes for bears during summer and fall as well as spring.

Fruits and berries are staples for black bears during summer and fall, although they continue feeding on insects and grass. Other favored fall foods for black bears are nuts from oak, beech, and pine trees.

Once a food source has been located, find the largest chunk of heavy cover nearby where bears are likely to lay up during most of the day. Select a spot to put a bait along the edge of heavy cover or in an opening somewhere inside the cover. Baits situated along the edge of heavy cover are sometimes best because visibility is usually better than in a swamp or heavy timber. Black bears will usually always approach from a known direction, from within heavy cover, when baits are on the edge, whereas they may approach from any direction when a bait is in security cover.

However, bears may show up earlier at baits surrounded by thick stuff than they will on edges. In addition, there is less chance of other hunters stumbling across a bait in heavy cover versus on the edge of it. Hunters have to weigh the pros and cons themselves to determine what type of bait site is best. If one option doesn't work, the bait can be moved at a later date. In mountainous or hilly terrain with a scarcity of evergreen trees, bears often bed down on ridgetops, hilltops, and upslope on mountains.

Locations where there is a good supply of natural food and plenty of heavy cover near a lake or river are ideal for baits. There doesn't have to be food available at the time a bait is placed in an area for it to produce results, as long as there is something that is expected to eventually bring bears into the

Bait can be hung in gunny sacks from ropes in trees or from a rope between two trees, as shown here. Note tree stand in the background.

area such as apples, wild cherries, or acorns that are not yet ripe, but have been utilized by bears in the past.

A good way to locate potential bait sites is to drive woods roads and walk overgrown trails or railroad grades, while constantly watching for bear sign and possible sources of bear food. Once a spot with potential is identified, check it out as thoroughly as possible. You may find a place or two with bear sign, but no food supply readily apparent. These could be bear crossings, locations that one or more bears frequently travel through within their home range. Bear crossings can be good bait sites, but bait should be placed as far from roads as possible where the animals are likely to find it and other hunters aren't.

Topographical maps can be used to help find bait sites. Look for large tracts of roadless country, plus larger-than-normal swamps or patches of timber. These types of areas are sure to be used by black bears. Areas that have been logged off are worth checking because fruit trees and berry bushes frequently grow in the openings created by logging, and the remaining stumps and logs often contain insects that attract hungry bears.

Wildlife biologists and game wardens or conservation officers can also be helpful sources of information in trying to locate bait sites. They spend a lot of time in the field and can sometimes direct hunters to areas where they've seen black bears or their sign. Loggers fit in the same category, along with other people who spend a lot of time in the outdoors such as fishermen and trappers.

Hunters who find spots that look as if they should be good bait sites, but can find no bear sign, can place a bait there anyway to test it. If black bears are in the area or pass through, they will find it eventually, although it may be weeks before they do. Baits in ideal sites should be hit in a week or less, but it can take longer if placed in areas where a natural food supply isn't being used.

Although most baiting of black bears is done on foot, some hunters use canoes or boats to run baits along rivers or around lakes. This is a very effective approach. The only drawback when baiting around lakes by boat is that the sites become inaccessible during periods of rough weather. However, hunting over bait isn't usually the best under those conditions anyway.

Baits should be a minimum of 100 yards from a road or trail to reduce the chances of disturbance when being hunted. I locate most of my baits at least a quarter of a mile from roads. This ends up being a lot of work hauling bait in and getting bears out, but I feel it's worth it. The farther from roads baits are, the more comfortable bears are going to feel about feeding there before shooting light fades.

The above advice applies to public land, of course, not necessarily private land or areas with no competition. The last black bear I shot was in Colorado while hunting with guide Jim Jarvis from Montrose. We bowhunted leased land and, consequently, didn't have to worry about being disturbed. We were able to drive right up to the bait I hunted, which was situated along a little-used tote road. I saw four or five different bears on that bait in two days before I tagged a dark brown adult male.

In Wisconsin, the game laws say bait has to go in a hole in the ground. The hole can be covered with logs big enough to prevent smaller animals such as skunks and raccoons from getting at the bait. Hunters using this method will know a bear has been there if the logs are moved.

Where baiting restrictions such as this don't exist, hunters can choose how to leave bait at sites. The practice in Wisconsin is certainly one alternative. However, more popular procedures are to put bait in bags or containers to hang or fasten to trees. Fifty-gallon drums are popular bait containers because they are sturdy and hold a lot of food. However, it's tough to lug those containers far from a road. I've used the smaller, lighter, metal garbage cans with good success. Garbage cans are easier to carry than the larger drums.

Even smaller five-gallon buckets are used by some baiters, covering them with logs and other debris that bears have to remove to get at the bait. The tops of larger cans are also covered with logs to keep out critters other than bears. Although I've used cans to contain bear bait, I prefer to hang bait from tree limbs.

Bait is placed in plastic garbage bags, then tied to suitable limbs that are from chest to head high. I choose dead or damaged trees to hang bait whenever possible, although any tree with sturdy limbs at the desired level is satisfactory. Small limbs that may be strong enough to hold up a bag of bait are sometimes broken off by feeding bruins. Alternatives to garbage bags for hanging bait from trees are gunny or onion sacks that can be suspended by rope.

The latter choices are more porous, allowing plenty of scent to escape from the bait. To make sure scent dissipates from garbage bags I put holes in the bags once they are hung. I often take pieces of food from bags and place them on limbs or in tree crotches to give off scent when starting a bait.

Odor from the bait is how bears find it most often, so the presence of plenty of scent is important. When starting a bait I frequently use fish or meat, where legal, which becomes more odoriferous the longer it ages. Although not necessary, it's also a good idea to use a strong, long-lasting liquid scent in conjunction with bait when starting out. Anise or anise extract is good, but both are expensive for small quantities. Other liquids work as well and are cheaper.

Dan Brockman from Vesper, Wisconsin passed on some of his bear potion for my use that works. He's experimenting with a number of different scents, but the one I've tried so far and am happy with has vanilla concentrate, cinnamon and anise as basic ingredients. Other scents he is experimenting with have fruit-flavored syrups as bases such as cherry, strawberry, and orange. All of these scents have sweet aromas.

Guide Wayne Bosowicz swears by scents for attracting black bears to baits. He uses sweet-smelling scent for fall, and a liquid that has a more "rank and rancid" odor during spring. Scent Wayne uses for fall baiting has a beaver castor base and a "sweetener." This guide also uses a lot of anise, buying it in gallon containers. Hunters can also try some of the commercial scents on the market.

Liquid scent can simply be applied to a tree or stump at the bait site or put on a scent pad made of cloth or cotton and hung in a tree. Dan Brockman uses an empty 35mm film container with a small hole in it as a scent dispenser.

Another trick is to leave scent trails leading to a site. This can be done by dragging fish heads or fat on a rope away from the bait, then back to it along the same course. To make sure plenty of scent is left, I smear fish or fat on logs and rocks en route to the bait site. On occasion I will put fat, grease, or something else with appealing odor on the bottom of my boots to leave a scent trail rather than drag something behind me.

Scent trails can be made as long as you want, but I seldom extend them over a mile in one direction, with one-quarter to one-half mile about average. Scent trails can be left in as many different directions as desired. Black bears that come in contact with scent trails usually follow them right to the bait just like a hound dog would.

After a bear has found the bait and is coming regularly, I sometimes begin dumping the bait on the ground, knowing that bears will get most of the food. Some baiters such as Bosowicz and Jarvis place bait on the ground to begin with. Animals other than bears have easy access to bait on the ground. Small critters don't often eat enough to make a difference, but larger ones like wolves or coyotes can. Wolves may be attracted to baits in Canada and northern Minnesota, whereas coyotes are found in many of the areas occupied by black bears.

Bosowicz tries to discourage wolves and coyotes from feeding on his baits

Scent trails can be left
with fish or fat to attract
black bears to baits.
Canvas backpacks are
handy for carrying bear
bait.

because they consume large quantities of food and he has had coyotes chase
black bears from baits. Wolves may also keep bears away from baits. What
Wayne does is to leave an item at the bait that retains a lot of human odor such
as a shoe. Other items such as socks or tee shirts might work equally well. The
presence of these items doesn't bother black bears.

Hunters who plan to bowhunt over bait and either place food in a barrel or
on the ground can increase the chances of getting angling-away shots at
feeding bruins by controlling the position animals stand in to get at the food.
If using barrels, they can be tied to trees leaning in one direction, based on
stand location, so bears have to stand where you want them to reach in the
barrel. If putting food on the ground, it can be placed in a position where the
animal can only get at it from one direction. When natural obstructions aren't
available, a V-shaped structure can be constructed with logs and bait put at
the intersection of the two sides. I highly recommend the use of cribs and
anchored bait barrels for bowhunters to increase their chances of getting the

best shots possible. The sides of cribs don't have to be high or sturdy. Pieces of wood and logs can simply be piled on top of one another to make the sides.

It's generally easy to determine what animals are using bear baits by the sign they leave. Black bears generally leave plenty of droppings and claw marks on trees, if bait is hung. And if bait is covered with big logs or rocks, bears are probably the only animals that can move them. Coyote and wolf scats taper to points at the ends while bear scat is more uniformly rounded or may appear as variable-shaped piles of loose dung.

Raccoons, pine martens, and fishers will leave claw marks on bait trees, too, but their claws generally leave light scratches that usually don't penetrate through tree bark. Claw marks from bears, on the other hand, leave deep scars in the bark and lighter colored inner wood is normally visible. Ravens will also feed at bear baits, leaving white splashings on vegetation and the ground from their droppings.

Ravens can be used to the hunter's advantage on baits in areas where these scavenging birds are common. Whenever ravens find a source of food, they call to each other, making a lot of noise. Other scavengers such as black bears that hear feeding calls of ravens often come to investigate. So when starting a bear bait, leave some food on the ground in the open for ravens to see, while covering or hanging the rest of the bait for bears.

When a black bear has been at a bait, the vegetation in the vicinity of the food is often trampled from the animals walking and laying on it. And if there is any food remaining when the animal is full, it will sometimes cover it with leaves, ferns, or other vegetation that is handy. Bear tracks may also be visible in the vicinity. If there isn't soft sand or mud near a bait, hunters can dig a quantity of soil and leave it around the bait to register tracks. I use a lot of bread for bait, which is good for saving impressions of bear tracks because the animals often step on uneaten slices that fall on the ground.

Hair is another clue to look for at bait sites to determine what is visiting there. Look for strands of it on bait trees, especially on stubs of broken limbs, and on the undersides of low hanging limbs or fallen trees that bears might walk under. Bear hairs are long and uniform in color, either black, brown, white or whatever, depending on the dominant color phase in the area being hunted. Raccoon hairs are brown and tipped with black.

I've already mentioned a few items that can be used for bear bait such as fish, fat from cattle or pigs, meat scraps, and bread. Check local regulations to determine what can and cannot be used. Meat and honey can't be used in Wisconsin, for example. Bears have a sweet tooth, so any items that have sugar such as donuts, cakes, pies, and candy are great for bait. They will also eat cheeses, fruits, vegetables, and grains.

Basically, meats and sweets are the staples of black bear baits any time of the year. Fat and meat scraps can be obtained from butcher shops, grocery stores, and slaughter houses. If you know a farmer who has livestock, you may be able to get animal carcasses for bait. Beaver carcasses make great bait during spring seasons, although be sure this is legal before using them. Most states prohibit the use of carcasses of game animals such as deer for bear bait.

Bakeries and donut shops are good sources for obtaining bread and sweets no longer suitable for human consumption. Some bakeries sell bags of stale bread as animal food. Plain bread can be spiced up by adding grease, gravy, syrup or molasses to it. Molasses and oats can also be used for bear bait.

Restaurants can be another good source for bear bait. These establishments throw away quantities of old food of all types, including meat, potatoes, gravies, soups, breads and more that black bears absolutely love. As far as fish, I generally use the heads and viscera from gamefish caught on hook and line, although I sometimes obtain larger quantities from commercial fishing operations. Even though I may start a bait with fish, I use this type of bait as little as possible once a bait is active because many black bears prefer other foods to raw fish, sometimes abandoning a bait that contains only fish, or leaving fish to rot when they have a choice of other foods at a bait. Bears will eat cooked fish more readily than raw.

If possible, use a variety of items at baits. Bears will occasionally get tired of one type of food and look for something else. I prefer using bread and sweet goods because they are light and easier to carry than other items. Jim Jarvis uses a lot of candy at his baits, but he's fortunate enough to live near a candy factory and can get quantities that are unsalable and would normally be thrown away. Otherwise, the cost of obtaining candy for bear bait would be prohibitive.

Fruits such as apples sometimes make good additions to baits. These can usually be gathered from trees in abandoned orchards and other locations. Spots with one or more apple trees can be good bait sites if they are far enough from roads and don't receive much human traffic.

When using any type of bait, but especially meat and fish, the fresher it is, the better. Black bears will eat ripe and rotted meat and fish when they are hungry, perhaps as much for the insect larvae and insects on it as anything else. When they have a choice though, such as when plenty of food is available, they prefer fresh food. If bait gets too ripe in barrels, empty it and replace it with fresh food. Holes should be put in the bottom of bait barrels to permit water and other liquids to drain out.

When using meat and fish for bait during hot weather I freeze them first and carry them into the woods frozen. They thaw quickly and will be fresher when a bear finds them. Meat and fish are often easier to handle when frozen.

I use large canvas backpacks to carry food to bait sites. The type I'm using most often now is a duffel bag with shoulder straps purchased at an Army/Navy surplus store. If I have several bears on a bait or won't be returning for about a week, I carry as much bait as I can. Large quantities of bait aren't necessary though, if only feeding one bear or if the bait will be replenished every one or two days. Bosowicz generally carries what fits in a five-gallon pail, unless several bears are present. Bears normally eat less during the spring than fall. As a general rule, I replenish bait at active sites every day or two as hunting season approaches and when hunting, but on an irregular basis before then.

Whenever I go into a bait site I make plenty of noise going and coming, not trying to make my presence a secret. If alone, I whistle. If with someone, I talk freely. This gives any bears at the bait a warning that I'm coming and they can walk off without becoming surprised or alarmed. Before I started my whistling routine I surprised a number of bears at baits, scaring them, and in some cases they didn't return for days. Bears know full well that people are providing the food they are eating. Hunters who try to sneak into baits to keep their presence a secret in an effort to not spook bears may do just the opposite and aren't giving the animals enough credit. Many black bears visiting baits monitor hunter movements more closely than the hunters realize.

It is the bait hunter's responsibility to keep all baits clean of debris. All papers, plastic, bottles, cans, and boxes should be cleaned up at sites during each visit. Don't wait until the end of the season to do it. Avoid bringing as much litter to a bait site as possible in the first place.

When using barrels or buckets, only put edible food items in them. The same applies to bags and sacks hung in trees. Torn bags should be picked up and removed and replaced with fresh ones on each visit. If bones are used that are too large for bears to eat, these should also be removed.

Baiters in Wisconsin have no choice. The law prohibits the use of any paper, plastic, or boxes at bait sites. One of the major reasons the law was established there is because hunters were leaving messes at bait sites. There is no excuse for this. Hunters who find messy bait sites on public land should report them to game wardens or conservation officers so the responsible individuals can be ticketed.

Hunting black bears over bait is a controversial method to begin with and those who don't practice it properly don't help matters. Because of the technique's overall effectiveness there is an overriding feeling that it is easy or takes unfair advantage of black bears, primarily by people who haven't or won't try it, and therefore don't understand it. Although killing a bear over bait can be easy, on the average it isn't, as I hope to illustrate in the next chapter.

CHAPTER
10

Hunting Over Bait

My brother was once trying to fill a black bear tag by hunting over bait. We were using an old, roofless shack as a blind in a small clearing on the edge of thick cover. One to several bears were visiting the bait regularly. While Bruce peered out of a glassless window frame at the bait, I sat on the top of the opposite wall where the roof once was with a camera, hoping to get some action photos of Bruce shooting a bear.

A bruin eventually approached the bait, but my brother never saw him. The animal noiselessly slipped up to the edge of the opening and sat down. The distance that separated the bear and Bruce couldn't have been more than 50 feet. Thick growth of leafed saplings on the edge of the clearing blocked the animal from Bruce's view.

After testing the breeze, the cautious bruin picked up my brother's scent and slowly faded out of my sight, never having made a single sound to give away its presence. If I hadn't been there, Bruce would not have known a bear had been within miles. Black bears have excellent hearing and a super sense of smell, often enabling them to detect the presence of a hunter watching a bait without giving hunters any clue of their presence. Once bears sense a person at a bait, they may leave the area entirely or revert to nocturnal visits, at least for a while.

Bear hunting over bait is little different than trying to ambush them at natural food supplies when it comes to the animals' ability to detect and avoid the presence of a hunter. In fact, there is a greater chance of bears pinpointing hunters at bait sites than elsewhere because human scent is frequently encountered at bait sites and bears are apt to approach them more cautiously than sources of natural food.

It isn't unusual for bruins to circle a bait before approaching to feed. Other animals may sit down just out of sight listening and testing air currents with their noses for up to half-an-hour before deciding to show themselves. In either case, if a bear picks up a hunter's scent or the hunter makes a noise that tips the bear off, such as slapping a mosquito or coughing, good-bye bear.

The next time the same bear visits that bait it will be even more cautious. If the wind is right, the hunter is in the right position and he doesn't blow it, there is a chance of scoring. As it turned out, Bruce eventually killed a bear at the site I mentioned. What made the difference is that he changed position to the other side of the clearing where the breeze was more favorable for him, considering the bruin's approach.

Stand selection is obviously important when hunting black bears over bait. Try to position yourself downwind from the bait, as well as from the area bears are expected to approach. Elevated positions like those in trees, where legal, can be an advantage, reducing the chances of bears winding hunters, but they certainly don't eliminate the possibility and won't if they aren't in the right location. Stands on the ground can be good, too, provided the wind is right and there is enough cover.

A black bear's eyesight is its weakest sense, so a lot of cover isn't necessary to remain unseen as long as movement is kept to a minimum. Bears see

A bowhunter takes aim at a black bear angling away from him as it feeds on bait.

movement more readily than stationary forms and can identify its source in a hurry. When hunting from the ground I use natural cover as much as possible, often simply sitting against a tree trunk to break my outline. Ferns, blow-downs, stumps, rocks, or old buildings can be used as blinds that are part of the natural surroundings. If you prefer, a blind can be constructed to your liking to reduce the chances of being seen.

When hunting from the ground, try to select a stand where a bear isn't likely to approach from the rear. Some positions that are generally good for this are against a rock wall, along the edge of a lake or in an opening overlooking the edge of heavy cover. If hunting with a rifle and the cover is open enough, it may be possible to sit up to 200 yards from a bait where the chances of being smelled, heard, or seen are slim. I know a number of people who have done this, setting up a rest to shoot from at their stand to ensure accurate bullet placement.

In many cases it won't be possible to wait for a bear to arrive at a bait from that distance. The terrain and cover usually dictate much closer shooting. Fifty yards is probably average for most rifle shots at black bears over bait. I would want to be within 30 yards when hunting with musket, shotgun, or handgun. Twenty yards is the maximum distance I recommend for bowhunt-ing at bait sites. The closer the better is my philosophy when hunting with bow and arrow from baited stands, with 10 yards my preferred distance.

Blinds or stands should be constructed or positioned in advance of open-ing day to give bears a chance to get used to them. Hunters may even want to leave clothing with their scent on it in blinds, so bruins will grow accustomed to human scent in that location. If bait activity drops off when this is done, forget it. Don't worry if unable to put a stand up ahead of time. I've positioned them the day before I hunted as well as the same day I hunted and enjoyed success.

Some black bears become so accustomed to ground blinds and tree stands positioned ahead of the season that they take a liking to them, either crawling or climbing into them out of curiosity or to use them for taking a nap. I know of a number of cases where this has happened both before and during hunting seasons. When in tree stands I've had black bears stand up against the base of my tree a number of times, as if thinking about joining me, although they may have just been checking my scent out on the tree trunk itself. In none of the cases did the bears actually try to climb the tree. I attempted to photograph one of the animals and it simply walked off, pausing to look back at me over its shoulder before walking out of sight.

Black bears that do climb into ground blinds or toward tree stands aren't necessarily interested in their occupants. The animals may simply be curious or may be repeating what they did before, using the stands previously when unoccupied. I'm convinced that due to the poor eyesight of black bears, they sometimes mistake hunters in trees for other bears, especially if the wind isn't in their favor.

Make yourself as comfortable as possible at your stand to reduce the amount of movement necessary during the long hours you may be there. It's

Hunter constructs a blind to hide any movements he might make while waiting for a bruin
at a bait.

okay to shift positions occasionally. Just do so slowly and as quietly as
possible when you don't think a bear is nearby. I sometimes take advantage of
the noise created by a passing jet or a gust of wind to shift positions so if I do
make some noise, it won't be as obvious.

Camouflage clothing is a good choice for stand hunting, although any
garments that blend in with your surroundings are fine. Michigan is one state
that requires bear hunters using firearms to wear a hat, vest, or coat of
fluorescent orange material. Hunters who wear bright-colored clothes won't
have to worry about being seen by bears if they are properly positioned
utilizing available or manipulated cover. Wear garments made of soft, non-
abrasive material that won't make noise when you move.

Mosquitoes and black flies can sometimes be a problem when hunting
over bait during warm weather, especially in the spring. Black flies are
notorious for climbing up pant legs and sleeves, so be sure to take measures to
prevent this from happening by closing them off with rubber bands or tape, or
tuck pant legs in the tops of boots. Light cotton gloves can be worn on hands
that also pull over the ends of sleeves. Headnets will protect face and neck.
Repellent can be used as added protection or by hunters who choose not to
wear gloves and headnet. Bosowicz recommends the use of either Muskol or
Ben's 100 as insect repellent while black bear hunting. He said they are
effective at keeping insects at bay, plus are relatively odorless.

Hunters concerned about their scent or that of an insect repellent may
want to use a cover scent. Bosowicz markets a scent called Pro Cover origi-

nally developed for deer hunting that is also widely used for bear hunting. More information can be obtained from Bosowicz himself at R.F.D. #2, Box 103, Dover-Foxcroft, Maine 04426. Skunk perfume is another effective cover scent because skunks are often attracted to bear baits. Black bears are occasionally exposed to essence of skunk at baits, as Jim Haveman once observed firsthand. Jim Jarvis uses anise or anise extract as a cover scent while he and his hunters are watching baits.

I prefer portable tree stands to permanent ones because if one position doesn't work, it's a simple matter to move to another. With time, bears using a bait may learn where hunters are usually stationed in permanent stands, and won't show themselves during shooting hours. A hunter who waits in a new place under these circumstances can sometimes claim the makings for a rug. Tree stands for black bear hunting need not be anymore than 10-to-15 feet above the ground.

One problem with portable climbing stands like Bakers, which I use, is they can make a lot of racket going up and down the tree when hunters come and go. A way to avoid this is to install steps in or on the tree trunk so it is possible to climb in and out of the stand without making unnecessary noise, especially at the end of the day.

There is no question that more black bears are shot at bait sites during afternoon and evening than any other times of day. Those hours are prime feeding times for bruins.

However, another reason most bears are shot then is that's when most hunters are hunting. Morning hunting for black bears over bait is underrated, in my opinion. I've seen bears at baits virtually every hour of the day and have had excellent success during mornings, and midday can be good, too.

Most hunters who don't hunt mornings claim they are concerned about scaring bears off the bait when approaching at that time of day, concerned the animals won't return. Hunters who follow my recommendations in the preceding chapter about whistling or talking as they approach a bait don't have to worry about that regardless of what time of day it is. Bears *will* leave the bait when hearing a hunter approach, but they will return if nothing appears out of order. If a bruin was at your bait when you arrived, it may simply wait until it thinks you're gone then return to check out what's new. If all goes well, you should get a shot.

One morning I dropped a bowhunter off at a bait and left whistling as I always do. The archer later told me that I wasn't even out of earshot when a black bear appeared to investigate what I left behind.

Baits that are routinely replenished during morning hours are most likely to be visited by bears during mornings, and the same with baits checked during afternoons or evenings. Although it can work the other way, too, depending on each particular bear's normal feeding time. To take the best advantage of my hunting time, I always try to hunt three or four hours during the morning, take a break, then return sometime in the afternoon. If the bait has been hit during my absence I make it a point to hunt through midday the following day, providing I don't connect before dark.

If I had a choice, I would much rather shoot a bear during the morning

Bowhunter watches for a bear from portable Baker tree stand overlooking bait. These stands are more versatile than permanent stands.

than evening. The light is generally better, and there's plenty of daylight remaining to track a bear, if necessary, and get the carcass out of the woods. Bait hunters who insist morning hunting is a waste of time can do what they like, but I can't help chuckling to myself when I hear or read words to that effect. I know better.

Whenever I'm going to be occupying a bait stand for a long period I make it a point to carry a plastic bottle with me to urinate in. I refrain from urinating at a bait site either before or during the hunting season. It makes little sense to use scents to attract black bears to a spot then deposit scent that may be offensive to them.

While waiting at a bait for a bear to appear it is best to remain constantly alert. Become familiar with the sights and sounds of your surroundings. A black spot that wasn't there before may be a bear lurking just out of sight. An unusual sound may mean the same thing.

Black bears can be amazingly quiet while moving through thick brush. It isn't unusual to see them before you hear them, if you hear them at all. Their thick pads are like cushions, permitting the animals to walk noiselessly, if they choose to. A sound to listen for that can be a good hint that a bruin is nearby is a snapping twig. As the animals cautiously approach a bait they sometimes step on twigs or branches that won't support their weight, giving away their presence to hunters who know how to interpret such sounds.

Occasionally, a bear will make a noisy approach to a bait, making no attempt at caution, breaking branches and rustling leaves with every step. As a general rule, these are dominant animals and have not had any bad experiences at that bait or any others. Bruins that are cautious and nervous may have been shot at before or are subordinates and want to avoid an unpleasant experience with a hunter or a larger bear that is also using the bait.

If a yearling or average-size bear shows up at a bait and is antsy, it may be because of other, bigger bears in the area. Some subordinate bears grab a mouthful of food and leave right away to avoid a confrontation. Hunters who hope to bag a better-than-average bear should be patient when observing this type of behavior. If hunting during June, a small to average-size bear may be a sow in heat and will soon be followed by a boar.

In situations where sows with cubs are involved, they are generally together during the spring, coming into a bait at the same time. By fall, it isn't unusual for cubs to arrive at a bait before their mother. Jim Haveman had a pair of cubs come to a bait he was watching in the fall, and was convinced they were orphans when their mother finally showed herself a full 15 minutes later.

Keep this in mind when hunting a state or province where cubs are protected. The size of bears can be difficult to judge at times, but if an animal looks small, it's best to be safe rather than sorry, so don't shoot. Sows with cubs are almost universally protected during spring seasons.

Some cubs are mistakenly shot as legal bears every year due to the difficulty in judging the size of some animals in some situations. However, I think there are also some legal bears left in the woods because hunters don't know how to tell the difference between a cub and yearling once bagged. Size alone isn't the only, or always the best, criterion to judge by. Some yearling sows are as small as male cubs.

The easiest way to tell the difference between a cub and yearling is to look at the teeth. If the animal has canine teeth in the front of both jaws, it's a yearling. Cubs have smaller milk teeth in place of canines.

There are other sounds to listen for besides those bears themselves might make that may serve as clues that a bruin is nearby. Bluejays, for instance, have tipped me off about an incoming bear a number of times. A group of jays will make a big fuss when they see a black bear, although they will do the same when observing other predators, too, both the landbound and winged types. Red squirrels will also chatter and scold bears from safe perches in trees.

If a bait has been hit by one or more bears regularly before the season, but you fail to see a bruin after a day or two of hunting, try not to get discouraged. Persistence often pays off when black bear hunting. It may simply require a change in the weather before a bear presents itself for a shot.

If possible, don't hunt when there is a strong wind that is constantly changing directions. The odds of going undetected by a bear under these conditions are slim to none. It is also best to forget hunting during heavy rain because black bears don't generally move then. Days with little or no wind are great for bear hunting over bait. A light rain doesn't hurt either. Times before and after storms or unsettled weather can be terrific for bear hunting over bait.

One year I hunted a hot bait for five days in a row before I finally saw a bear and tagged it. The bait was only hit at night until that fifth day when an animal strolled into view two or three hours before sunset. If you are unwilling to wait for the weather to change or are convinced bears are feeding primarily at night, the use of something really appealing to the animals such as candy or honey, where legal, might lure them into view.

Baits are sometimes abandoned by bears for any number of reasons. A hunter's presence at a bait or hunting pressure in general sometimes causes bruins to change their habits. The sudden availability of a natural food supply also may lure bears away from bait. In the spring, for example, bears may leave baits to feed on grass for about a week, then return to baits. Availability of apples, acorns, or beech nuts may affect baiting during the fall. There's no question that baiting success is better during years with a scarcity of natural food. Bears will generally return to baits they've left after hunting pressure subsides or their taste for natural groceries is satisfied, but it may be a while.

It is normally a good idea to prepare one or two alternate bait sites in case something happens at a preferred location to reduce the chances of success.

Most hunters like bait sites that haven't been hunted before, but previous hunting pressure may not make any difference, especially on baits being visited by a number of black bears. The bait I hunted with Jim Jarvis in Colorado last spring is a prime example. Another bowhunter killed a bear from the bait I hunted the week before I arrived. I nailed one of four or five different bears seen on that bait in two days, and two days after I connected another bear was taken from that bait.

All three animals killed there were boars. Some locations are simply attractive to bears for one reason or another and hold lots of animals at certain times of the year. Bruins that are shot are sometimes replaced by others. In Colorado last spring, a breeding sow may have been responsible for attracting males to that particular bait. Good bait sites usually remain that way year after year, unless too many animals are harvested from the area or something happens to change the habitat. I know of some baits that produce at least six bear kills a year.

Michigan bow-maker and bowhunter Phil Grable probably holds the record for the most black bears shot at a bait in the shortest period of time. He bagged four bruins at the exceptional bait with bow and arrow over a span of

42 minutes. This took place in Ontario about 15 years ago according to Grable, and there was no limit on black bears in the province, or at least where he was hunting, at the time. Grable was testing some new bowhunting equipment on that hunt and took advantage of the liberal limits to give it a good workout and it performed well.

Two of the four bruins Phil shot that evening dropped where hit, and a third only ran a short distance before dropping when still in Phil's sight. The bear that dropped in sight after running a short distance was the first one for the evening and others that came in later smelled the dead bear, but the carcass didn't bother them. The fourth and last bruin for the evening was the only one that made it into nearby cover before going down.

If a black bear is hit at a bait, but not hurt seriously, the animal may return, giving the hunter another chance. I can think of two cases where this has happened. One year Bruce Wood hunted a bait with me on opening day of Michigan's bear season. He was using archery equipment and hit a bear first thing in the morning.

We trailed the animal for a long distance with little blood and eventually lost the trail. The following evening I was hunting the bait by myself when a bear cautiously stuck its head into view by the bait, then moved ahead so I could see its shoulder. I anchored the sow on the spot with a .30-06 and, upon examining the animal, found Bruce's broadhead imbedded in her skull. It was in heavy bone where it didn't do any damage, not penetrating far enough to reach the brain.

Francis McCarthy hit a bear with an arrow that ricocheted along its ribs,

Black bear skull with a broadhead imbedded in it, from Bruce Wood. I shot the animal the next day with a rifle. Bears that aren't seriously injured will sometimes return to a bait. It isn't unusual for a number of hunters to connect from the same stand.

although at the time he thought the arrow penetrated the body cavity. I tried, unsuccessfully, to locate that bear with one of my hounds. Some time later the same animal gave Fran another chance and he made good on it.

When shooting light fades and I'm ready to leave a tree stand for the day I often whistle when climbing down on the chance a bear might be nearby. The whistle prevents the animal from approaching any closer than it already is without alarming it. If using a ground blind, I may simply walk away as quietly as possible. However, if I have reason to suspect a bear is nearby I will whistle as I depart. Arrangements can also be made for one hunter to pick up a partner, whistling as he approaches the bait, then both can leave together without making any bears in the area overly suspicious. The buddy system is especially useful in situations where a bruin appears as a hunter is getting ready to leave and it's too dark to shoot. The bear will leave when the partner approaches without the hunter having to give himself away.

Some seasoned black bears know what's happening at a bait at all times, aware that hunters are stationed there during hours of daylight, regardless of

Baiting can be done by boat or canoe as well as on foot. Gene Ballew and Rich Scott use a canoe to get a bear to a road. Gene bagged it with bow and arrow.

what precautions are taken. These animals may simply approach a bait so close, then wait for darkness and the departure of resident hunters before moving in to feed. One of the biggest black bears I've encountered did this to me.

It was late in the season when I started baiting him. An experienced hunter had seen him earlier and estimated his weight at 600 pounds. The sign he left confirmed that he was big. The animal was eating everything I put out on a daily basis. After several days of consistent action on the bait I decided to try for him, using a Hawken .50 caliber muzzleloader made by Thompson/Center Arms. It was loaded with a 370-grain maxi-ball.

I was sitting on the ground about 20 yards from the bait on the edge of a swamp. It must have been 20 to 30 minutes before shooting light faded when I heard subtle sounds that I was sure was a bear approaching. However, nothing showed by the time shooting time ended, so I had to leave. The hammer on the rifle was cocked, with a cap in my hand ready to put on the nipple when and if the bear appeared.

Before standing to leave I lowered the hammer, which clicked twice. At the sound, the bear, which had been waiting just out of sight, made a bound or two deeper into the swamp, then started pacing back and forth grumbling and growling and breaking branches. In general, making a lot of noise in an effort to intimidate me. That bear was hungry and wanted me out of the way so he could eat. It worked. I left in a hurry with my hackles raised.

That was the closest I came to that bear. After that evening he either waited until full darkness to approach the bait or patiently remained quiet when it came time for me to leave. However, he kept visiting the bait at night. I could have had another crack at that trophy size animal though if I would have organized a hunt with hounds. In fact, that may have been the best way to try for that bruiser in the first place, but the season ended before such a hunt could be arranged.

CHAPTER
11

Bear-Dog Basics

Black bear hunting with hounds is a darn exciting way of trying to fill a tag, whether trophy hunting or after any legal bruin. The excitement is often high during any chase regardless of whether the bear is actually seen. The chase is the major part of the hunt. Some of the most exciting and enjoyable bear hunts with hounds that I've been on have been during training or pursuit seasons when guns or bows are not permitted, just cameras, and the bear's survival to run another day is guaranteed.

Enjoyment of the chase is really heightened when one or more of the dogs on a bear's trail is yours. Friendly rivalry among houndmen based on whose dog is alleged to be putting on the best performance is very much a part of this type of hunting. The hounds and their owners are what makes dogging bears what it is. It takes special hounds with the nose, endurance, courage, brains, and sometimes speed to make good bear dogs. And it also takes special people to raise and run these hounds. I'm pleased to say I've known both special dogs and special people who practice this specialized approach to black bear hunting.

The breeds of hounds generally used to hunt black bears are Plotts, Walkers, blueticks, black and tans, and redbones. Plotts are among the most popular of these bear hunting breeds today, but there are some fine bear dogs representing other breeds, too. Not all of the best bear dogs are purebreds. A couple of the best hounds I've seen in action are owned by Lawrence Edwards and they are part Airedale, although they look like Plotts. Some houndmen also breed pit bull into their dogs.

The best bear dogs generally weigh between 40 and 65 pounds. Hounds in that weight range are generally quick and agile enough to harass a bear at

Plott hounds, like this one belonging to Lawrence Edwards, are one of the most popular
breeds for dogging bears. These hounds often
have a brindle coat, but can be all black.

close quarters and dodge out of the way when necessary, plus they are usually
fast enough to catch a bear in the first place. Hounds heavier than 65 pounds
tend to be slower and have a better chance of getting hurt or killed in a bear
fight. D. DeMoss claims to have killed 2,000 black bears in front of hounds,
most of them in Washington when working for timber companies on damage
control programs, and a couple of his better dogs were females weighing 42
and 43 pounds.

There are exceptions to weight limitations though. A Plott named Tiger
Two and owned by Leo Dollins is an example. The male was a big dog,
weighing 80 to 85 pounds, and he delighted in chasing big bears, according to

Leo. It was a big bear that eventually killed Tiger Two when he was seven years old.

A perfect bear dog would have a nose good enough to smell scent that is at least ten hours old and have the ability to follow an old trail until the bear is jumped, then tree the animal and keep him treed until hunters arrive, even if it takes them hours to get there.

Such a dog would also have a steady, loud mouth, enabling hunters to locate the tree. There are some hounds used for bear hunting that have these abilities, but they aren't encountered everyday, by any means. Although one dog can tree a black bear, and it has been done many times, it usually takes teamwork on the part of a number of dogs to see a bear chase to a successful conclusion.

Anywhere from three to six dogs are good dog pack sizes for chasing black bears. In situations where more than three hounds are used, one to several members of the pack are often young dogs in the process of learning from their more experienced packmates. It is possible to use too many dogs on a chase, sometimes resulting in confusion and a hunt that ends sooner than it should, while the bear remains safe and sound. In cases where large packs of dogs bay a bear on the ground and there's a fight, a hound or two may be hurt unnecessarily because their packmates got in their way when trying to dodge out of the bear's way. States such as Michigan and Wisconsin have laws limiting bear dog pack size to six, with no relaying of dogs permitted.

A treed bear is the desired outcome of most dog races, but this certainly does not always happen by any means. Some bears simply refuse to climb, and in other cases the dogs don't have what it takes to force a bear up a tree. It generally takes pressure to make bears climb, which translates into constant barking on a bruin's heels or in its face and/or biting the bear's flanks whenever possible.

The combination of hunters and hounds is sometimes what it takes to put a bear up. A bruin that encounters people ahead of it with dogs close behind may tree. Lawrence Edwards has helped his dogs tree bears a number of times in a different manner in an effort to help clients he was guiding bag a bear. He said the technique he uses works 60 to 70 percent of the time.

Edwards employs this unique approach on animals his dogs have at bay, usually after the client has tired and can't keep up with the chase. When the guide catches the hounds and bear he charges at the bruin while hollering and firing a handgun in the air. That's more than most bears can take. As a result, they run as hard as they can, tire quickly, then climb a tree.

Unless pressured in this fashion some bears, especially bigger-than-average animals, travel at a leisurely pace ahead of hounds, stopping occasionally to face the dogs, and never tire. Lawrence said he has helped tree eight to 10 bears by pulling this trick. One of those bears was the heaviest any of his clients have tagged, weighing 540 pounds.

"That bear let me come from here to the tent [about 15 to 20 feet]," Edwards said. "All the time he was looking over his shoulder right at me. It looked like he was never gonna break. Then he just mowed a path out of there."

Black and tans like these are also good bear dogs.

The big bear went out of sight over a ridge and climbed an "enormous white pine" tree not far on the other side.

It takes an exceptional pack of dogs, and hunters to match, to consistently tree black bears. By consistently I don't mean on every race. Houndmen who average a bear for every three chases, whether treed or shot on the ground, are doing terrific. A lot of training and conditioning are required to produce a topnotch pack of hounds.

That's where pursuit or training seasons come in. The more practice dogs

Most bear hounds are transported in pickup trucks in dog boxes like the one in the bed of this truck. A lot of ventilation is important for use in hot weather.

get chasing bears before hunting season opens, the better condition they will be in once it's time to hunt seriously, and the better they will be able to perform. The same applies to hunters. Short of actual field experience, hounds can be conditioned for bear hunting by "roading them," which involves letting them run ahead of or behind a vehicle for exercise until they tire. In many cases it is best to get dogs accustomed to running both in front of and behind hunting vehicles on woods roads that don't have much traffic.

The reason for this is that in a hunting situation a good way to start a chase is to let an experienced and trustworthy dog go ahead of vehicles to locate where a bear crossed. When roading dogs in front of a vehicle let them go at their own pace. Hunters can set a faster pace when roading dogs behind a vehicle.

There are opportunities to condition bear dogs in other ways, too. I've heard about one houndman who hooks his dogs up to a merry-go-round type arrangement in his backyard for exercise. The hounds run in circles for hours at a time, toughening pads plus building muscles and endurance.

When it comes to training pups to hunt black bears, the best approach is to turn them loose with seasoned veterans. Experienced hounds make good teachers. It is important for pups to get as much exposure to other dogs as possible, so they will become accustomed to hunting with them as a team. Males that have a tendency to fight with other dogs at any time detract from a pack's effectiveness and can ruin a hunt. Fortunately, most hounds are easy-going.

D. DeMoss with customized bear hunting rig. A rig dog is in front, with hood removed, and dogs in back have holes in the top of compartments so they can stick their heads out to get fresh air.

In situations where a dog shows fighting tendencies, efforts should be made to discourage this behavior. One option is to expose the hound to others while on a long rope so a fight can be ended quickly and the dog disciplined, should a fight start. A shocking collar can also be used to discourage fighting.

You should also discourage dogs from chasing or showing interest in nontarget animals such as deer and porcupines. Shocking collars are widely used for breaking hounds on deer.

Pups that are taught the meaning of the word "no" can be discouraged from chasing species such as deer by repeated use of the word when exposing them to deer scent.

Bear dogs are often wrongfully accused of chasing deer when whitetails are seen running out of an area where hounds are driving. In most cases, deer are simply disturbed by the barking of dogs on a bear's trail and leave the area as the sound draws close to them. A bruin may cross a road a long distance ahead of hounds and when deer cross in the same area just ahead of dogs it is easy to get the wrong impression. Hounds that prefer chasing deer to a bear are of no value to bear hunters and are quickly removed from a pack.

Many a bear dog has gotten its start on raccoons. Raccoons are good for training pups because they tree readily and don't travel as far as most bears will. The best time to train pups on raccoons is when there is snow on the ground, either during early fall or spring when raccoons are active. Under

Radio collars are being used on bear dogs with increased frequency to protect the hounds from becoming lost for days. Hounds that may be killed by a bear can also be recovered with the aid of these devices, so hunters don't continue looking for animals for days without knowing what happened. This was never possible before. Some of the better hounds are extremely valuable and it makes sense to protect the investment.

these conditions the dog handler can see tracks and encourage the hound to follow the right course in addition to helping the dog get back on the right track if it wanders off the trail.

Once a 'coon is treed, the dog should be praised and encouraged to bark as long as possible. It helps to bring a treat to give the hound at that point. A way to train dogs to tree for greater lengths of time after they learn to trail on their own is to delay arrival at the tree. Stop when still out of sight and hearing of the dog and wait five or 10 minutes before going to the hound to praise it and perhaps give it a reward. The time it takes to reach a tree can be gradually lengthened until you are confident that a hound will stay treed for an hour or more, and it can take that long in a hunting situation for hunters to arrive. Exercises of this type also build the dog's confidence in its master, knowing the master will eventually show up with a reward.

A technique for getting pups interested in following bear scent is to leave a scent trail by dragging a piece of bear hide or a head. Be sure to make several turns rather than going in a straight line, so the dog will learn to check for changes in direction, which bears in the wild do constantly. Make sure the hound is out of sight when leaving the scent trail and hide the item at the end of the trail. Start the dog at the beginning of the trail and encourage it to follow, then reward the dog if successful in the trailing effort. Try to avoid leaving the scent trail in the same manner and the same place every time. Otherwise a dog may simply run to the location where it expects the head or hide to be hidden.

Most hunters don't have the space, time or money to train and keep large packs of bear dogs. However, if each member of a group of hunters who routinely hunt together houses one to several hounds, there should be enough dogs to hunt with, plus some reserves.

Hunters who haven't tried dogging bears, but would like to get involved, should try to arrange to go along on a hunt with someone in their area. Joining one of the bear hunter organizations listed in the back of this book would be a good first step toward getting to know dog hunters, if not already acquainted with some. Most groups of recreational hunters are willing to show a newcomer the ropes, and some guides may be willing to take a novice along in exchange for assistance while handling clients. If you don't live in bear country where hunting with hounds is permitted, you may want to hire a guide to introduce you to this fascinating and sometimes frustrating bear hunting technique.

I was fortunate enough to be able to tag along with a group of dog hunters in the Munising area of Michigan's Upper Peninsula to get my feet wet in the pursuit of black bears with hounds. And I did, indeed, get my feet wet, both literally and figuratively, as well as a camera, on my introductory hunt when wading across a river to follow the dogs. Hunts with Dan Flynn and crew were usually weekend family affairs with children and wives often going along, which is not an unusual situation among dog hunting groups. This fact reflects the universal appeal and satisfaction provided by participating in this form of bear hunting. Dogs aren't the only members of the chase that work as a team. The dog handlers and other members of the party do, too. It's one big team effort.

If a bear is solidly treed, word goes out to everyone on the hunt, and no action is taken until everyone arrives at the tree who wants to be there. As a general rule, the first hunter to the tree can claim the bear. However, on social hunts of the type I participated in at Munising, group members who had never bagged a black bear were designated as shooters.

It isn't unusual for some houndmen to lead their dogs away from a treed bear to let the animal run another day. In situations where the bear is taken, the kill is generally earned. Even though only one tag is filled in such a situation, each member of the party usually feels a measure of success no matter what role they played. This is one way that bear hunting with hounds differs from most other techniques.

A bear bagged over bait, for instance, usually gives the greatest sense of

Transmitters in collars give off a signal that can be picked up
by an antenna and receiving unit carried by hunters.

accomplishment to one hunter, the person who tagged it, although one or two others who helped in the endeavor may share in the warm feelings that go with success. The bruin bagged in front of hounds may be reason for celebration for as many as 10 hunters or more, which spreads the recreational benefits provided by a bear, no matter how intangible, a lot further.

There are plenty of ways to transport hounds on a hunt. Pickup trucks probably transport more bear dogs than any other type of vehicle. On rigs with caps, dogs may simply be left loose in the back. More often though, hounds are chained or tied in pickup beds to prevent fighting and possibly keep dogs out of gear. One method I've seen used is extending chains across the width of the bed that have short pieces of chains with clips extending from them, far enough apart to allow for spacing of dogs. Hounds in open pickup beds must be secured on short ropes or chains to prevent them from jumping out and hanging themselves.

Dog boxes of various sizes and shapes with any number of compartments are often fashioned to fit in pickup beds on the backs of hunting vehicles. Most of these are homemade to suit the owner's fancy. I've even seen them constructed for use in the backs of hatchback economy cars. Regardless of the design of dog boxes it is critical that they have plenty of ventilation if they will be used during hot weather, to protect hounds from suffocating. If improperly ventilated to let heat escape and the flow of fresh air, the temperature inside boxes can reach intolerable levels when dogs are placed inside after a hard run on a hot day. I know of a number of bear dogs that have died needlessly in boxes. Pickup campers can be a problem, too. Dogs should be checked regularly when in boxes during hot weather and then removed and chained outside as soon as possible when overheating develops.

D. DeMoss uses a specialized rig for hunting with hounds consisting of a modified Volkswagen with a Pinto engine that has a fiberglass shell on the back for carrying dogs. The shell is divided into compartments, with holes in the top of each just big enough for hounds to stick their heads through.

Heavy, wide collars of leather or other sturdy materials, with metal name plates attached, are used on most bear dogs for a number of reasons. The collars protect hounds from serious neck injuries if they tangle with a bear. More than one bear dog's life has been saved by its collar. Name plates identify the dog's owner along with his telephone number and address, should hounds become lost, which isn't unusual. Some collars are bright orange in color and/or have light reflecting tape on them to increase a hound's visibility during day and night, decreasing the chances they will be mistakenly shot in the woods or hit by a car on a road.

"We really appreciate it when someone picks up one of our dogs for us," Dan Flynn said. "It saves us a lot of time and effort looking. Even if they don't want to take a dog into their car, if they just tell us where they saw the dog it's a big help. We're usually driving roads looking for lost dogs near where a chase ended and they are expected to come out."

Radio tracking collars are being used by houndmen on their most valuable bear dogs in addition to their regular collars during recent years, in an effort to reduce the chances of losing dogs and relocating them when they become lost. The collars give off radio signals picked up as beeps by a receiving unit hunters switch on when hounds are lost. Receivers are attached to antennas that pick up collar signals. These collars are very similar to those used by wildlife biologists to monitor the movements of black bears and other wildlife.

Although some people are critical of the use of radio-collared dogs to hunt black bears because they feel they give hunters an unfair advantage, these arguments have no more validity than criticisms of CB radios and four wheel drive vehicles, in my opinion. A discussion on these pieces of equipment is included in the next chapter. It only makes sense for houndmen to use tracking collars to protect their investments. Bear dogs can be expensive to keep and hunt, with some hounds valued at thousands of dollars. Even if a dog is killed, radio collars enable owners to locate the carcass rather than anguishing over the hounds whereabouts and spending days on end searching for the animal in vain. Individuals who don't know much about this form of hunting and seldom take the effort to learn, are often responsible for unnecessary criticism of helpful hunting aids as well as hunting methods.

At least one Michigan hunter who had tracking collars on his hounds was able to locate one of them that was shot and killed intentionally. The collar also enabled him to determine who was responsible for the dog's death and, through court action, he was able to recover damages for the lost dog in the amount of $2,000. In most areas where dogging bears is permitted, it is illegal to shoot hunting dogs, which only makes sense.

CHAPTER
12

Hunting with Hounds

The first order of business for the day on any black bear hunt with hounds is to find the freshest scent trail possible left by a bruin since the previous day. In most cases, hound hunters try to locate spoor from the biggest bear possible, although it is sometimes difficult to control the size bear that is run.

When starting from a bait, for example, it can be difficult to determine what size bear was there most recently, unless a track can be located or it is known that a big boy is frequenting the area. Hunters who hope to start a chase from baits should check them for activity the evening before the hunt. Then it should be easy to tell if a bear has been there when checked again the following morning. One to three experienced dogs are normally led to a bait that has been hit and released to sort out the scent and start the chase. If the bear scent is fresh enough and the veterans start away on it, additional dogs are often released to join them for support. Support dogs learn to go to the barking of packmates.

There is usually even less opportunity to be selective about the size bear that is run when starting a chase by roading a dog in front of vehicles. The hound will follow the first bear scent encountered that is fresh enough. Hunters should take note of where the dog left the road to look for bear tracks upon reaching that point, as confirmation the dog is going in the right direction. The scent is often just as strong on both sides of a road a bear crosses and hounds sometimes start in the wrong direction, although smart dogs usually soon realize their mistake and return to the road to head off the right way. Confirming a track's direction prevents releasing support dogs to follow a trail backwards.

To save wear and tear on strike dogs, they are often positioned in the open

121

This hound is being roaded ahead of hunters in vehicles in an effort to get a bear chase started. The hound will follow the scent of a bear that may have crossed the road, and other dogs will be released to follow once the trail is straightened out.

bed of a pickup or on the front or top of one, to smell for bear scent as the vehicle is driven slowly along woods roads. When the dog or dogs smell bear they bark. This method of starting a hunt enables houndmen to be selective about the bear they chase. Once a dog strikes, bear tracks can usually be located where the animal crossed the road and a rough idea of its size determined. We generally used this method with good success when I hunted with Lawrence Edwards and his hounds in Ontario, normally passing by sows with cubs plus yearlings, and turning loose on mature bruins.

D. DeMoss and a Plott named "Lucky" jointly developed the use of "rig dogs," which is what hounds that strike from a vehicle are called, by accident years ago in Washington. After roading Lucky until he tired, DeMoss would put the dog in the back of his pickup untied. When the dog smelled a bear he would jump out and start a chase, sometimes without his master realizing it until later. DeMoss then started tying Lucky in the truck bed to prevent this from happening and the hound responded by barking when he scented bear. That's how the use of rig dogs developed.

Dune buggies like this are used by some dog hunters to save on gas. A rig dog rests in a box up front to smell for bear scent.

One more method of locating a bear to run with hounds depends on the hunters' eyes. A party of houndmen may split up into small groups and each group is assigned a sandy road to drive slowly while looking for bear tracks. Spotters may ride on the hoods of vehicles for better visibility. As economical measures to save gas, some houndmen use motorcycles, three wheelers or dune buggies to look for bear tracks. Once a good track is located and the place where tracks leave the road is identified, a strike dog is started on the trail at that point, then support is added if the track proves runnable.

Bear hunting parties who rely on visual location of tracks to run rather than strike dogs, often "drag" roads in the evening that will be searched for prints the following morning. This is usually accomplished by pulling a treetop, log, old bedspring, or something similar behind a vehicle, sweeping the road of old tracks and making new ones easier to see. This practice has gotten out of hand in some cases, resulting in damage to some U.S. Forest Service roads, and could be outlawed if abuses continue.

Occasionally, a bear will actually be seen crossing a road while hunters are looking for tracks or trying to strike bear scent, which ensures a hot chase. In situations where there is an opportunity to shoot a bruin on the spot, hound hunters normally pass up the shot in preference to running the animal with the dogs. This happened on a hunt sponsored by the Michigan Bear Hunters Association a number of years ago.

Members of the party searched for a bear track fresh enough to run all morning and into the afternoon without luck. Finally, two hunters with the

Hounds and bear cross railroad tracks during a race.

group saw a bear in a two-track woods road. The pair watched the animal amble down the road for some distance, during which time there was ample opportunity to take a shot at the bruin, until it finally disappeared into heavy cover.

The two assembled party members as quickly as possible and the hunt was on. The dogs chased that bear until dark without anyone getting another glimpse of the quarry. However, there was a lot of excitement and anticipation involved in that chase, especially when several members got close to bear and dogs a couple of times as the bear temporarily stopped to fight. That experience, which everyone relished after long hours with little activity, would have been missed had the party members killed the bear when they initially saw it. This is but one example of how the chase is more important than the kill when bear hunting with hounds.

It is also worth noting that this form of black bear hunting is not all adrenalin-pumping action and excitement. There are a lot of boring and frustrating hours spent trying to get a chase going and looking for lost dogs. On some days no chase develops at all, with the entire time spent looking for tracks, to no avail. Then the next day, hunters may have their choice of running four or five bears in the same area. Bears simply don't move or are relatively inactive on some days, and on others they're everywhere.

Although most dog hunters start their search for a fresh track early in the morning, the animals or their spoor can be encountered at any time of day. However, it's generally not a good idea to start a race too late in the day due to loss of shooting light and the chances of losing dogs. While hunting with hounds in Ontario during the spring we've frequently struck hot scent during the middle of the day. It is practically impossible to hunt with hounds on days when heavy rain is falling because scent is washed out as fast as it's laid down. Bruins will often be active after the rain stops though. Windy days are bad, too, because the dogs can't be heard for any distance.

Once a chase gets underway, one to several members of the party often attempt to follow the dogs on foot, while others try to anticipate the bear's course of travel and intercept it ahead of the dogs as it crosses a road or simply try to keep the chase in hearing to be in position to go into the action if a bear bays on the ground or trees. At least one hunter usually stays where the chase started on the chance the race circles back in that direction or it abruptly ends for one reason or another and the dogs return to the starting point. Once the hounds fade out of hearing, hunters in the rear usually move ahead.

Hunters who attempt to follow a bear chase on foot must be in good physical condition, better than many people realize, because black bears often lead hounds for miles cross-country through some of the thickest, most rugged terrain in North America. Even hunters in the best of shape are sometimes left behind as the baying of fast-moving hounds moves out of hearing in minutes. In the event that happens, the best course of action is to take a compass reading on the direction the dogs were last heard and continue on that heading. Carrying a compass is a must when following bear dogs and having a map of the area is a good idea, too. In mountainous country, the position of baying hounds can sometimes be relocated from a high point in the direction they were last heard. If contact with the hounds isn't regained by the time a road is reached, hunters usually wait to be picked up by another member of the party.

Hunters on foot normally carry walkie talkies with them and can radio for a ride once on a road. Chances are someone else in the group has contact with the chase, and runners can get back in the hunt once picked up. In situations where runners manage to stay within hearing of the action, they use radios to keep other party members appraised of how the chase is progressing. Runners routinely carry a leash or two with them, wearing them over a shoulder, for later use if dogs have to be led out of the woods.

The use of 4x4 vehicles enables hunters to take part in such a hunt that they otherwise wouldn't be able to due to physical limitations. Some men, women and children fit in this category. Even physically fit hunters would be

Fresh hounds are sometimes released to join the chase
where a bear crosses a road, provided there are fewer
hounds in use than legal.

totally left out of some hunts without the use of vehicles due to the distances
traveled in short order by bear and dogs, which would increase the difficulty of
recovering dogs.

The biggest benefit CB radios provide is they save on gas consumption,
enabling party members to communicate with one another. At least one
participant usually always knows where the dogs are and passes the word
along to others. Otherwise, hunters out of touch with what is happening would
be forced to expend the time, effort and fuel to locate others in the group to find
out what was going on. On some hunts without radios, hunters could conceiv-
ably spend more time chasing after each other than bears.

Communication between hunt participants by radio is especially important when it comes to preventing those on foot from getting lost or perhaps
locating and helping someone who gets stuck or injured. It's easy to lose track

of your position when on foot, but a call on a walkie talkie can result in assistance in the form of honking horns or shots to direct hunters to the nearest road.

I recall one hound hunt on which a group of people could have been spared a sleepless night and a lot of worry when three hunters headed toward a treed bear without a radio. The trio became lost and ended up spending the night on a dry hummock in a large swamp. If they would have taken a radio with them they could have either been directed out to a road, or, at the very least, notified other participants on the hunt that they were alright and would find their way out at daylight. As it was, those who searched or waited for the missing threesome feared the worst.

Hunter moves in on a bayed black bear. A bluetick hound is in the foreground. Hunters should move in quietly and against the wind to avoid spooking the bear. Hunters must also wait for an opening to shoot when hounds aren't in the way. (*Photo by Michigan Department of Natural Resources*)

Radios and 4x4s don't help houndmen kill many, if any, more black bears than they otherwise would. Good dogs and experienced hunters are the key ingredients it takes to tag any bruins, much less numbers of them, when employing this hunting method. A fact worth noting is that in most states and provinces where bear hunting with hounds is permitted, houndmen using radios and four wheel drive vehicles don't harvest enough animals to adversely affect black bear populations, provided hunting is done legally. Many experienced houndmen estimate that it takes five to 10 chases to bag a bear. Some groups do better than this, but they are the exception rather than the rule.

There are probably as many black bears killed on the ground ahead of hounds, either as they cross a road or when bayed, and perhaps more, than those that are treed. It depends on who you hunt with though. Leo Dollins, for instance, is a houndman who feels if his dogs can't bay or tree a bear, it deserves to live. For years he did not allow hunters with him to shoot bears on the ground unless bayed, and some bears got away because of that personal conviction. However, Leo told me recently he is considering relaxing that restriction due to changes in his dogpack.

Black bears have favorite crossings on roads when pursued by hounds. These are perfect places to post to intercept bears, for hunters familiar with them. When hunting unfamiliar country, progress of the chase will generally dictate where to post. Bruins often cross roads in low areas where there's water or heavy cover, but they will travel through upland habitat, too.

Blackie may be a long distance ahead of dogs, so posted hunters should be

Treed black bears like this one don't always stay put; they sometimes bail out when hunters arrive. It is possible to miss treed bears, too.

constantly alert when hounds are headed their way. Hunters hoping to intercept a bear should wait on the edge of woods on either side of a road so shots
can be directed into the cover either as a bear enters a road or leaves it.
Out-of-place noises can turn a bear intent on crossing a road, so standers
should remain as quiet as possible during their vigil.

Standers who hear hounds coming their way are often treated to excitement and suspense not knowing where, when or if a bear will appear. These
sensations become more intense as the baying of dogs comes closer and closer.
In situations where a walking or fighting bear is involved, the animal may
appear just ahead of the dogs or at the same time as hounds, and in some cases
a dog or two may reach a road or railroad grade before the bear does, so
hunters in this position shouldn't be overanxious to shoot, being sure of their
target. If bear and dogs are together, a shot might not be possible if there is a
chance of hitting a hound. Bears that do approach a road to cross can sometimes be heard coming, giving hunters a brief time to get ready to shoot.

In situations where a bear gets across a road unscathed and there isn't
already a full complement of dogs on the chase, it can be a good opportunity to
release one or more fresh hounds. The added pressure from new blood may
increase the chances a bruin will make a fatal mistake. If the bear doesn't tree,
it could stop to fight, or take refuge on the ground, with hounds baying
excitedly while facing their adversary.

Moving in on a bayed bear is a one-of-a-kind experience charged with
excitement. Locations bruins pick to stop and face their pursuers are usually
in extremely thick cover where visibility may be limited to a matter of feet. The
trick is to maneuver into position for a shot without being detected. For this
reason, a cautious approach is generally called for that is as quiet as possible
and downwind from the action. Bears that hear or smell incoming hunters
sometimes leave the scene, although they may not go far before baying again.

Hunters who get close enough to see a ground fight will generally be
treated to a spectacle they won't soon forget. The bear will probably be in a
mean disposition with ears laid back, hackles raised and jaws working,
clicking teeth together. Bruins are normally backed against something to
protect their rear and may lunge toward dogs that get too close.

Once a bear is in sight, the trick is to take a shot that will miss dogs and
kill the bruin instantly. Head shots are best for this purpose. Since most
shooting in these situations is at very close range, many houndmen prefer
houndguns, big caliber handguns, for their maneuverability. There is potential danger to hunters under these circumstances as well as to dogs, so they
should have their wits about them, shooting fast and straight when an
opening develops. In some cases it may be necessary to administer the coup de
grace at point-blank range.

The closest call DeMoss had with a bear in his many years of hunting
them was one that was bayed. It was under a vine maple and he said he
thought the animal was a yearling, so he wasn't as careful as he should have
been. He moved in for a closer look and the bruin came at him. DeMoss had
time for one quick shot from his .45/70, which clipped the bear's neck, before
the animal hit him, knocking him down and stunning him.

When the houndman came to, the bruin was standing on his legs and about to bite him in the stomach when one of his dogs—Lucky—intervened, pulling the bear off him. Before DeMoss could shoot the black again, it died from blood loss. His bullet ruptured the jugular vein. He was fortunate enough to walk away from there with only puncture wounds in a leg and a scratched forehead from the bear's initial blow to his head with a paw. That bear weighed 200-plus pounds.

Leo Dollins received a couple of scratches on a hand one time when he got too close to a big bear his hounds were fighting. In another close quarters affair a bear grabbed the barrel of Leo's .444 rifle, leaving marks from its teeth in the metal before he freed the rifle and shoved the bore against the animal to kill it.

Houndmen are sometimes more concerned about their hounds than themselves in a bear fight, and rightly so, because the dogs usually stand a better chance of getting hurt than hunters. If a hunter should get in trouble, dogs are usually quick to distract a bear, as DeMoss' experience illustrates.

Injury and death to hounds by black bears is one of the drawbacks or least appealing aspects of this type of hunting. Good dogs that are fast and smart may hunt for years without a scratch, but it's generally only a matter of time before they make a mistake or slow down as they grow older, that Blackie takes his toll. Fortunately, there's only a small percentage of bruins that choose to fight the dogs rather than run ahead of them. However, those few can be real hard on hounds, and it isn't just big boars that become defiant. Many a sow in the 125 to 150-pound class has left her mark on bear dog packs across North America.

Treed bears don't always stay treed and shooting a bruin out of a tree may not be as easy as you think. The bear sometimes climbs a tree, then reconsiders its options and bails out. The animals sometimes do this on their own or when detecting an incoming hunter. For this reason, it is usually a good idea for hunters to approach treed bears the same way they would animals bayed on the ground, unless it's obvious the bear is way up a tree and isn't likely to come down.

I got an unexpected surprise when the first black bear jumped out of a tree on me. The chase had been going for about four hours when I got close enough to get my dog, a black and tan named Drew, in on the action. Not long after Drew joined the chase, the bear treed, and since I was close, I headed toward the excited hounds, only carrying cameras and a walkie talkie. As soon as I arrived at the base of the tree and the bear saw me, it started the descent.

My voice joined that of the dogs and I beat on the tree in an effort to make the bruin change its mind. However, it kept coming, staring down at me with a blank expression as it slid toward the ground. I started backing away from the tree when the bear got close. After taking a few steps backward I tripped and fell flat on my back. My eyes were glued on the bear rather than watching where my feet were going.

The bear leaped from the tree away from me, and as soon as it hit the ground, the dogs were all over it. From a sitting position I tried to get my cameras into play, but before I got the straps untangled, bear and hounds faded into the swamp. About an hour later the dogs bayed the bear on the ground and a couple of other members of the party carrying .44 magnum handguns dispatched the bruin. It was a boar with a dressed weight of 175 pounds.

Every effort is made to kill treed bears that stay treed, as quickly and cleanly as possible, unless a decision is made to spare the animal. Head shots are generally the rule when shots are taken, unless a trophy bear is involved or the bear's position prohibits it. All dogs are customarily tied to trees in the vicinity, away from where a treed bear is expected to fall, before any shots are fired to protect them from injury if a bruin isn't dead when it hits the ground. Hounds have been killed when bears fell on them under a tree, too. Backup shooters are usually designated to finish bears when they hit the ground, if they're not dead.

It is possible to miss or wound a treed bear. Lawrence Edwards had a serious problem with the marksmanship and behavior of a trio of hunters he once guided. Two of his best dogs were seriously injured and another badly shaken as a result. On the first day of hunting, the dogs treed a bear and a pair of the hunters reached the tree before Edwards and the third hunter.

Without taking the time to catch and tie the dogs away from the tree, one of the two men at the tree took a shot at the bear and missed. The pair stood and watched as the bruin started down the tree toward the screaming pack of hounds. Lawrence arrived before the bear hit the ground and hollered at them to kill the animal. Another shot rang out and the black bear dropped among the dogs, very much alive.

The bear grabbed Buck, one of Lawrence's best Plott hounds, and knocked him around. Then the bear broke the jaw of Bob, a key dog that was in his prime at the time. Edwards had to wade in among dogs and bear to kill the animal before it did any more damage. Buck was scared, but not hurt. Bob's jaw healed after being wired together.

The next bear that treed on that hunt was only 10 feet up. The sow popped her teeth at the dogs as she glared down at them. Lawrence figured she would jump out if she heard or saw him and his hunter. He got one of the trio to within 30 yards for a shot—another miss. The sow dropped out of the tree onto the dogs. Buck was there again and she grabbed him.

Lawrence killed the bear at point-blank range after she released Buck. Fortunately for the hound, he escaped injury again.

Two days later a similar situation occurred. This sow was only eight feet up in a birch tree, ready to make a quick getaway. The third hunter was about to take a shot offhand when Lawrence insisted he rest his rifle against a handy jack pine tree. His shot still only wounded the sow.

Guess which dog that bear got her paws on first? Buck again. Then the sow turned her attention to a female hound and relocated half of her face. The guide had to kill that bear, too, to protect his hounds from further damage.

Once again, Buck escaped injury, but those three thrashings didn't do him any good. Buck would have been an "outstanding" bear dog, in his owner's estimation, if it weren't for those experiences. The hound is still better than most.

Hunters going into a tree or ground fight should always take a gun with them, even if they know someone else is carrying one. I violated that rule the time that bear jumped out of the tree on me, and that animal may have gotten away as a result. That alone wouldn't have been a major loss, but either the dogs or myself could have gotten into trouble, as happened in a couple of other cases.

One time Leo Dollins' dogs treed a small bear near a road in Canada. Not wanting to shoot the animal, he walked in without a gun to retrieve his hounds. The bear unexpectedly dropped out of the tree among the dogs and grabbed one of them by the neck. Leo beat on the bruin's head with a club in an effort to get it to release its grip, and it eventually did, running between Leo's legs.

As the bear was going between the hunter's legs, a dog grabbed the animal by the rear. At the moment, Leo was concerned that his leg was really going to get chewed up. However, after the episode was over, he only had bite marks on a leg and lost part of a pant leg. The whole incident could have been stopped short had Leo brought a gun with him.

On another Lawrence Edwards hunt, a hunter and hound were injured because the party of four or five hunters only brought one rifle to a tree. The bear was about 12 feet off the ground when the first shot was taken with a .30-30, grazing the animal's neck, and it moved out of the shooter's view to the opposite side of the tree. The hunter with the rifle was in a depression at the base of a tree and remained there when handing his rifle to another party member to shoot the bear again.

At the shot, the bear dropped in the depression with the original shooter and the dogs. The bruin was still alive, so the rifle was passed back to its owner and he put the rifle up to the bear's ribs, firing the third and last round in the rifle. That shot didn't phase the bear, which weighed an estimated 260 to 280 pounds, so, when realizing the rifle was empty, the hunter threw it to Lawrence for reloading. The guy thought Lawrence also had a .30-30 with him on that hunt, which he usually carries, and would have shells of that caliber in his pockets.

However, Edwards had a different caliber rifle with him. At the same time the gun owner threw his rifle, he tried to climb out of the bowl to get away from the bear, but the bruin grabbed his leg. Then Lawrence informed his partner in a none-too-casual tone that he didn't have any bullets and the guy desperately dug one out of his pocket and threw it to Edwards. Lawrence put that slug in the bear's head after getting it in the rifle, ending the episode. Fortunately, the hunter was not seriously hurt.

When following hounds or going to a treed bear, it's a good idea to carry plenty of shells to go with a gun, too. The firearms become excess baggage without enough ammunition. Lawrence only carried three .30-30 shells with him on one chase to backup a hunter he was guiding. However, the hunter eventually tired and insisted on remaining where he was while Lawrence

Not all treed bears are shot. When they are, every effort is made
for a clean kill.

continued after the dogs. The hounds treed the bear once, but the bruin jumped
out before they arrived.

Lawrence finally reached a point where he was sure he last heard the dogs
barking, but all was quiet. So he hollered and fired a shot in the air in an effort
to get a response from the dogs. They did have the bear treed nearby and had
quit barking because they were tired. The shot got them going again and
Lawrence went to the tree, but he only had two shells left at that point. He took
careful aim at the 300 pound male in an effort to break its neck, but missed the
backbone. With one bullet remaining the guide went for the head and connected. If that bullet hadn't done the job, Lawrence would have really been in
a predicament.

Most black bears bagged on dog hunts are taken with guns, but some have been brought down with bows and arrows, and there's potential for more bowhunters to fill bear tags in this way. The major drawback to bowhunting black bears with dogs is that archers are basically restricted to shooting at treed bears.

Bow shots at treed bears are not always easy, due to the steep angles sometimes involved, so archers interested in connecting in this fashion should practice accordingly. I was on a hunt during which Randy Hamilton bow-bagged a treed bruin in Ontario. Although the shot was not an easy one in my estimation, Randy made a good hit, thanks to hours of preparation for that shot. And Tom Nelson took a trophy bear with a bow ahead of a pack of Walkers with guide Dave Powers in Idaho during a recent spring hunt.

The type of clothing worn on hound hunts isn't a major consideration, as long as it conforms with the law, plus is warm and comfortable. Try to avoid wearing noisy fabrics though. Runners generally dress lighter than standers to avoid overheating, although a sweatshirt or coat can come in handy after a chase is over, during cool weather.

Boots are a more important consideration for those who follow hounds. The best boots for this type of hunting are combat styles with leather bottoms and canvas tops available at military surplus stores. These boots have holes on the insoles that are great for draining water after wading creeks and rivers or crossing bogs and marshes.

Boots made by L. L. Bean that are little higher than ankle level are also good for dog hunts because they are lightweight and have rubber bottoms with leather tops. Waterproofed leather boots are another option, but don't wear all-rubber boots if possible. That's what I wore on my first bear hunt with hounds and they filled with water, doubling the weight I was carrying on my feet. Although tennis shoes can be worn, they don't offer any ankle support or protection, so aren't the best choice.

In the event dogs are lost, they usually filter out to roads after they tire and quit the chase. If not picked up, they may stop at the first house they encounter. Some hounds routinely return to the point where the chase started when they are done hunting. For this reason, at least one hunter usually remains at the starting point to wait for dogs while others drive roads to look for missing hounds. If all canines aren't accounted for by the end of the day, a coat or blanket with familiar scent is sometimes left at the starting point for homing dogs to lay on until picked up. These items are left inside the woods where they won't be visible to passing motorists or other hunters.

Fresh dog tracks going down a gravel or sandy road are a sure sign that hounds are out of the woods. Animals can usually be located by following the tracks. Hounds that are extremely tired when they quit may rest before venturing out to a road and may not turn up for two days or more. The use of tracking collars enables hunters to locate these dogs quickly and easily.

There are more ways for black bears to escape hunters and hounds than there is for them to be caught. In many cases, bears are simply too tough for the hounds and will stay ahead of them all day until the dogs tire. Other times, bears might lead hounds into areas where hunters can't follow or aren't able to get into soon enough, and even if a bear trees, hounds eventually leave the tree before hunters arrive.

These hunts are team efforts, not only among members of a dogpack, but between hunters and hounds, too. Dogs and hunters work together to occasionally accomplish something that neither could normally do alone. If one segment of the team either doesn't or isn't able to come through on their end of the hunt, the bear benefits. When this often happens it is beyond the control of hunters or hounds, having simply been beaten by the bear that has control of the situation.

Black bears have plenty of tricks to throw hounds off their trail. They may swim across a river, pond, or lake or walk down a creek, using water to erase their scent. This sometimes happens naturally, too, when it starts to pour during a chase. Bruins frequently walk logs, too, either jumping off to the side or up in the air to reach them where it can be difficult for dogs to piece together what happened. Some bears are also good at backtracking, retracing their steps then jumping off to the side. A good way for hunters to get an idea of how tricky black bears can be when pursued is to follow their tracks in the snow, which is a hunting technique covered in the next chapter.

Sometimes when a chase blows up or fizzles out, hunters can only guess at what happened. A hunt I shared with Lawrence Edwards and Gary Lohman in Ontario is an example. We were using Lawrence's hounds, and were trying for a big bear we knew was in the area. We found his huge tracks on two different days, but they were too old for the dogs to follow. The third time we found the big boy's prints they were fresh enough to run.

The bear was jumped in short order and my two partners got a glimpse of it as it bounded across a road in front of the dogs. The chase sounded so good they went in after the hounds and bear, only to have the experienced canines quit. Lawrence made an unsuccessful effort to restart the race, leaving us all scratching our heads about what happened. It seemed as though the bear vanished into thin air. We knew that didn't happen, of course. The bruin obviously pulled a sneaky maneuver that baffled the hounds, or, as Lawrence theorized, a moose may have crossed between the bear and dogs, throwing the canines for a loss.

CHAPTER
13

Other Techniques

You don't have to use bait or dogs, and it's not legal everywhere, to score on black bears. Other tactics include hunting natural feeding areas or waterholes, bringing bears in with calls, spotting and stalking them, making drives and tracking them in the snow.

Hunting feeding areas is a good way to tag a bear and hunters who try this method should become familiar with the types of foods black bears prefer at different times of year and where supplies of these foods are located. Food sources in or near bear habitat, which consists of timbered mountainous terrain, hardwood ridges, riverbottoms with lots of heavy cover and other locations that afford bears plenty of protection, such as expansive swamps, are naturally those most likely to be visited by the animals. The presence of black bear sign will be the final evidence hunters need to determine exactly where bruins are feeding, and perhaps the approximate size of the animals involved.

If a spot with an abundance of sign is located where there's still plenty of food remaining, it is usually a good idea to select a stand nearby and post there early and late in the day, although other times of day can produce action, too. Before selecting a stand, look for trails indicating from where bears are approaching, and use this information, plus the prevailing wind direction, to make the best stand site selection.

Hunters who feel bears aren't arriving at feeding grounds until after shooting hours can try to sit somewhere along their approach path, trying to get closer to what might be a bedding area. This practice, incidentally, can

Dave Pietro points to direction trophy black bear took after he shot it with a .270 as it came in to feed on apples from tree next to him.

also be used to ambush night feeding bears on baits or those that wait just out of sight from a bait for darkness to fall.

Michigan hunter Dave Pietro bagged a trophy black bear one fall by building a blind overlooking an apple tree where the animal was dining. Pietro actually saw the animal several times not far from his home before bear season opened. The size of the bruin impressed him and he decided to try for it once the season opened.

He located the apple tree where he figured the animal was feeding not far from where he saw the bear. There were other apple trees in the area, but this one contained the freshest sign. It was also closest to a swamp and the tree

I pose with a bruin I collected in an apple orchard as it came in to feed. An abundance of bear sign led me to where the bears were feeding.

had plenty of fruit left.

Dave saw an average-size bear on opening day and passed it up, hopeful he would get a crack at the big one. He eventually got the shot he wanted on the fifth evening of his vigil. When the bear was weighed it tipped the scales at 499 pounds.

Don't overlook farming areas in bear country as potential magnets for hungry bruins. Black bears love corn and grains such as oats and wheat when they ripen. Hunters who can locate farmers with corn or oat fields being raided by bears stand a good chance of getting permission to hunt. Local game wardens or conservation officers can be good contacts to learn which farms might be getting hit because these men often handle damage complaints.

Ray Juetten bagged a better-than-average bear one year that was visiting a cornfield. After scouting the area for sign and places to take stands, Ray said he and a partner estimated there were eight bruins using the field. There were a lot of trails entering the corn, but most of them ended in short order. Juetten finally found the main trail and watched it in the evening, bagging a bruin that dressed at 280 pounds. Ray's partner got a shot at a bear, but it got away. A third person hunting that cornfield tagged a trophy that had a dressed weight between 460 and 470 pounds.

If bear sign is distributed over a wide area in correspondence with scattered patches of food, a better way to get a look at a bear may be to stillhunt into the wind or crosswind from one patch of food to another, perhaps stopping to watch each spot for a few minutes before moving on. A group of four friends of mine enjoyed tremendous success one fall by stillhunting through stands of beech and chokecherry trees. The group included Mike Hogan and his son, Brian, Dr. Tom Porn and Paul Myron. They saw a total of 20 bears between them during five or six trips afield, with the father and son connecting and the other two getting shooting.

Myron stumbled on one of the hotspots for bear while grouse hunting. He was walking along a woods road when he saw a bruin climb down a beech tree. The animals often climb beeches to get at the nuts. A short time later, Paul saw three more bears. Those sightings were enough incentive for Paul to exchange his shotgun for a rifle, and upon returning to the area he eventually saw a fifth bear descend a beech tree, and took several shots at it but missed.

Brian was the first member of the party to score. He and his father came upon four bears feeding on fallen cherries in an opening. The younger Hogan sighted on the largest of the four, which was 50 yards away, and filled his tag with a 150-pounder. Mike got a bear the same size as his son's the following week as it slid down a beech tree and started to run off.

Black bears are fond of agricultural crops such as corn, and can be ambushed along trails leading into fields.

Dr. Porn was nearby when Mike connected, and when Tom heard his partner shoot, he headed that way. Before he reached Mike's position he jumped two more bears, missing one of them. On another hunt that season, Tom had a cub approach to within a matter of feet from him. He didn't shoot, of course, because cubs are protected in Michigan.

Stalking can also come into play when one vantage point offers hunters a view of a large area where bears may emerge to feed. Once an animal is spotted that a hunter wants, he or she can try to move into position for a shot and claim the prize. Variations of stillhunting and stalking are possible from boats or canoes on protected bays of oceans or lakes, plus rivers, and from trail bikes or all-terrain vehicles on logging roads or woods trails.

Is stillhunting or stalking to within bow range of black bears possible? You bet it is. Bob DeJong from Sitka, Alaska can tell you all about it. He and friend Bill Burgess each bow-bagged 200-pound bears on the same fall evening while hunting along a stream where salmon were spawning, and the animals were feeding on the abundant fish.

In Bob's case, he was fortunate enough to have the bear close the gap between them to bow range after he started a stalk toward the animal. He made his killing shot at 30 yards. Bill crept to within 20 yards of his bear before shooting it, having covered the last 100 yards on hands and knees. Bill was able to put a second arrow into his bruin at 40 yards.

Black bears can also be stillhunted or stalked while feeding on berries in alpine areas or clearcuts during the fall in Alaska, according to Bob. The same can be done in other areas where the same situations exist. During spring seasons, Bob said he stalks black bears on beach fringes and tideflats where they graze on grass. In one evening last spring he counted 13 bruins on a large tideflat.

One of Michigan's longtime bowhunters—Loren Willie—has bagged a number of black bears while stillhunting or stalking them as they fed on blueberries or cherries. When stillhunting among cherry trees he always listened for the telltale sound of limbs breaking to give away a bear's location. Then he would take off his shoes or boots and pull on heavy socks over those already on, to protect his feet during the stalk. The socks made walking quieter than with normal footwear. The bears were so preoccupied with filling their bellies, in many cases, and making lots of noise in the process, that he was able to sneak in close enough for the kill.

Gun hunters as well as bowhunters should use their ears plus their eyes when looking for black bears. They are noisy eaters, often breaking limbs on all types of fruit and nut trees that they feed on. When grazing on grass, the sound of them biting or pulling mouthfuls of the green stuff can be heard, although not from far away. Bears feeding on spawning fish usually make plenty of noise by splashing in the water.

Hunters who anticipate watching large areas for feeding bears should carry a good pair of binoculars, or even a spotting scope, with them. And before setting out on a long stalk, check out the animal's location carefully first by noting landmarks to help guide you. Surroundings are going to look much different when closing in on your quarry. If hunting with a partner or two, work out a set of hand signals to help direct one of you to the bear. Always try to keep the wind in your favor on a stalk, too, by moving into or across it.

In the arid southwestern U.S. where water is limited, black bears are sometimes ambushed at waterholes. Leo LaPaz, a Mescalero Apache Indian hunting guide from New Mexico, told me that watching waterholes is a good bear hunting tactic there. As it so happens, D. DeMoss killed his first black bear while it was "taking a bath" in a pothole in New Mexico. DeMoss was raised in that state and was 14 years old at the time he shot his first bear. He said he saw a lot of bear sign in the area of the pothole, which led him to hunt there.

As predators, black bears will respond to calls of animals in distress such as rabbits and fawns. Calls that imitate the screams of rabbits and bleats of fawns can be and have been used to bring bruins to hunters, both intention-

Stillhunting through oak or beech woods can sometimes result in a shot like this.

ally and accidentally. Most successful hunters who have called bears in have done so with calls that imitate the cries of rabbits, either cottontails or jack-rabbits, by calling early and late in the day. However, DeMoss said he knows of some hunters who have had good success luring black bears into view with deer calls that sound like fawns. Deer calls would be most effective in the spring when fawns are present.

For calling to work, a bear obviously has to be within hearing. Select calling sites in areas with lots of bear sign or try calling bruins that are spotted and are too far away for a shot or go out of sight before a shot is possible. A call could be the ticket for producing a chance at a bear that might otherwise have been missed.

The only bear I called in was at Montana's Glacier National Park. I was trying to locate some of the animals to photograph when one crossed a road in front of my vehicle. I visually marked the spot where the bear left the road and pulled over with my window open and cameras ready, as I made like an injured rabbit. A couple of minutes later I heard, then saw, the animal return-ing. It came close, but was mostly screened by brush, then started circling me and walked back into the road behind me.

Because I knew this bear was close, probably 100 yards or less, I cupped my hands over the call to muffle the sound so it wouldn't be too loud. This wouldn't be necessary when animals are farther away. It can take as much as an hour or more for bears to reach a caller in some situations because they

In areas where high vantage points offer a view of slopes where black bears feed, spotting animals like this one from a distance is possible. Then a stalk can be planned to try for a shot.

When being followed, black bears often walk on logs, as this animal is doing, or on rocks and in water. They also backtrack.

usually approach slowly, often stopping between calls, so hunters serious about trying to call in a bear shouldn't leave stands too soon. Callers should also make sure they have good visibility around them to prevent a bear from sneaking in close without being detected. Hunting with a partner reduces the chances of being surprised by Blackie.

Since black bears sometimes don't bed down far from bait sites, I've often thought calling might work well at or near these locations, perhaps trying it late in the morning or during early afternoon. In situations where no bears have been seen at active baits after several days of hunting, calling might be worth a try during prime feeding times. The calls may just get an animal or two to abandon their normal caution and show themselves during shooting hours. Although I've tried calling from bait sites a few times without success, I haven't done it enough to determine the technique's effectiveness at these locations.

Drives are a popular method of trying to fill bear tags in Pennsylvania, although other tactics are also employed. Groups of hunters usually drive swamps in the same fashion they would when deer hunting. Some members of the party post in locations where they think jumped bears will go, while drivers move toward them trying to move any bruins they may encounter toward standers. Pennsylvania bear biologist Gary Alt said black bears normally leave a swamp at a point closest to the next patch of security cover. Locations that fit this description make good stand sites during drives.

Young bruins are more susceptible to drives than older animals, according to Alt, because they tend to panic and run into hunters. He said older, more experienced bears tend to stay put during drives or circle back behind drives, refusing to leave a swamp. A hunter or two following behind drivers stand a good chance of getting a crack at bears that try to circle drivers.

Black bears that are old-timers may also seek shelter in small patches of thick cover not normally hunted, to avoid detection. One of the biggest black bears tagged in Pennsylvania, which was bagged in 1983, was in a small pothole swamp that a group of hunters drove as an afterthought after pushing larger swamps in the area with no success. That bear, a boar, proved to be 18 years old and had a dressed weight of 572 pounds.

In states and provinces where deer and bear seasons are open at the same time, some black bears are shot on deer drives. The first bruin I bagged was pushed into me by my brother during gun deer season in Michigan. Bruce came upon the yearling male as it was rummaging for acorns, and spooked it. The bruin stopped some distance away from my stand with its head behind a tree when I took the first shot, which I think missed the animal. Confused about which direction the shot had come from, the bear ran toward me until about 20 yards away, when it turned broadside. My second shot was on target, but the animal stayed on its feet. My third shot caught up to the bear before he traveled another 10 yards, putting him down.

There was a light covering of snow the morning I collected that bear and I saw his tracks, or those of another animal similar in size, on the way to my stand. I could have followed those tracks and might have been able to get a shot at the animal that way. Trailing bears is certainly a viable technique for filling a tag in areas where the season is open when snow blankets the ground. A lot of snow isn't necessary to see tracks to follow, although when there is an inch or more of snow on the ground the white stuff usually makes for quiet walking, deadening the sound of leaves and twigs underfoot, increasing the chances a hunter can get close enough to a bruin for a shot before being detected.

However, it's no easy task to successfully trail and tag a healthy black bear regardless of how much snow is on the ground. It may be necessary to follow a bear for miles through thick, rugged terrain before catching up to it. With this in mind, hunters who hope to try for a bruin in this fashion should be in good physical condition and be comfortable in the woods, carrying a compass to find their way and being prepared to spend a night in the woods, if necessary, with waterproof matches and snacks in pack or pockets.

Black bears that know they are being followed often pull tricks that will test a hunter's tracking ability, in addition to shedding light on what hounds sometimes have to unravel when on the trail of a black bear. Gary Alt tracked a mature male that was wearing a radio collar a distance of 14½ miles in two days and got some insight into how difficult it can be for trailing hunters to get a look at their quarry. On the first day of tracking, Gary got close enough to hear the animal run off through a swamp when he jumped it at one point, but he didn't realize it was the bear at the time.

The bruin had made a loop and was laying 50 feet from its backtrail, watching it. Gary didn't realize it was the bear he heard until following its tracks around the loop. By then the animal was well ahead of him. Several times during the second day of tracking, Gary's father monitored the bear's location from his airplane to check how far the animal was from the tracker. The average distance between Gary and the bruin was 1.4 miles.

Looping back to watch his backtrail was only one of the tricks the bear pulled. On the second day, it went so far as to circle in Gary's tracks, leading him to wonder who was tracking whom. Blackie also entered a stream a number of times, sometimes leaving on the same side it entered and other times walking in the water for a distance before returning to dry ground, occasionally going in the opposite direction than headed when entering the water. The bear also backtracked a number of times, then jumped off to the side of its original trail before continuing on. The first time this happened, it caught Gary by surprise and it took him awhile to figure out what happened.

"He went over this hill into open woods and all of a sudden his tracks just ended," Alt said. "I thought he probably jumped up a tree or something . . . but there weren't any trees around. Then I thought I was on Candid Camera and I was waiting for Allen Funt to turn up. Finally, I concluded that Captain Kirk had beamed him aboard his starship Enterprise. I mean it was pretty hilarious. I was alone. I was looking around and I was laughing to myself and I thought, 'Where the hell did this bear go,' because these tracks went nowhere.

"Then I got down on my knees. I was thinking of praying, but it didn't get that bad yet. I looked in the tracks and saw toe marks in both ends of the tracks. Then I realized he had turned around. But in the process of turning around he never slid sideways or anything. His tracks were perfect," Alt said.

One last trick the large male pulled was to jump from one snowless rock to another, resulting in an absence of tracks until the bear ran out of rocks within stepping or jumping distance.

Although tracking and tagging a black bear can be difficult, it isn't impossible, especially if the animal doesn't know it's being followed until it's too late. Michigan hunter Jerry Weigold has bagged seven bruins after tracking them to their beds. Each of them were collected at the time they were initially jumped or encountered, when the element of surprise was in his favor. He said he has never been able to connect on bears that were jumped and got away, because they knew they were being followed. Weigold reported bears that knew they were being trailed pulled tricks similar to those that Alt experienced.

Jerry was just as puzzled as Gary had been when a bear started backtracking on him. One particular animal that did this didn't want to leave the swamp where Weigold jumped it.

"He would walk up to trees and scratch the bark off to confuse me," he said. "That bear would always go up to great big white pine trees so you'd swear he would be way up in the top where you'd never see him. He had me going back and looking up in those trees for a long time. The first two times he did this I figured he had to be up there for sure, but he walked so carefully backwards in his tracks that you couldn't see where he turned around or anything. He walked about 40 feet back and made one big jump on the other side of a windfall so you couldn't see his track."

In addition to walking on rocks, the bears Jerry tracked frequently walked on logs, jumping or stepping from one log to another, when possible. Seven miles is the farthest he trailed a bear that he bagged. Most of them were jumped in swamps at a distance of 20 to 25 feet, although some bears were found bedded in stands of hemlock trees. The bruins Jerry shot while tracking them averaged 200 pounds. In addition to the animals he shot, Weigold has tracked others to dens and left them undisturbed. Shooting denned black bears is unsportsmanlike and unethical, if not illegal. The practice is, indeed, illegal in many states.

Tracking black bears in the snow is a hunting technique some hunters enjoy because of the challenge involved, and they choose to do it for that reason. Trailing bruins that are hit and run off poses a different kind of challenge, one that all black bear hunters should be prepared to meet.

CHAPTER
14

Trailing Wounded Bears

But the most important aspects of trailing bears come before and as a shot is taken. The factor that determines more than any other how easy or difficult a trailing job will be and how far a black bear will have to be trailed is shot placement. Far too many hunters take shots at black bears they shouldn't, and I've been in on the trailing of enough poorly hit bruins to know.

Part of the problem is many bear hunters are already successful deer hunters and they assume shots that put deer down quickly will work on black bears. This is true to some extent, but not in every case. One major difference between deer and bear that gets hunters into trouble is the size and position of lungs. The lungs of most black bears are smaller and positioned farther forward in the chest cavity than they are in deer, according to my experience.

So before going on a black bear hunt, hunters should become familiar with where to best place their shots. Ask guides and other experienced bear hunters for their advice.

Bowhunters can do one more thing to prepare for a tracking job by obtaining and using a string tracker. In most cases, these tracking aids enable bowhunters to follow arrowed bruins, even if there is no blood, and I highly recommend their use. The reason I do is that black bears do not bleed as freely as deer, sometimes not leaving any blood trail at all, or one that may not start until the animal has covered 50 to 100 yards. The layers of fat on a black bear's body, especially during the fall, and the long-haired hides, retard blood flow.

There are a number of string trackers on the market, but the one I've found to be best for bear hunting is a model called the Game Tracker. These models come with a larger volume of line than others I'm aware of and have white line, which is easy to follow at night with a light as well as during hours

Proper shot placement is one of the most important aspects of trailing wounded bears. Animals seldom go far when properly hit.

String tracking devices like the one Gene Ballew is using here are recommended for bowhunters because bears don't bleed as freely as deer.

of daylight. Game Tracker line comes in both 17 and 22-pound test. The heavier line is best for bear hunting.

The tracker line is attached to arrows by fastening it at the end of the shaft, holding it in place between the back of screw-in broadheads and the shaft. The line should be taped to the end of the shaft for added insurance on the chance the head unscrews as a bear runs. Arrow trajectory isn't affected out to about 30 yards on bows of at least 50-pound pull, well within the range of most bow shots at black bears. However, hunters should test the devices before hunting to make sure they work properly.

If using a string tracker with small capacity spools be sure to hunt with a full spool or one that is almost full. A bowhunter who was bear hunting with me one year was using a model containing small spools of orange line. He had taken several practice shots with the gadget, leaving little line on the spool. When the man took a shot at a nice bear the remaining line balled up and was too large to feed through the opening in the container. The arrow had enough force to snap the line and went on to hit the bear. However, the arrow used so much energy breaking the line that there was little penetration, not enough to seriously hurt the bruin.

String trackers are not infallible. Sometimes the line breaks soon after a bear is hit, or the arrow may pull out and the line comes with it. But when they do work properly and the line proves helpful in locating a bear, they are worth their weight in gold. In my opinion, their advantages outweigh the disadvantages by a long shot. They prove valuable even on missed shots by enabling bowhunters to quickly and easily locate their arrows. And when a bear is shot,

Tom (left) and Bud Jarvis with tracker string picked up from a bear I shot in Colorado. The bear dropped by the log behind Bud. Bait is on the other side of the opening in the timber.

hunters need not worry about finding their way back to where they started from. The line will lead them to their trophy and back again.

I used a Game Tracker when I connected on my brown black bear in Colorado, hunting with guide Jim Jarvis. The device worked perfectly, feeding line out with the running bear for the 50 to 75 yards it covered before piling up. My arrow passed completely through the bear, leaving a double line to follow. The line went from my bow to the bear and back to my arrow where it imbedded in a tree trunk at the bait.

Hunters who use string trackers must accept the responsibility of picking up used string at the conclusion of a hunt. Failure to do so is the same as littering.

Bear hunters who familiarize themselves with proper shot placement, taking only shots they should, and bowhunters who employ string trackers, are a step or two ahead of those who don't when it comes to trailing a bruin they hit. The procedure to follow immediately after a hit varies, depending on whether firearms or bow and arrow are used. As a general rule, gun hunters should follow up shots immediately and aggressively, with the exception of those using single-shot firearms, such as muskets, and bowhunters should be passive, waiting before taking up the bear's trail.

Gun hunters should be ready to put a second slug into a bear after the initial shot, and should do so if the animal shows any sign of life. If the animal drops, rolls, or runs out of sight after hit, move up to the point where it was last seen as quickly as possible or at least to a spot where the bear is once again visible, and use a second bullet if the animal is not yet dead.

Hunters using firearms will have to rely on their ears to determine the next course of action when bears are out of sight upon reaching the point where the animals were standing when shot. Listen carefully for any sound such as crashing brush, coughing, or moaning that may give away a bruin's location or line of travel. Visually and mentally mark the location of any telltale sound by picking out a distinctive feature such as a nearby tree for reference.

If there is a lot of commotion in one location, the bear is probably down, but not yet dead. Proceed to that spot quickly and finish the animal. As black bears die, they sometimes moan loudly when air is expelled from their lungs. The sound isn't pleasant, and has sent chills up the spine of more than one novice black bear hunter, but hunters who know what it means can proceed directly to the spot where the sound came from to claim their kill. Lung-shot bruins will sometimes make coughing or gurgling sounds as they expire.

Sounds of a running bear may also be heard. Black bears usually crash through branches and brush on a dead run when shot, making lots of noise. Mark the spot where the last sounds are heard as best as possible. The animal either dropped at that point, slowed to a walk, reached an opening or stopped to lay down. If sure of a good hit, the animal is probably dead and the hunter can move to the spot where the animal was last heard to find the carcass. Hunters who are unsure of the hit or uncomfortable about following up on a bear by themselves, should go get help then return, making sure the spots where the bear was hit and last heard are carefully marked before leaving.

When returning to recover the bear, make sure you have something with you to mark a blood trail with such as tissue, surveyor's tape, or a spool of Game Tracker line. Tracker line is the best choice of all, in my opinion, because the line leaves a continuous trail rather than a broken one to refer back to when looking ahead for new blood sign and can be followed out more easily once you're done tracking. There are 2,500 feet of line on a spool of 17-pound test. This is one way that gun hunters can make use of archery equipment. If it is dark, or will be soon, bring flashlights with fresh batteries or a lantern to help in locating a bear. Under these circumstances, leave guns and bows in the vehicle. It is illegal to have either in the woods after shooting hours end.

If a dead bear is not located where the animal was last heard, search the area for signs of its passing such as blood, tracks, and broken brush. Look on the sides of saplings, trees, and brush below waist level for blood that may have wiped off as a bear passed them, as well as on the ground. Blood will be left on both sides of the animal if the bullet exited, but only on the side of entry if it didn't. A running bear often leaves noticeable scuff marks on the ground

A hound on a leash is unbeatable for locating an injured
black bear or a dead one that didn't leave a blood trail.
I've got Charlie on a leash here, trailing a wounded bear.

where it lands between strides, if not clearly defined tracks. Freshly broken branches, bent or broken saplings, turned leaves, crushed logs and damaged stumps may be other clues of a bear's passing.

Once the bear's trail has been located, mark it, then move ahead, marking each additional track or spot of blood, unless there is a steady flow that is easy to follow. Frothy blood is a sure sign of a lung hit and a short blood trail. Bright red blood may mean a heart shot or arterial wound. Dark red blood usually originates from the liver. Intestinal matter mixed with blood is an indication of a gut shot. If hit in the evening and the weather permits, trailing a gut-shot bear should be resumed first thing the following morning. If hit in the morning, wait at least four hours.

In situations where the bear's course of travel can't be located in the vicinity where it was last heard, return to where it was hit and try to work the trail out from there, circling back and forth across the bruin's probable path until locating blood. There should at least be hair at the spot where the bear stood when hit and blood is often present, too. Follow blood trails as far as possible, keeping noise to a minimum to avoid scaring the bear off if it is still alive, and to be better able to hear the animal should it move. If trailing during hours of daylight and a bear is jumped, try to shoot the bear again to finish it. If it stays too far ahead, wait several hours or until the next day to resume trailing.

A bruin hit with a firearm that goes a quarter mile or more without laying down is probably not hurt seriously. One that is properly hit certainly won't go that far. Nonfatal injuries may leave plenty of blood initially then gradually taper off to nothing. A poor blood trail may not be an indication of a poor hit though. Most bleeding will be internal on hits high in the body when there isn't an exit wound, so don't give up too soon.

Under circumstances where no blood can be located or the blood trail ends after a short distance, hunters must do their best to relocate the trail or find the animal by covering as much ground as possible. Criss-cross the terrain in the direction the animal was headed until it is covered thoroughly. Wounded bears often travel downhill, but not always, when they have a choice and may go to water. Keep this in mind when coming to a deadend on a blood trail. If there are clearly defined trails where the blood stops, follow these as far as possible for further clues.

The absolute best way to find a bear when there is little or no blood is to rely on a hound. One that will follow bear scent doesn't need blood to determine where the bear went. I've used a hound on a leash as an ace in the hole to locate downed bears for years and have recovered some that would have been impossible to find any other way. My dogs have also made it possible to determine that bears not found were healthy enough to recover from their wounds by following the animals much farther than would have been possible going on blood sign alone.

All serious black bear hunters should own at least one hound for trailing purposes. Even in states and provinces where hunting with hounds is not permitted, allowances should be made for tracking dogs restrained on a leash.

Most game wardens would probably permit the practice, but hunters should inquire ahead of time to protect themselves. Wardens may want to go along, or at least be notified each time a dog is used to trail a bear.

When trailing a wounded black bear with a hound, proceed as you otherwise would. If the animal is still alive and jumped, mark the location and return later. Hounds with good noses can follow bear scent the following morning. The two dogs I've used for the purpose have done so. If more than one bear dog is available when a bear is jumped during shooting hours and hunting with hounds is legal, the hounds can be released in an effort to bay or tree the bear. A single dog stands a better chance of being hurt or killed by an injured bruin than two or three, but sometimes one hound can successfully tree or bay a wounded bear.

Last fall I brought my Plott hound, "Charlie," along to help trail a bruin that had been hit with a broadhead. The animal was shot at a bait in the evening and we took up the trail the following morning. There was plenty of blood to follow initially, but when we eventually jumped the animal where it had bedded for the night, the bleeding had stopped. I was convinced there was no way we would catch the bear by following it with the dog on a leash because the animal was healthy enough to move out ahead of us without us hearing or seeing it, so I let Charlie go on the bear's trail.

Always approach a downed black bear from the rear. Make sure its eyes are open and the animal isn't breathing before moving too close. If the eyelid closes when touched with a stick, the animal is still alive.

The dog was in good shape and I figured he would be able to stay out of the bear's way long enough for us to catch up and finish it, if the bruin bayed on the ground. As it turned out, the bear treed after about a half-mile chase and was finished with a firearm. There is no way that bear would have been trailed successfully and bagged any other way. As it turned out, the arrow wound wasn't serious, the broadhead having ricocheted off bone, simply going under the skin. If it weren't for Charlie, I'm sure that bear would have recovered from the injury.

On another occasion, a fellow I was guiding shot a bear with a .44 caliber rifle during the morning and was unable to find the animal. I put "Drew," a black and tan, on the trail several hours later to see what he could come up with. The dog led me toward a steep, rocky hillside several times and I didn't think an injured bear would climb it, so I kept stopping the dog short and went back to the bait to start over again. Eventually, I let the old hound have his way and the bear was on that hillside, hiding among the rocks.

There were a number of downed trees on the hillside, too, and when we got close to where the bear was hiding, Drew lunged ahead and jerked me into one of the trees, where I fell and lost my grip on the dog's leash. The hound ran ahead and I got back on my feet just in time to see the bear run downhill ahead of him. I threw a shot at the bruin, but missed. Drew bayed the injured bear at the bottom of the hill, out of my sight behind some big boulders.

I hobbled toward the action, having injured a knee, only to hear my dog start to move off before reaching the bottom of the hill. When I rounded the last boulder and saw what was happening I discovered the tables had been turned. The bear was chasing Drew at that point and the dog's leash was dragging on the ground. If the leash hung up on brush, the hound would be in trouble.

My next shot had to count, and it did, but I don't even remember aiming. When I shot, the bear dropped with a broken shoulder and I pumped two more rounds into the bruin to make sure it wasn't going to get up. Drew's chances of being hurt were increased because of his leash, but even a single hound without such a handicap may be hurt by a wounded bear.

On that particular day I was carrying a 12-gauge shotgun and slugs. Now I usually carry a .44 magnum handgun, freeing both hands to handle the dog.

All of the wounded bears I've jumped, with or without a dog, day or night, have run away. However, it always pays to be cautious. Wounded bears that are cornered have been known to turn on their pursuers, both hunters and hounds. If a bear did attack when trailing with a hound, it would make sense to release the dog to distract the bear. When trailing without a dog to let you know when you're getting close to a bruin, always keep an eye out ahead in an effort to avoid close contact with a bear that may still be alive.

Hunters who have access to a bear dog and hit a bear they are unable to trail shouldn't wait too long before putting the hound into service, especially if other bears are in the area. The presence of bear scent fresher than that from the wounded animal may distract a hound, reducing its effectiveness in following the right bear. Scent fades, too, with time. Rain and wind accelerate the process. Even under favorable conditions, trailing a bear with a dog should be started within 12 hours. If I'm having trouble with a trail, I try to put a dog in action within three to four hours so the scent is as fresh as possible.

If more than 12 hours elapse before a dog can be put on the trail of a wounded bear or the blood trail has been washed out, all is not lost. If a bruin is down within a reasonable distance of where it was shot, a hound can locate the carcass by winding it. A dog worked into the wind to check for the animal will sometimes find it.

The first black bear I shot with a black-powder rifle didn't leave a drop of blood I could find, although I was sure I connected. I aimed for the bruin's chest as it sat facing me. Since I was hunting close to home, I got Drew and we were on the bear's trail in about an hour. The bear had only gone about 50 yards before dying on its feet. My maxi-ball hit a little lower than I aimed, but still did a good job. The reason there was no blood was the slug didn't exit and the hole of entry was plugged with fat.

I probably would have found that bear without the dog, but it would have taken longer, and there was a chance the carcass would have gone undetected. The animal went down in extremely thick cover in a swamp. With the dog, there was no question I was going to locate the bear, as I did. Any bear hunter can up his odds of finding bears they hit in the same way.

Any type of bear dog will do to trail wounded animals. Hounds that are on the small side such as females are best suited for the task because they are easier to handle on a leash. The dog I now use for trailing bears (Drew died several years ago), Charlie, weighs in around 80 pounds. Charlie is sometimes hard to control on a hot trail.

Not all hounds take to a blood trail willingly, so a little training is helpful. Take the dog on the trail of a number of bears that you may have already located or ones that leave an easy-to-follow blood trail. Then praise and reward the hound once the carcass is reached.

Whenever the carcass of a black bear is located always approach from the rear and look for signs of breathing. Also look at the eyes. The eyelids are open on a dead bear. If they are closed, the animal is probably still alive and should be shot again.

Hunters using single-shot firearms should reload as quickly as possible, then follow the same procedures for trailing bears outlined above. The reloading process for front-loading rifles can take minutes to complete, so hunters using them may want to listen to determine what course a bear takes, if it does run off, before starting to reload.

In most cases when a black bear is hit with a broadhead, the animal runs off so fast there is no time for a second shot. However, on occasion a second shot is possible, and bowhunters should be ready to take advantage of the opportunity should it arise. Fellow bowhunter Dave Bigelow hit one of the first bears he tagged with two shafts, dropping it in sight. The animal spun around in a circle when hit with the first arrow, giving Dave enough time to nock a second arrow and put it in the bear's boiler room.

Michigan bear hunter and taxidermist Jim Haveman once grazed a nice

Where guns and bows are legal at the same time for bear, bowhunters may want to have someone along with a gun while trailing a bear on the chance it is still alive. Wounded bears should be finished with a gun if it isn't possible to get another arrow into them.

boar with his first arrow and it ran a short distance and then stopped, giving him a 10-yard shot broadside. Haveman's second broadhead sliced through one of the animal's lungs, redeeming the bowhunter.

When a bear is arrowed, bowhunters should try to see where the shaft hits. Although this is not always possible, when it is, the knowledge can be useful in deciding how long to wait before beginning tracking. Solid chest/lung hits will kill quickly, but to be on the safe side, hunters should wait a minimum of 30 minutes before starting on the trail. Wait at least an hour after a liver hit, which is located about in the middle of a bear's body. At least four hours should elapse before following a gut-shot bear.

Archers using string trackers will get an idea of how good a hit they made by watching how the line pays out, provided the device works properly. If line uncoils rapidly for a number of seconds then stops and moves again, but at a much slower pace before stopping for good, that's a good sign. It's not a good sign if line keeps unraveling until the spool is empty. In situations where the animal is still heard running and the line stops moving, the arrow either pulled out or the line broke. Under those circumstances, hunters should try to mark the location where the departing bear was last heard.

Bowhunters not using string trackers should note at what point a bear goes out of sight, the direction of travel the animal is taking, and where the bruin is last heard. Unlike gun hunters, bowhunters should remain in place quietly for about five minutes to look and listen for any further clues to where the bear may have gone. After a short wait with no new developments, leave the area as quietly as possible. It is important to be quiet on the chance the bear laid down nearby. Any disturbance may cause it to get up and move off, making the recovery process more difficult.

Don't wait if an animal is paralyzed from a spine shot, but still alive. Try to get another arrow into the animal from your blind or stand. If the animal starts dragging itself off, and this isn't possible, go after it to put an arrow into its lungs immediately. A hunter Lawrence Edwards guided last fall hit a bruin in this fashion and didn't attempt to finish the animal. It was hours later before the guide arrived and they followed blood to where the bear stopped to rest. From that point on there was no blood and the bruin was lost. The paralysis was apparently temporary, the rest giving the animal an opportunity to recover.

Once an appropriate amount of time has passed on most bow hits, return to the spot where the bear was hit and begin trailing the animal by following the string or as described earlier. If following tracking string and it begins to move, the bear may still be alive and the best thing to do is back off for an hour or more before starting after the bruin again.

Since both firearms and archery equipment are legal during most bear seasons, bowhunters can often have a partner carrying a gun accompany them when tracking, provided it's during shooting hours. My brother Bruce was my backup when trailing the first couple of black bears I shot with bow and arrow. A gun is most useful if a bear proves to still be alive and it isn't possible to get another arrow into it.

Under these circumstances, it is the hunter's responsibility to finish the bear as quickly as possible with a bullet. Hunters who insist on pursuing a wounded bear with a bow when the odds of getting a decent shot are against them are unethical and unsportsmanlike, in my opinion, being more concerned about their ego than the quarry. The chances of recovering a wounded black bear are reduced by simply relying on bow and arrow.

If hunting during a bow-only season, the hunter has little choice, and must try to finish the job with archery equipment, unless a game warden or conservation officer can be contacted and is willing to assist with a firearm or give hunters permission to use a gun. When night trailing, hunters must leave guns and bows behind, of course. The best course of action to follow when a bow-shot bear is jumped, whether day or night, is to mark the area carefully so it can be located again and quietly back off, waiting a number of hours before returning. The animal probably won't go far if pursuit is broken off right away.

In situations where there isn't much blood, hunters can sometimes see what little there is better by getting down on hands and knees. Rust spots and red pigment on leaves can sometimes be mistaken for blood. Blood spots that have dried wipe off easily with a wet finger. Rust and red pigment won't. Crushed berries sometimes leave blood-like stains on vegetation, too, so be aware of it and try not to be led astray by these possible distractions.

Three people are ideal for following a blood trail, with one person assigned to mark spots of blood and other sign, remaining on the last clue until another is located. When only two people are present, both can search for clues, marking each one when located. If more than three people are on hand to follow a wounded bear, one person should be in charge to conduct an organized search. Too many hunters, some who may not know what to look for, can trample blood sign or tracks before they are recognized.

Bowhunters who have made good hits should find their bear within 200 to 300 yards, but keep trailing as far as possible until the bruin is either located or you are convinced it wasn't seriously hurt. Even minor wounds may yield a long blood trail, but bleeding may be heavy at first then taper off or be sparse the entire time. Bow hits can sometimes be difficult to judge visually based on blood sign, and where it appeared that the arrow struck. Arrows that sometimes look like they go into the chest cavity slide along the outside of the ribs, especially on angling away shots. In most cases, the lungs were missed if a bear goes beyond 200 or 300 yards.

If there's no blood or string to follow, use a hound to trail bow-shot bears. Drew made the difference in recovering two bow kills that would never have been found otherwise and I've already mentioned an example in which Charlie did the same thing. One of the animals Drew located was gut shot and the other was hit a little too far back in the chest, missing the lungs. Both animals were hit in the evening and we night trailed them until we jumped them, then marked trails back to the baits, returning in the morning to try again. The gut-shot bruin was dead and the other was finished with a gun.

There are several reasons why I feel it is important to locate bears as soon as possible after they are shot, which sometimes results in trailing them during hours of darkness. There's always the chance of rain, and sometimes snow, to wash out a blood trail. Hunters should do their best to trail a bear as soon as possible in the event it starts to rain or snow, or it is expected to soon.

Dead bears that are left in the woods overnight may be eaten by other bears or wolves. I've only had this happen once, but Wayne Bosowicz reports it has happened a number of times to kills made by his hunters. In some cases, the entire carcass has been devoured.

In addition, the longer a bear carcass lays without removing the viscera and allowing the meat to cool, the greater the chances of spoilage of both meat and hide. Heavy bear hides hold heat in, resulting in fast spoilage in warm weather. Bear meat is excellent eating, if handled properly, and hides are great trophies, so both are worth preserving.

CHAPTER
15

Caring for Your Trophy

A black bear is dressed or gutted much the same way a deer is. The procedure is relatively simple. Hunters should make it a point to carry sharp knives with them afield to be prepared for this chore. A long-bladed knife isn't necessary. Pocketknives work just fine, as long as the blade is sharp. The knife I use is a folding model made by Buck with a 3¾-inch locking blade that I carry on my belt. I've dressed lots of black bears with that knife and look forward to doing many more.

There are a couple of ways to open the body cavity for removal of the viscera. Before you start though, it is usually a good idea to roll up sleeves and put wrist watches in a pocket to protect them from blood. The animal should be resting on its back, with the head uphill, if possible, for dressing.

I usually start cutting in the abdominal area where the hair is thin, making a small horizontal cut through the skin, fat, and muscles into the body cavity, being careful not to cut deeply enough to damage intestines. Then I use the two fingers next to the thumb on my left hand (I'm right-handed) to hold the body tissue above the viscera and I start a vertical cut that will open the body cavity, keeping the knife blade between my two fingers as I slice toward the chest.

Once I reach the ribs I grip the knife with both hands and continue cutting through the ribs to the neck. Blades on pocketknives may not be suitable for cutting ribs, and if that is the case, this step can be skipped. I prefer to cut the ribs because it makes it easier to remove heart and lungs and aids in cooling. After ribs are cut I may return to where I started and extend the cut downward to the pelvic area, and if it's a male, remove the penis and testicles.

Some states such as Colorado require that proof of sex be left intact on a

Use your fingers to hold the skin above viscera and guide the knifeblade when making the major cut to open the body cavity.

bear carcass, at least until the animals have been registered. If that is the case, the genitals will have to remain until later.

Another way to open the body cavity of black bears for gutting is to start the cut at the sternum, which is at the bottom of the ribs in the center of the body. There is a gap at this point between viscera and the body cavity wall, enabling hunters to stick the knifepoint downward into the cavity without damaging internal organs or the stomach. Then the cut can be extended to the pelvis, using two fingers to guide the knifeblade and hold the tissue you are cutting clear of viscera. Slice through the ribs, if possible, once done with the lower part of the body.

After the carcass is open I usually cut the diaphragm first, which is a thin muscle separating the chest cavity from the lower body cavity. Cut it as close to ribs and backbone as possible. The stomach generally has to be held out of the way to get at the diaphragm. Stomach, liver, and intestines can be pulled to the side and rolled out on the ground after the diaphragm is cut. There may be other strands of connective tissue holding the viscera, which can be severed as you go.

Next, I reach up above the heart and lungs into the neck, grasping the windpipe and pulling it tight. Then the windpipe is cut above my hand, being careful to avoid slicing fingers in the process. Once the windpipe is cut, pull it out and the heart and lungs will come with it.

The final step in the dressing process is cutting around the anus and removing the lower digestive tract. After the bowel is removed, check the passageway to make sure it is free of obstructions to allow drainage of blood and heat to escape. If fat is present, remove it. Some hunters take care of cutting around the anus before removing the viscera. The individual stages of dressing a bear can be done in any order desired.

When all of the viscera has been removed and the anal area cleaned, I take a few minutes to remove kidneys, excess fat, and any of the diaphragm remaining. Successful black bear hunters in Pennsylvania may want to leave part of the diaphragm in the body cavity because pieces of this muscle are usually taken at check stations to test for trichinosis. If stomach or intestines have been ruptured, clean as much of the material out of the carcass as possible. Meat that has been soiled should be cut away and discarded.

The heart and liver are good to eat, provided they haven't been damaged by bullets or broadheads. Bear livers are much lighter in color than those from deer, sort of reddish-brown, and have green, fluid-filled gall bladders attached. The liver is separated into several lobes and is connected to the diaphragm. A plastic bag is handy to put heart and liver in to carry out of the woods.

The prevailing circumstances will determine what course of action to take next. The carcass will have to be transported from the spot where it fell to a point where it can be loaded in a vehicle. How and when this will be accomplished must be decided. If a road is nearby, dragging the animal the short distance there may be the best thing to do. When there's a long haul ahead, however, and it's late, the best option may be to hang the bear in the woods and return to get it out the following morning.

That is how we handled two bruins bagged last fall. One was dropped about an hour before dark, but by the time two of us dragged it up a steep hill it was dark and there was still a quarter mile to go, so we hung the animal from the sturdy limb of a hemlock tree with a rope. A piece of wood was used to prop open the chest cavity to aid in cooling the carcass. That was a gun kill.

The second bear was bagged with bow and arrow about a half hour before dark using a Game Tracker string. We returned to our cabin and ate dinner, then the five of us hunting together went to trail the bear well after dark. We

A block and tackle is the
answer for hoisting
heavy black bears like
this one off the ground—
or even for lifting
average-size animals
when alone.

found a 300-pounder at the end of the line within 100 yards of where it was hit.
Rather than trying to manhandle the carcass out of the woods that night, we
hung it from a nearby tree and got it out of the woods the following morning.
Coincidentally, the fellow who tagged that bear is Bob Eastman from Flush-
ing, Michigan, a long-time bowhunter and owner of the company that makes
Game Trackers. Rock star Ted Nugent was also on that hunt.

When hunting alone or in the event a big bear is bagged that you want to
hang in the woods overnight, a block and tackle is the best way to hoist
carcasses off the ground. We had to use a block and tackle to hang a big male
that bowhunter Gary Lohman got one year. We were never able to have the
carcass weighed, but I estimated the dressed carcass went over 400 pounds.

If there is concern about other bears or wolves tampering with a bear
carcass, the best thing to do may be to get it out of the woods right away. A
piece of clothing or item with human scent on it will keep wolves away from a
carcass, but I'm not sure about other bears. One fall a big boar made off with a

Black bears can be carried out of woods on a pole, but the pole should be tied close to the body rather than simply to the feet to prevent the animal from swinging back and forth.

small bear a group of hunters camped in Michigan's Upper Peninsula had hanging near their tent.

In the event temperatures are warm, above 60 degrees, bears should be taken out of the woods and skinned as soon as possible. Under circumstances where a big bear is involved and there is no way to reach the carcass with a vehicle, the best thing to do is skin the animal first, then quarter the carcass and carry it out piece-by-piece. All-terrain vehicles are great for hauling bears out of the woods, provided one is available and it can reach the carcass.

Most of the bear hauling I've been involved with has been by hand, either carrying or dragging the carcass. Small to average bears, those that dress around 150 pounds or less, can be carried with front and back legs draped across shoulders. If someone isn't along to help get the bear on the carrier's shoulders, the carcass may have to be pulled up on a stump or log to get it in a position to carry. I watched one hunter carry a bear over his shoulders that weighed a minimum of 150 pounds.

Jim Jarvis did the same thing, only he had each front leg over a shoulder and leaned forward as he stood up to get the hind legs off the ground behind him, then walked toward the road with the load. The bear Charlie treed last fall after being hit with bow and arrow was carried out in the same fashion. That bruin had a dressed weight of 160 pounds.

Another way to carry small bears is to tie a hind foot to a front foot on the opposite side of the body, forming a sling. This bear-leg sling can be slung over either shoulder to carry an animal out of the woods.

Still one more method of carrying bears out of the woods is to tie them to a pole. A strong pole longer than the bear is necessary so the ends can be put on carriers' shoulders. When tying a carcass to the pole, secure it between the legs next to the body to prevent it from swinging back and forth. My brother and I once carried a 140-pound bear he shot by simply tying its feet to a pole. The weight of the swinging carcass constantly upset our balance, and we ended up dragging the bruin most of the way to the road.

I do not recommend carrying bears in areas where there are other hunters, for reasons of safety, unless it's after dark or the carcass is wrapped with hunter orange material.

To drag black bears, use a strong rope with one end around the bear's head and the other attached to a sturdy stick or pole to hang onto when dragging. The shorter the length of rope between the drag stick and bear the better, so part of the front quarters can be lifted off the ground while dragging to reduce friction. If a pole is used, hunters can push against it at waist-to-chest level like a yoke.

Rather than putting a rope around a bear's head for dragging purposes, Leland Stice puts a thick piece of wood in a bear's mouth, behind the canine teeth, using a piece long enough to protrude from both sides of the mouth. Then the mouth is tied shut and the middle of a rope or chain is secured to the protruding stick around the muzzle, leaving both ends for hunters to drag. This works well in thick cover where spaces between trees are too narrow for two people to get through together.

A third person can help drag in thick cover by attaching a second rope to a front or hind foot. Another way for three hunters to pull a bear in thick cover is to use three separate lengths of rope with one secured to each front leg and the third on the head. When dragging in open hardwoods, or along a trail, three or four people can pull simultaneously by using a long enough drag stick.

Take frequent breaks when dragging or carrying a bear out of the woods to avoid overexertion. It's surprising how easy even long drags can be if taken a short distance at a time. Lone hunters should always try to obtain help to get a bear out of the woods, unless planning on skinning and quartering the carcass.

A bear can be skinned just as easily in the woods as at camp or home, and the sooner it's done the better anyway, to allow maximum cooling of the meat.

Rope attached to a stout stick is handy for dragging black bears.

Start skinning with the animal on its back. If still laying where it was gutted, try to move the carcass far enough away from the viscera to avoid soiling hide or meat. A spot where the ground is level is best.

The first steps I take are to make all of the necessary cuts in the hide. If the pelt hasn't already been split from the neck to the tail for dressing, extend the main cut along the middle of the body. I usually start at the base of the legs

White line roughly marks where cuts should be made to skin a black bear.

and cut upward until reaching the feet. I've seen Lawrence Edwards start at the feet and slice down the leg to the body. It doesn't really matter which way it's done.

Incisions on hind legs should extend to heels and can be continued through the center of the pad to toes. End cuts on front legs partway into the center of pads forward of the wrists. Once these cuts are complete, start working the skin free from the carcass, one leg at a time. Use a sharp knife to cut tissue between hide and meat with one hand while pulling the hide with the other hand. Skin the inside of each leg first, remove the feet from the legs, leaving them attached to the hide, then the skin can be quickly peeled from the back side of the legs.

Front feet can be removed easiest at wrist joints. A knife is adequate for cutting the connective tissue, but a saw can also be used. If a saw is employed, take care not to cut the hide on either side of the joint. Once the bone is severed with a saw, complete the cut with a knife to avoid cutting the skin on top of the wrist.

Skin hind feet as far as the toes then cut across toe joints, leaving toes and pad attached to the hide. If in a hurry, hind legs can be skinned to the heel and the entire foot removed by cutting at the ankle joint.

Attention can be turned toward the body after the legs are skinned. Remove the hide from one side first, as far as the middle of the back, by rolling the carcass on its side. Then do the other side. The already skinned hide protects the carcass from dirt to some extent as it is rolled from one side to the other.

Eventually, the entire pelt will be free from the carcass, with the exception of the head. At this point, the head can be removed from the carcass with the hide attached by either cutting or sawing somewhere along the neck.

Under more favorable circumstances, such as at home or camp, black bears can also be skinned while hanging by their hind legs. The lower portion of hind legs and feet must be skinned first before a bear can be hung in this fashion. Take care not to cut the tendons that attach to the back of heels while skinning hind legs. Once hide is removed from lower legs, make a cut between those tendons and the leg bone for insertion of a sturdy pole. The pole or branch used doesn't have to be long, but it will have to be strong enough to support the weight of the bear carcass.

Put one end of the pole through a gambrel, then hoist the carcass to a sturdy tree limb, meatpole, or some other support so the pole can be placed over the top of it and inserted through the remaining gambrel. Hanging a black bear in this way is relatively easy from the bed of a pickup truck. Once hung, the skinning can be completed. The job is often easier on a hanging bear than one on the ground because it is possible to work all the way around the carcass. It is also possible to peel some of the hide from the carcass once there is enough loose skin to hang onto. In addition, there is less chance of getting dirt on a carcass that is hung. Unfortunately, it is not always possible or convenient to hang a bear for skinning.

Terry Frint carries skinned hide from a bear he bagged in Ontario. Skinning the animal on the spot made it easier to get the carcass out of the woods rather than attempting to take it out in one piece.

After a bear is skinned, the shoulders and hams can be removed to carry out of the woods. The same process is followed when butchering a bear yourself. Cut hind legs or hams from the carcass at the end of the heavy leg bone where it joins the pelvis. A knife is sufficient to cut through connective tissue at that joint. Front legs with shoulders attached can be removed from the carcass by cutting between the shoulder blade and ribs with a knife.

These hunks of meat can be put in meat bags or garbage bags to carry on a packframe or in a large canvas pack. The canvas packs I use to carry bait are large enough for this purpose. If meat is put in garbage bags for the carry out, be sure to remove it from them as soon as the road is reached if the weather is warm because the meat will not cool and may even spoil in plastic bags. Lay meat on top of plastic in the shade, either in a vehicle or outside until ready to leave the area.

Hunters who wish to de-bone bear meat on the spot will be able to reduce the weight of their load considerably and may be able to carry it all in one trip. Cut as much fat as possible from the pieces of meat before deboning to reduce the weight further. Hindquarters will have thick layers of fat during the fall.

Two other cuts of meat to remove from a bear carcass, which will be boneless, are the loins and tenderloins. There are two of each. The tenderloins are long, narrow muscles that taper to a point at each end. They are on the inside of the body cavity along the lower part of the backbone. These choice pieces of meat may be covered with fat and it will have to be trimmed off to see the tenderloins clearly.

Jim Jarvis, Bob Eastman and George Gardner (left to right) hold up skinned hide of a brown black bear I bagged in Colorado.

Remove tenderloins by cutting along them next to the backbone. Then grasp one end of the muscle and pull away from the backbone while using the knife blade to finish freeing it all along its length. I like to eat tenderloins when they are fresh, refrigerating them until prepared for a meal.

The loins or backstraps are long, narrow muscles on both sides of the backbone that are removed from the bear's back. Loins extend from near the rump to the base of the neck. Remove as much fat as possible that is covering that portion of the back before extracting the loins.

Follow basically the same procedure used to free tenderloins to obtain the longer loins. Cut as deeply as possible on both sides of the backbone, slice one end of the loin free from the carcass and pull away from the body while making final cuts along the length of the loin.

The four quarters and the loins comprise the bulk of the meat on a black bear, other than the neck. Ribs are usually too fatty for my liking, but there is some meat on them. What I normally do is cook the ribs and other scraps from a bear carcass that I don't want to eat for my dog. I boil bear meat intended for my dog because he is as susceptible to trichinosis as I am. Odd pieces of usable meat salvaged from the carcass are used for stews, casseroles, or ground into burger.

When transporting meat and hide long distances by car or airplane, dry ice is best for keeping them cold. It helps if they are frozen when starting out. Heavy-duty boxes available from moving and storage companies are great for packing meat, hide and dry ice together. Pat Jarvis and I packed the meat and hide from my Colorado bear in such a box with 10 pounds of dry ice. Newspapers were than used to fill in empty spaces before sealing the box with heavy-duty tape. When I got home late the following day, everything was still frozen solid.

One or two large coolers can also come in handy for transporting meat and hide home. If dry ice isn't available to keep these items cold, chunks of regular ice will have to do, although the supply will have to be replenished at regular intervals, depending upon the temperature. Plastic garbage bags can be used to transport meat and hides with ice for day trips, if coolers or boxes are not available.

If a black bear carcass is taken out of the woods whole and the weather is cool (daytime temperatures less than 45 degrees), or the animal can be put in a cooler, it can be hung several days without skinning. When it's warmer, the carcass should be skinned and butchered within 24 hours. If a bear is hung outside, make sure it stays in the shade. Direct sunlight will ruin bear meat and hides in no time. If it's warm enough for flies to be a problem, don't delay skinning and butchering. Flies can be discouraged from laying eggs on the meat for a short time by sprinkling pepper inside the carcass liberally, as well as on any open wounds, in the anal opening and in the nostrils. If flies do lay eggs on bear meat in little white clusters, the eggs should be removed as soon as possible to avoid damage to the meat.

The first step in butchering a black bear after the major pieces have been removed from the carcass is to slice away as much fat as possible, while

Most of the meat on a black bear is contained on front legs and shoulders (top), hind legs below those and loins at the bottom of photo. Neck can be used as a roast or muscles removed for burger or stew. Other scraps can also be salvaged for casseroles, stews and burger.

getting rid of hair and dirt. Fat will reduce the effective freezer life of meat, so it is important to eliminate it. Less freezer space will be required for de-fatted meat, too, and de-boning is a good idea for the same reason. Fat will be trimmed throughout the butchering process, as deposits inside the meat become easier to reach. Due to all of the fat trimming necessary on bear meat, especially in the fall, it is helpful to have a couple of sharp knives to work with or a sharpening tool to touch up the blade on a single knife.

Before starting to break down hams and shoulders into steaks, roasts, and other cuts you should also have a supply of freezer paper, freezer bags, or heavy-duty aluminum foil to wrap meat in. I have used heavy-duty foil for years to wrap bear meat in with excellent results. A large cutting board is handy to work on, and two big bowls are helpful to separate meat that will be used for stews or casseroles and burger.

When butchering a bear, try to cut away bloodshot meat. I usually give these pieces to my dog after boiling them with ribs, but meat that isn't too bloody can be salvaged by soaking it in saltwater.

Hunters should also have an idea what cuts of meat and how much of each they will want and use. Some people I know grind most of their bear meat into burger, only using the choicest pieces of meat for steaks and chops. That's a far better way to go about it than the person who puts roasts in the freezer, but never finds the time to prepare them. My wife and I reduce a carcass to roasts, steaks, chops, stew meat, and burger because we like it prepared in a variety of ways, which helps prevent the meals prepared with it from becoming boring.

To speed up the butchering process, I usually trim and cut the meat while Lucy separates it into meal-size packages and labels them. I normally try to get four roasts from a bear. One from each shoulder and one from each ham. Roasts are also possible from the neck, but I prefer to use neck muscles in stews or burger. If in a hurry, I sometimes leave the shoulder blade in shoulder roasts, deboning everything else. Steaks can also be cut from shoulders instead of roasts.

Meat from the lower portions of all four legs (below the knees) is used for stews or burger. Thin, outer muscles on hams are used the same way. Larger muscles on hams are separated and cut into steaks or left as roasts. Meat that is firmed up from being chilled or partially frozen is easiest to work with for butchering, but that isn't always possible.

Loins can be cut into small chops, if you prefer, or they can be separated into larger steaks, as I do. Remove as much fat and connective tissue as possible from cuts before they are wrapped. It isn't necessary to get every scrap of fat from steaks, chops and roasts though. Final trimming can be taken care of once the meat is thawed and ready to prepare a meal. However, all fat should be eliminated from meat that will be ground into burger.

If you don't have a meat grinder, butchers at most supermarkets will grind bear meat into burger for you. Call ahead to be sure, and find out when it's convenient for the butcher. Some hunters insist that beef suet or pork fat be added to burger in a ratio of one pound of fat to anywhere from five to 10 pounds of meat. It's okay to do this, but it is not absolutely necessary. I leave my burger as pure, lean bear meat and it eats just fine, thank you.

Because I'm normally in a rush when butchering a bear, I generally freeze two or three pounds of stew meat in chunks. Then I cut it into bite-size pieces before adding it to a stew or casserole. Hunters who prefer to have ready-to-cook stew meat in the freezer can take care of final cutting before freezing.

Whichever material is used to wrap bear meat, be sure it is wrapped tightly around the meat, eliminating air pockets. One layer of heavy-duty aluminum foil adequately protects meat. Some hunters double-wrap their meat in freezer paper or use Ziploc bags for one layer and freezer paper for the other. All packages of meat should be labeled as to type and cut along with the date. I use masking tape to label foil packages, writing the information on the tape in ink before putting it on the foil. I simply use B for bear rather than writing out the word, followed by steak, roast, stew, or whatever, and the date.

When packages of meat are put in the freezer try to spread them out initially rather than stacking them on top of one another, to accelerate freezing. The colder your freezer is, the faster meat will freeze. Storage life of frozen meat can be extended the colder a freezer is. A temperature of 0 degrees F is better than 10, and readings below zero are better yet.

Now that the meat from your bear is taken care of, let's return attention to the hide. Thusfar it has been skinned, with the exception of the head. If the hide is to be turned over to a local taxidermist for processing the day it is skinned, no further work is necessary. If more than a day will elapse before head and hide can be left with a taxidermist, place them in the freezer right away and bring them to the shop frozen when convenient. Fold hides loosely and put them in one or two garbage bags for freezing. It helps to turn freezers up to their coldest settings, if they aren't already, to insure that hides freeze solidly. Don't apply salt to bear hides that are to be frozen because salt will keep it from freezing.

Hunters who plan on shipping bear hides to taxidermists or a tannery will have to skin the head and flesh the hide themselves. Remove the skull first. If you are interested in having a rug made, cut the hide along the underside of the neck and throat to a point two or three inches short of the end of the lower jaw. Hunters who are considering a full or head mount should not cut the head skin any farther than the base of the neck. The head can be skinned by inverting the skin over the skull.

Either way, be extremely careful when skinning the head. When the ears are reached, cut them from the head flush with the skull. The skin around the eyes must also be cut flush with the skull around eye sockets, as should the lips. Cut the cartilage on the nose an inch or two back from the tip.

Once the head is skinned, the entire hide must be fleshed and salted. Bear hides contain large quantities of fat. All of it must be removed in order to protect the pelt from spoilage. Feet and a number of points on the head require special attention.

Scrape away all flesh and cartilage from the feet. Also remove flesh from the base of ears and skin the back of the ears, being careful while doing so. Then shave the lips down as thin as possible without cutting the hide.

Once all of these steps are taken care of, the hide is ready for a liberal application of salt. Use fine table or pickling salt to rub into all parts of the pelt. Make sure plenty of salt is applied to feet, ears, and lips.

Then let the hide dry in the shade outside or on the floor of a shed or basement while resting on newspapers to absorb moisture. Keep hides out of direct sunlight because the sun will burn a bear hide. Moisture will come out of the pelt as it cures. The hide can be shipped, preferably in a burlap bag, but some carriers require that hides be contained in plastic bags, after it is completely dry.

While skinning a black bear or fleshing the hide, there is always a chance of cutting a finger or hand. However, the odds of doing so are reduced by working slowly and carefully. If the job gets tedious it is better to take a short break rather than risk injuring yourself or the trophy you worked so hard to get.

Any cuts that are suffered, small or large, while working on a black bear should be thoroughly cleaned and disinfected once the work is done. Germs have a way of getting into the smallest of cuts. I once neglected to take care of a small nick in one of my fingers after skinning a bear in hot weather. A serious infection developed as a result and a hospital visit was necessary to clear it up.

Hunters who follow the steps outlined in this chapter to care for black bears they bag can look forward to a beautiful rug or mount to remind them of a memorable moment in their big game hunting experience, as well as some fine eating.

CHAPTER
16
Cooking Ideas

Most people eating their first sample of bear meat that has been properly cared for are often surprised at how good it tastes. A fellow who got his first bear last fall remarked about how great the meat was after having had several meals of it. He said it tasted like beef. Other hunters have told me they like bear meat better than venison.

Sound different than what you've heard about the meat from black bears? It may. There's as much misinformation floating around about the meat from these bears as there is about the animals themselves. The truth is it can be great eating, whether from a spring or fall bear.

It is also true that some bruins have trichinosis, resulting from trichina larvae in their muscle tissue, which can be passed on to humans who eat infected meat that is improperly cooked. Pigs are also carriers of trichinosis along with raccoons, red foxes, coyotes, and wolves. The percentage of black bears that have trichinosis in hunted populations is very low, between two and three percent. In remote areas the rate of occurrence may be slightly higher.

The odds of bagging a black bear that has trichinosis are not high. To be on the safe side though, all meat from bears should be cooked thoroughly, which will kill any trichina larvae present. Bear meat should be cooked so the inside of the meat reaches a temperature of approximately 140 degrees F for a few minutes. To ensure that the meat is thoroughly heated inside, steaks and chops should be sliced thinner than venison.

There is no information available on how freezing affects trichina larvae in meat from wild game, according to Dr. Jerry Shad in Pennsylvania. However, he said that the larvae are killed in pork after being frozen solidly at 5

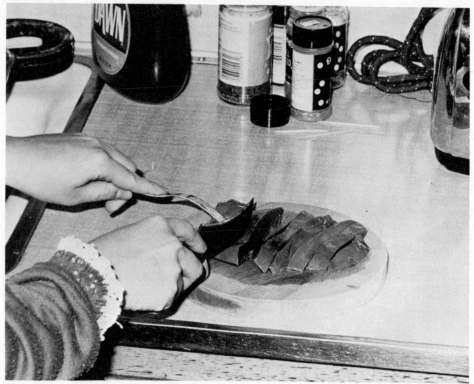

Bear liver being sliced into small pieces to prepare a meal.

degrees F to −10 between two and three weeks, with the longer period required for the warmer temperature.

The fact that black bears are fatty animals, especially during the fall, turns some people off on the meat. I can't understand why, because you don't eat the fat, just the lean meat. Like any other big game, it is important to remove every speck of fat possible from black bear meat before it's cooked. Most of the fat should be removed during the butchering process before meat is packaged and frozen. Fat does not freeze well and will reduce the quality of meat it is on the longer it remains frozen. When meat is thawed for a meal, any last little bits of fat should be removed as a first step in preparing the meat for cooking.

Roasts are the toughest cuts to free of fat with a knife. What I usually do is break a roast down into smaller chunks of meat to get at as much fat as possible. However, there is an easier way to remove the last traces of fat from roasts—parboiling. By parboiling a roast for 20 to 30 minutes at medium to high heat before putting it in the oven or crock pot, fat marbled in the meat is boiled off.

The age and weight of black bears doesn't appear to affect the quality of the meat either. A fellow I know who killed a male that dressed over 500 pounds said the meat was so tender he could cut it with a fork. That animal had been eating apples. I ate meat from another male that was over 400 pounds and that tasted as good as any other bear meat I've eaten. A friend of mine bagged a sow that was about 16 years old and the meat proved to be fine from that one, too.

Because bear meat should be cooked thoroughly, steps should be taken to ensure that it stays moist. Sauces, soups, and broths all work for this purpose. In some cases, small amounts of water can be used to steam meat. No moisture at all is necessary when broiling steaks, including tenderloins, or chops. It doesn't take long for these cuts to cook thoroughly at 375 to 400 degrees and the inside of the meat retains plenty of moisture.

Most of the cooking my wife and I do with bear meat involves quick and simple recipes. Lucy deserves credit for developing most of the recipes we use for preparing bear meat. We use very little seasoning, enjoying the natural flavor of the meat rather than trying to mask it, although we do use a lot of soups. When frying steaks and chops, a little butter or margarine is melted in the fry pan, then the meat is browned. Once the meat is browned, a cup of water or beef broth is added and the pan covered to keep steam in while the cooking process is completed at medium heat for about 20 minutes.

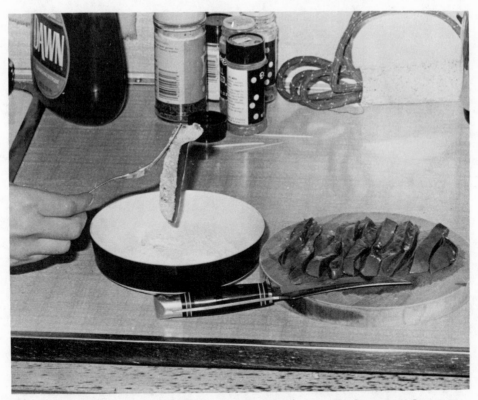

Pieces of liver can be coated with seasoned flour or cooked uncoated.

Liver or heart are prepared the same way. Slice them thin, being careful to remove all of the fat from the heart, brown in butter or margarine, then add water and cover the pan. Pieces of liver and heart can be dipped in seasoned flour before browning, if desired. I usually slice a medium to large onion or two to cook with both liver and heart.

Ted Nugent did most of the cooking during a week of bear hunting last fall and at least one of the meals he prepared included the heart from a bruin that had been bagged. His simple recipe involved heating cooking oil with a touch of butter in a fry pan, then adding sliced pieces of heart dipped in seasoned flour and cooking them for 15 minutes. Ted usually seasons flour with pepper and garlic. He also said that he sometimes marinates pieces of heart in Half & Half for 30 minutes before cooking them.

Black bear liver is a different consistency than the same organ from deer, being very tender when cooked. Bear liver is the best I've eaten, and it is high in vitamin B.

Burger from black bear meat is as versatile as ground beef or venison. It can be used in meatloaf, sausage, chili, spaghetti, casseroles, sloppy joes, and plain hamburgers. If beef or pork fat is mixed with bear burger, grease should be drained after the meat is cooked before adding other ingredients. As mentioned in the chapter on "Caring for Your Trophy," we keep bear burger as

Bear casserole is one of our favorites. This dish is also popular among our friends at potluck dinners.

lean as possible, melting margarine in a fry pan to cook burger with to keep it from sticking to the pan, then drain off the margarine and any traces of grease once the meat is cooked.

One of our favorite meals with bear burger is burger stroganoff. Between one and two pounds of ground meat is cooked and grease drained. Then cans of cream of chicken and cream of mushroom soup are added to the meat and mixed together. A third can of soup of either kind is added when using more meat than normal, to achieve the proper consistency of the mixture. Meat and soup are cooked for about 30 minutes at medium heat, then served over hot casserole noodles.

When making spaghetti, tomato sauce is added to cooked and drained meat in the desired quantity to produce a meaty sauce. Then diced onions or onion powder are added, along with garlic powder, to suit our taste.

Friends Jim and Sarah Haveman passed along their recipe for bear summer sausage. Mix three pounds of burger thoroughly with ¼ teaspoon each of onion powder, garlic powder, and pepper; 1½ teaspoons liquid smoke, three tablespoons of Mortons Tender Quick and a cup of water. Roll into three sausages and wrap each in aluminum foil. Refrigerate them for 24 hours, then bake at 300 degrees for 1½ hours. Punch holes in the bottom of foil before baking.

We make another stroganoff dish using various cuts of meat from stew to round steak. This recipe and another one to follow are great for using odd bits and pieces of meat sometimes left over after butchering a black bear, so don't discard any scraps of lean meat from a carcass. The meat, between one and two pounds, is cut into bite-size pieces than browned in margarine. Cans of consommé and onion with beef broth soups are added to the meat and cooked for about 25 minutes at medium heat. Here again, a third can of soup of either kind is sometimes added if two cans don't match the amount of meat. A small can of drained mushrooms is added with the soup.

After about 25 minutes, the mixture is brought to a boil and a small container of sour cream is mixed in. Cook for five more minutes then serve over minute rice in bowls. Spoons are recommended for eating this meal due to its soupy consistency.

Bear casserole is a hit with us as well as our friends at potluck dinners. Meat is cut into bite-size pieces and browned. Meat and any broth is then transferred to a deep casserole dish along with cans of cream of celery and cream of mushroom soup. A drained can of mushrooms is sometimes added, too. This combination is baked at 350 degrees for two hours and served over noodles.

To make pepper steak, cut bear steaks into narrow strips approximately two inches long by one-half-inch wide and brown them in margarine. Add a can or two of beef consommé soup along with a diced onion or two and one or two green peppers sliced into strips. Simmer at medium heat until meat and vegetables are tender (about 20 minutes), reduce heat, then add tomato wedges and serve over rice after a few minutes.

Sweet and sour bear is one of Lucy's favorites. Cut meat into strips the

Adding tomato wedges to pan for pepper steak, the last step in preparation of the meal.

same as for pepper steak and brown in margarine. Once meat is browned add a can of chicken broth, cover pan, and simmer for about 20 minutes. Meanwhile, drain the liquid from a 20-ounce can of pineapple chunks, saving the liquid. Then mix ¼ cup each of brown sugar and vinegar, two tablespoons of cornstarch, and three teaspoons of soy sauce with the pineapple syrup in a sauce pan. Heat this mixture until thick and bubbly, stirring continuously.

Combine sauce with meat and chicken broth, then add ⅓ cup of thinly sliced onion, three carrots cut into curls and a large green pepper cut into

Pepper steak tastes great served over rice.

strips. Simmer until veggies are tender, reduce heat, and add tomato wedges from two large tomatoes for a few minutes before serving over rice.

For Smith bear stew, cut two pounds of de-fatted meat into pieces and brown in margarine. Put browned meat in a three-quart pot along with two cans of onion soup, two cans of water, three or four sliced carrots, five or six small to medium potatoes, and three onions. Cook at a gentle boil for about an hour with the pot covered.

Haveman stew can be prepared in a regular pot or crock pot. Mix two pounds of seasoned meat chunks with a cup of carrots, celery and water, plus a diced potato and onion, a can of stewed tomatoes, and $\frac{1}{3}$ cup of tapioca. Mix well and cook at 250 degrees for five hours.

One of the best ways to prepare bear roasts is baked in barbecue sauce. Parboil first, if desired, than put in a roasting pan and cover with barbecue sauce. To make the sauce, combine a 15-ounce can of tomato sauce, an envelope of Italian dressing, $\frac{1}{4}$ cup each of vinegar and light molasses, two tablespoons of salad oil, one tablespoon of wet mustard and $1\frac{1}{2}$ cups of water in a sauce pan. Boil the sauce for three minutes while stirring. Once the sauce is added, bake for $1\frac{1}{2}$-2 hours at 350 degrees. Baste at regular intervals with sauce in pan. Add water as needed if sauce begins to dry out.

That's the method Lucy and I use for preparing barbecued bear roast. The Havemans use a different sauce. It's composed of $\frac{1}{4}$ cup of vinegar, $\frac{1}{2}$ cup water, two tablespoons sugar, one teaspoon each of dry mustard and chili powder, five squirts Tabasco sauce, $\frac{1}{2}$ teaspoon pepper, $1\frac{1}{2}$ teaspoons salt, $\frac{1}{4}$ teaspoon garlic powder, one tablespoon lemon juice, a diced onion, and $\frac{1}{4}$ cup salad oil. These ingredients are mixed in a sauce pan and simmered for 20 minutes uncovered. Then $\frac{1}{2}$ cup of catsup and two tablespoons of Worcestershire sauce are added, and the sauce is brought to a boil.

Meanwhile, the roast is being baked at 325 degrees. When the meat is well glazed it is basted with the sauce. The roast is basted frequently over three to four hours until done.

CHAPTER
17

Hiring a Guide

Hiring a black bear guide is a lot like preparing for a hunt on your own. You have to do your homework to end up with what you want. However, in this case, hunters must select an experienced person who can help put them in position for a shot at a black bear. Hunters who don't take the time to choose guides carefully can end up dissatisfied, disappointed, or worse.

All persons claiming the title of black bear guide are not deserving of the title, although I know many of them who are. Some who aren't are simply in it for the money, knowing little or nothing about black bears and how to hunt them. Others may try hard, but lack the experience or area to produce consistently, and still more rely on illegal hunting methods to fill their clients' tags.

So-called guides that fit in the above categories can generally be weeded out in the selection process, if done properly. One of the first steps in this process is deciding how you want to hunt and what services you desire from a guide. A corresponding consideration is how much money you are willing to spend for a guide's services. The services of quality guides don't generally come cheap, but there are some bargain black bear hunts available for hunters who require little assistance during a hunt.

There are bear guides available who specialize in hunting with hounds, baiting, spotting and stalking, and calling. Some use a combination of techniques in an effort to bring clients and bears together. Lawrence Edwards and Wayne Bosowicz, for example, employ both bait and hounds in their hunting. Lawrence primarily relies on his hounds, but during days when there has been no success with dogs during the morning, he puts hunters on stands overlooking baits in the evening. Most of Wayne's hunts are over bait, but he also maintains hounds for hunters who prefer to hunt in that fashion.

One of the first steps in deciding on a guide is to make a list of those who may offer what you want. Names can be obtained from magazines and books like the *NRA's Hunter's Planning Guide and Directory*.

Some guides provide transportation, while others expect hunters to use their own vehicles. Meals and lodging may be included as part of the package available from guides, which is the case with the hunts Jim Jarvis offers. Others may simply provide lodging or expect hunters to make arrangements for their own meals and lodging, only taking care of details dealing with the actual hunt.

One of the simplest and cheapest guide services offered deals with baiting, where a guide baits a location until the hunter arrives. Once the hunter is taken to the bait, he's on his own. The potential for problems is greatest on a hunt of this type, although no guided hunt is exempt from misunderstandings and less-than-expected services. For this reason, hunters who hire a bear guide should select the person they plan to hunt with carefully and clarify what they will be getting for their money in advance.

Once you know what type of black bear hunt you want and how much you can spend, start compiling a list of guides who may offer what you are looking for. Many guides advertise in magazines that publish hunting material, and some names can be obtained from the pages of these periodicals. State and provincial agencies that manage black bears maintain names and addresses of guides in some cases, so check with them in an effort to obtain possible additions to your list. Taxidermists can also be good contacts to get names of guides.

The National Rifle Association, 1600 Rhode Island Ave., NW, Washington, D.C. 20036, has listings of guides by state and province in the *NRA Hunter's Planning Guide and Directory*, which is updated every year or two. The North American Hunting Club, P.O. Box 35557, Minneapolis, MN 55435, also maintains a list of guides for its members along with reports, both good and bad, on hunter experiences with guides. Additions to a list of potential black bear guides can be obtained from friends and acquaintances who have hunted with guides.

Recommendations of reputable guides from friends are often the most valuable because acquaintances can provide a first-hand account of a guide's performance and services, giving hunters an accurate account of what can be expected. The reason I selected Jim Jarvis for my Colorado bear hunt was due to recommendations from friends George Gardner and Ann Clark, who had hunted with him the previous fall. Recent experiences of friends are the most valuable, of course. A guide's services as well as the quality of hunts offered can change over a period of years, either for better or worse.

Never assume guides with ads in national magazines are reputable. Anyone with enough money can place such an ad regardless of their credentials. The advertising departments of most magazines don't investigate guides who purchase space, nor should they be expected to. It is the responsibility of hunters who wish to employ guides to check them out.

Narrow your list of possible guides as much as possible, based on available information, then make an initial contact by mail or telephone. The guide selection process, by the way, is something that should be done as far in advance of hunting season as possible. Starting preparations for a guided hunt a year or more in advance is not unusual. This may be necessary in situations where licenses are limited and have to be applied for well in advance. Popular guides often book all of the hunters they can handle early, too.

Don't ask guides for their life story on the initial contact. The services they provide, their average success, what they charge and if they have any openings are the primary bits of information that will be most helpful in determining which guide best fits your needs. Query letters to guides might go something like this:

Dear Bear Guide:

I'm in the process of planning a spring (or fall) black bear hunt with bow
and arrow (or rifle, musket, handgun) and am interested in the hunts you
offer. Could you please send me information about the services you provide
and how much they cost? I am also interested in the rate of success your
hunters have enjoyed during recent years and what part of the season usually
offers the best hunting. Please include this information with your reply.

Sincerely,

J. Bear Hunter

The best letters are brief and to the point. Guides don't like to read long
letters any more than they like to write them. In fact, some guides may reply
by telephone rather than writing, so be sure to include your telephone number
and your address in your letter. Give guides at least a month to reply by mail,
and longer if you write during hunting season when they are busiest. You may
want to phone guides who are slow to respond, or eliminate them from consideration if a suitable guide has already been located.

Keep in mind when gathering this type of information that quality black
bear hunts cost from $600 to $1,000 in 1984. Guides that charge less are

Recommendations of friends can also be valuable in deciding on a black bear
guide, as was the case when I hunted with Jim Jarvis in Colorado. Here Jim
gives me a congratulatory handshake for bear I bagged while hunting with
him.

probably providing less services, although some good part-time guides may charge less. Most guides require a deposit of up to 50 percent of the hunt cost to confirm dates. Some charge hunters who don't connect less than those who do. When corresponding with guides in Canada, find out if their rates are in Canadian or U.S. funds.

As far as rate of success, any guide who averages 50 percent or better is doing terrific. In all fairness to guides, the success ratio need not only include bears that were actually tagged. Bears that are wounded and not recovered should have been dead bears in most cases and are the individual hunter's responsibility, therefore shouldn't be held against the guide, unless he was negligent in attempts to find the animals. Missed shots are generally not the guide's fault either.

So guides who put at least half of their clients in position for shots at bears are doing good. Guides who report lower rates of success, only including actual kills in their percentages, are still doing a good job, and are being honest. Not all guides are honest, with some inflating their success ratios to attract more clients.

If there are questions remaining in your mind about services, fees, or success of guides after they've responded to your initial letter, give them a call or write again to clarify the points in question. More information can usually be gathered over the phone much faster than by mail. If you do call guides with specific questions, write them down before placing the call, leaving room to write answers, so they won't be forgotten.

There are a number of important questions to ask of guides who will simply be baiting a spot for hunters until their arrival, then turning it over to them. One is, "Will the bait be active," meaning will the site be visited regularly by at least one legal black bear? Hunters should also determine if additional bait will be provided once the existing supply is gone, if alternate sites will be available if the bait becomes inactive or is only being visited after shooting hours, and if assistance will be provided to trail wounded animals, plus get bagged bruins out of the woods.

Once you've narrowed your list of possible guides to candidates that are seriously being considered, ask them for references, hunters who have hunted with them during recent years. Ask for names, addresses and telephone numbers of unsuccessful as well as successful hunters. Try to obtain references that live as close to you as possible, then contact them by letter or telephone for their comments about the guide. Also ask them for names of other hunters you can contact. I recommend using the phone to check out references. If you do so by mail, be sure to include stamped, self-addressed envelopes for replies.

By the time references are checked you should know who you want to book a hunt with. Send in your deposit for the desired dates, requesting a receipt, and ask any last-minute questions you might have such as what distance to sight your gun or bow in for and what type of clothing or footwear to bring. You should already know what your license is going to cost, plus where and when one can be obtained. Don't forget to ask if there are any special regulations or provisions you should know about. In Colorado, for instance, anyone born after January 1, 1949 is supposed to have a hunter safety card to obtain a hunting license.

If you are only interested in a trophy bear, this should have been mentioned in your initial contact. You should also spell out what you mean by a trophy. The word means something different to many hunters. It may be a bruin that weighs at least 300 pounds, one that measures six feet in length or an animal with a skull that scores at least 19 inches by Pope and Young and Boone and Crockett standards.

If you book a hunt with hounds, plan on doing some pre-hunt conditioning to prepare for the strenuous exercise that often comes with such a hunt. Hunters who are in poor physical shape are doing both themselves and the guide a disservice by booking a hunt with hounds. Hunters who have any handicaps, physical problems, or special requirements should inform the guide of these when booking a hunt, not after you arrive.

An alternative to going through the process of selecting a black bear guide yourself is using a booking agent such as Jack Atcheson, 3210 Ottawa, Butte, MT 59701, or Safari Travel International, 3505 Hart Ave., Rosemead, CA 91770. You tell them what type of hunt you want and they arrange a hunt for you with a reputable guide. Booking agents usually receive commissions from guides, so their services shouldn't cost hunters anything extra, but check to be sure.

After a black bear hunt is booked with a guide you are satisfied with and you arrive on your hunt, trust your guide's judgment. He's obviously highly recommended for a reason. The man should know how, where, and when to hunt black bears in his area better than you do, so don't try something he recommends against. The biggest mistake some hunters make on guided hunts is not having confidence in their guides or not following a guide's instructions.

Some guides who use bait only hunt evenings, reserving mornings for trailing wounded bears or checking baits. Unless special arrangements have been made to hunt at other times, hunt when the guide says it's best. On days when conditions are adverse for hunting, a guide may recommend not hunting at all, with good reason. Trust your guide's judgment. I've been a guide and have hunted with guides, so I speak from experience. Some hunters simply don't give their guides enough credit once they've hired them.

And although most good guides try their hardest to get every hunter a shot at a black bear, it can't always be done. He usually has no control over the weather and, in many cases, other hunting pressure. And even though your guide may be knowledgeable about black bears, the animals aren't always predictable.

Guides can make mistakes or choices that turn out to be the wrong ones at a later date. However, they are human like everyone else and hunters have no right to expect super-human results from them.

To increase the chances of success, hunters should plan on booking five to seven-day hunts. It isn't unusual to lose a day or two to weather during some weeks. Even if the weather is favorable, it may take that long to get a look at a bear. Hunters who book two and three-day hunts limit their chances of success from the start, although, in many cases, that is enough time to score.

Hunters who don't see action on the first day or two of their hunt shouldn't become discouraged. It often takes patience and persistence to get a chance at a bear, whether hunting with a guide or on your own. Hunters who become discouraged simply don't hunt properly and reduce their chances of success regardless of their guide's performance.

A bowhunter I know was hunting over bait, and when he didn't see anything his first two days on stand, he lost his enthusiasm. The man left his stand an hour before dark, which was prime hunting time, on the first evening of his hunt. When a nice bear finally showed on the third evening, he was totally unprepared, sitting in his tree stand with his legs dangling in the air. When the bowhunter tried to bring his bow into play he bumped it on the stand, alerting the bear. He still got a shot as the bear walked off, but missed. If that hunter had been on his feet prepared to shoot, as he should have been, I'm sure he could have bagged that bruin.

Proper selection of a black bear guide can be a simple matter, if going on the recommendation of a friend or using the services of a booking agent. However, when doing it yourself, the process can take a lot of time and effort, as much as planning a do-it-yourself hunt. You're sure to reap the benefits of doing your homework though, when it comes time to take part in the guided black bear hunt you've chosen. That is, if you have confidence in your guide and are persistent.

CHAPTER
18

Record-Book Bears

There are two record books maintained to recognize outstanding big game kills. Bow and arrow kills are monitored by the Pope and Young Club. Exceptional animals taken with firearms are listed in *Records of North American Big Game* published by the Boone and Crockett Club. A black bear skull has to have a minimum score of 18 to qualify for listing in the *Bowhunting Big Game Records of North America* and 21 to be considered for the Boone and Crockett record book. A bow-bagged bear with a skull that scores at least 21 can be listed in both record books.

Black bear skulls are scored by measuring their length and width with the lower jaw detached, then combining the measurements. All muscle and tissue has to be removed from a skull before it can be scored, of course. A 60-day drying period is also required before the skull can be officially measured. Some shrinkage takes place during the drying period.

Flesh should be removed from any bear skull that is to be measured for record book consideration as soon as possible. Carve off as much muscle as possible with a knife first. Once that step is complete there are several ways to finish the process. The skull can be boiled to soften the remaining tissue for removal. This is a relatively fast method, but may result in some shrinkage of the skull if it is overboiled.

Hunters who decide to boil bear skulls should remember to remove the brain. It can be taken out in pieces through a hole in the base of the skull where the neck was once attached.

The other methods of skull cleaning leave the final process to insects and decay. Skulls can be buried in a convenient, well-marked location, allowing the remaining tissues to break down naturally with the help of bacteria in the

Boone and Crockett scorer Duaine Wenzel measures length of a big bear skull using two straight-edges and a yardstick. Calipers are often used by measurers to score skulls.

soil. The same thing will happen faster if the skull is left above ground, but it should be put in a location where it will be safe, yet the smell won't be offensive. If either of these alternatives are chosen to finish cleaning a skull, it should be enclosed in a wire cage or porous box to prevent neighborhood dogs and other animals from carrying it away or damaging it.

Some museums and universities may have still one other method of cleaning skulls for bear hunters to consider. Some of these institutions maintain beetle collections, which quickly clean flesh from bones. Establishments that have beetle collections may be able to save bear hunters the time and trouble of cleaning skulls themselves. A phone call is all it would take to inquire about the possibility, if a university or museum is nearby.

Calipers are usually used by official scorers to accurately measure the length and width of bear skulls to the nearest one-sixteenth of an inch. However, I watched Michigan measurer Duaine Wenzel score a black bear skull by placing it on a ruler, then using two straight edges to determine measurements. Hunters can do the same thing themselves. Hunters can also get a rough idea how skulls will score with a tape measure or ruler and a couple of blocks of wood. Simply put the skull, minus the lower jaw, on a flat, level surface, then place the pieces of wood parallel to each other against the widest points of the skull. The blocks of wood should be about as long as the skull, but taller and remain upright when resting on the bottom surface.

Then measure from the inside of one block to the inside of the other across the widest point. Once the width has been obtained, the pieces of wood can be positioned parallel to one another with one at the nose and the other across the back of the skull to determine the length. If the cumulative total comes close to 18 or 21, depending on whether the bear was bagged with bow or gun, an official scorer should be contacted for an accurate measurement.

A list of official scorers in the hunter's state can be obtained from Pope and Young and Boone and Crockett. Address inquiries for gun kills to Boone and Crockett Club, 205 South Patrick St., Alexandria, VA 22314. The address for the Pope and Young Club is Rt. 1, Box 147, Salmon, ID 83467.

Large black bear skulls that are found by hunters while afield and those turned up in barns, garages and attics are elligible for record book listing as well as those entered by hunters who bag big-headed bruins. Damaged skulls will not be considered, however, so hunters interested in having bear skulls considered should try to avoid shooting the animals in the head. Bears must also be taken under rules of fair chase for their skulls to qualify for listing in either record book. Bruins taken in front of hounds wearing radio collars can be entered.

The present world record black bear skull was found by Alma Lund and Merrill Daniels seven miles from their home in Ephraim, Utah in 1975. The skull scored 23 $^{10}/_{16}$, 1 $^{4}/_{16}$ inches better than the previous record holder, which

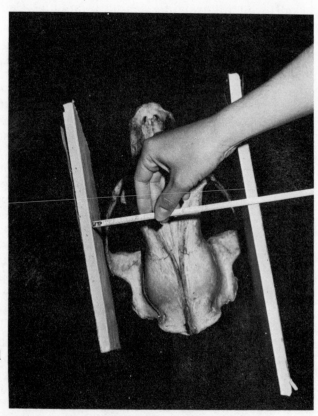

Hunters can get a general idea how a skull will score by taking measurements between two blocks of wood.

also came from Utah five years earlier. Rex Peterson and R.S. Hardy collected the former world record black bear while hunting with hounds, and the skull scored 22 $^6/_{16}$. Two more black bear skulls of that same size are now on record. One was collected in Arizona by Roy Stewart in 1978.

The second was bagged by John Whyne in Pennsylvania in 1983. Whyne said he was making a drive with companions on a mountain when he stopped to take a drink of water from a spring and got behind the other drivers. As he moved ahead after taking the drink, he spotted the record book bear 50 to 75 yards ahead looking downhill toward one of the other drivers. The animal had a dressed weight of 580 pounds, according to a scale at the check station, and it was determined to be nine years old. The skull from Whyne's bear was measured by a member of the Pennsylvania Game Commission.

At the end of the Boone and Crockett's 18th awards program in 1983, those three skulls each scoring 22 $^6/_{16}$ became third largest. A bruin bagged in Saskatchewan in 1977 by Calvin Parsons is $^2/_{16}$ of the inch larger with a score of 22 $^8/_{16}$.

Ray Cox holds the honor of having arrowed a black bear with the largest skull on record for a bowhunter at 22 $^4/_{16}$. The old male was treed by dogs in Colorado in 1978. Cox reported that the animal didn't have any teeth left. The number two bow-killed black bear was collected by Robert Faufau in Wisconsin in 1981 while hunting over bait. The skull from that bruin scored 21 $^{14}/_{16}$.

Sow black bears seldom grow heads large enough to qualify for record book recognition. Consequently, most of the skulls listed in the record books are from males. However, there are six skulls from females listed in the second edition of *Bowhunting Big Game Records* out of more than 500 entries. Two of the record book sows were taken in Wisconsin, two in Idaho, and one each from Minnesota and New Mexico. The score of the largest sow skull is 19 $^{15}/_{16}$.

Age, genetic background and diet are probably the three major factors that determine if any given bear will have a record book skull. There has to be a good mix of all three to produce a boar with an exceptional skull. Some males may be old and heavy due to an abundant food supply, but have skulls that won't score 21 because their genetic background does not favor large head growth.

The largest bear on record in Michigan, weightwise, is a prime example of this. The animal had a dressed weight of 613 pounds. That bruin's skull scored 20 $^{12}/_{16}$. A bowhunter, Hawley Rhew, bagged that bear, so it easily qualified for listing among the bowhunting records, but if a gun hunter had taken the animal, it would have been too small for the book.

On the other hand, a boar with a genetic makeup that favors head growth may never become record book material if his food intake is meager, and certainly if he doesn't live long enough. Black bears attain maximum skull growth by the time they are nine or 10 years old. The number of possibilities involving age, genetics and nutrition are numerous, but as a general rule, the heaviest black bears in a given area are the oldest and have the biggest heads. And boars average larger in size than sows. A 300-pound-plus sow is bigger-than-average and represents the top end of the weight scale for females. Boars attain weights upwards of 700 pounds; however, they become exceptional once they reach 400 to 500 pounds.

Body, head and track size are the best guidelines available for judging a black bear's record book potential in the field. Any bruin that leaves a front foot print that measures five to six inches or more across is definitely above average and would probably weigh a minimum of 300 pounds in the round, at least during the fall. The odds that such an animal would have a skull big enough to qualify for Pope and Young listing are excellent. Whether the animal's head would have at least another three inches of bone may depend on the animal's genetic background and age.

The best a hunter can do when hoping to bag a book bear is look for the biggest bear in the area being hunted and try for it. Big-bodied bruins are generally easy to distinguish from small-to-average animals. Their bodies are often deep from back to belly and long from head to tail. Fall bears will look thicker across the body than they will in the spring, of course. The heavy breathing of a fat bear is often audible within 20 or 30 yards, too, and their gait is slower and more swaggering than smaller animals.

The ears on the heads of small-to-average black bears will be prominent and snouts will have a pointed appearance. Ears will look shorter and smaller on bears with big heads and their snouts look rounded, giving a snub-nose appearance. It takes experience to judge the head and body size of black bears with any consistency, and even experienced hunters make mistakes in situations where the entire animal isn't visible or only brief glimpses of animals are possible.

A good thing for a hunter to do who has seen few black bears and plans to hunt them, is to visit a zoo that has the animals and look at them carefully. Estimate their weight and, if possible, check with the zookeeper to find out how much the animals actually weigh. Black bears are simply difficult to judge accurately. Most hunters overestimate the weight of black bears.

Bear hunters who are serious about getting their name in one of the record books should also study current record book listings on the state or continental level to get an idea what areas have produced the most big bear skulls. These locations can be good places to try for a book bear of your own. Arizona, Colorado, and Wisconsin, for example, lead all other states and provinces for the number of bears in Boone and Crockett listings through the 18th recording period by a wide margin. The first two have 20 listings each and Wisconsin has 19. California is next in line with 14. From there the most B&C bears from any state or province goes down to seven.

The most listings in the latest edition of the Pope and Young records are for Colorado (94), Ontario (89), Idaho (47), Maine (45) and Wisconsin (44). Also high in record book bow kills are Minnesota (36), California (31) and Michigan (20). A complete listing of the number of book bears presently on record for individual states and provinces is included in this chapter.

Although current record book listings provide valuable information, they in no way provide the total picture as far as book bears are concerned. Unlike large antlers, which are usually always saved and eventually end up being

The bear this hunter is aiming at looks like a trophy animal. The body is deep from back to belly and the ears appear small on the head, indicating that the skull is big.

measured for record book consideration, many big bear skulls have been left in the field or discarded and will never be recorded. States and provinces with the most listings probably reflect where the most bear hunting pressure is as much as where book bears are located. Included in this chapter is a method for cleaning and preserving skulls, developed by Donald Smith of the Minnesota Museum of Natural History.

I firmly believe that the book bear producing potential of a number of Canadian provinces is yet to be realized. Alberta, British Columbia, Mani-

Directions for Preparing Bear Skulls

1. Boil the skull until the meat is soft (the consistency of stewed meat).
   Make sure that the skull is completely covered with water; any part exposed to air during the boiling process will become permanently discolored.
   Adding a small amount of potassium carbonate will speed up the softening process. Beware of adding too much, as an excess will decalcify the bone. Use about ½ teaspoon per gallon of water.

2. Remove the softened flesh with fingers and a toothbrush.

3. Immerse the skull in a clear *glass* jar filled with a solution of pure Chlorox or Hilex bleach.
   Chlorinated bleach has a corrosive effect first on the cartilage, then on the bone. Cartilage such as in the turbinates and on the occipitals will dissolve off in a stream of bubbles. As soon as the cartilage has dissolved, the skull should be removed from the bleach and rinsed in cold water. If the skull is immersed in the bleach for more than 10 minutes, the bone itself will be attacked.

4. Place the skull in a 50-50 solution of 3% hydrogen peroxide and water in a clear glass jar. Adding a small amount of ammonia will speed up the bleaching process. If greater whiteness is desired, put the jar containing the skull and peroxide on a white piece of paper and set it in direct sunlight. Let the skull bleach for about six hours.

5. Rinse in cold water and dry.

6. Immerse the skull in carbon tetrachloride or gasoline to remove grease.

7. Dry.

8. Spread Duco cement on the teeth to prevent them from cracking, as they dry out with time. This *must* be done with carnivore skulls because their teeth are especially prone to crack.

9. Spray the skull with clear acrylic plastic (such as Krylon). This seals the bone surface and makes it impervious to dirt and oils which would otherwise stain it.

Developed by Donald Smith,
Minnesota Museum of Natural History

toba, and Saskatchewan all have excellent black bear populations, for example, but not many animals from those provinces are listed in the record book compared to some states with lower bear populations. A high percentage of the bears qualifying for the records that are listed for Canadian provinces were taken in the past 10 years. Ontario, with 89 entries in the P&Y records, is an example of the book bear potential in Canada.

I think the reason more black bears are not listed from most Canadian provinces is lack of hunter interest in them there at the present time. Many hunters who travel to these provinces to hunt from the United States have their sights set on larger and more glamorous game such as moose, sheep, elk, caribou, and grizzly bears. Many local hunters look on black bears as pests. For these reasons, black bears are largely overlooked in much of Canada. Hunters interested in a record book black should keep that in mind.

Any hunter who is serious about bagging a record book black bear has an excellent chance of doing so, especially with bow and arrow, not only in Canada, but in parts of the U.S. as well. To be successful in the search for an exceptional bruin, however, a hunter must be willing to pass up lesser animals and make the time to go on lengthy hunts. Although I've shot my share of black bears, I haven't gotten one with a skull large enough to qualify for record book listing, but that's something I hope to change soon.

My best bear to date is one I bagged with bow and arrow in Colorado last spring. The six-year-old male has a 17-inch skull, according to guide Jim Jarvis, who recently measured it for me. I've come close to nailing bears with bigger heads a few times, but something always prevented a shot.

While guiding bowhunter Gary Lohman from Grand Rapids, Michigan, I stood next to him as he shot a Pope and Young bear, which was perhaps more thrilling for me than Gary at the time because he didn't fully comprehend what he had accomplished until later. I knew there was a big bear on the bait we were hunting by the sign, and I saw the animal once. I didn't get a real good look at the animal though, so I couldn't be sure of its size, but I estimated its weight between 300 and 500 pounds. The upper limit was close.

I knew the bear was big when I saw it coming on the first evening of the season during the last minutes of daylight. The animal reminded me of a big, round barrel with legs. Gary drew his compound bow as the big bruin approached the bait and released the arrow as soon as the animal turned angling away, making a good hit that put the boar down in 50 to 60 yards.

I'm sure the animal had a dressed weight over 400 pounds. The skull scored $18^9/_{16}$ and will be listed in the next edition of *Bowhunting Big Game Records of North America*.

A trophy bear is a very personal thing. Each hunter sets his or her own standards for determining what is and is not a trophy. Hunters who have never bagged a black bear may consider any legal animal a trophy, especially if they only have one opportunity to hunt them in a lifetime. To others, a trophy might be one that weighs a minimum of 200 pounds. To me, any black bear with a dressed weight of 300 pounds or better is a trophy.

An animal with that body size may have a head large enough to make one or the other big game record books. If it did, it would be both a trophy and record book bear. If it didn't, it would simply be a trophy, which should be satisfaction enough for any hunter. One thing I want to make clear is that the bagging of a book bear does not necessarily mean that the hunter is among the most skillful or is a notch above other hunters, although it does sometimes take an exceptional measure of skill and persistence to bag a book bear. Just as often, luck is involved in such a kill, with the hunter simply being in the right place at the right time.

Number of Book Bears by State and Province

State	B&C Bears	P&Y Bears
Alaska	5	16
Arizona	20	3
California	14	31
Colorado	20	94
Idaho	2	47
Louisiana	1	—
Maine	—	45
Michigan	1	20
Minnesota	2	36
Montana	—	9
New Hampshire	—	1
New Mexico	1	12
New York	3	1
North Carolina	—	2
Oregon	2	9
Pennsylvania	4	—
Tennessee	2	4
Utah	4	6
Vermont	—	2
Virginia	2	1
Washington	6	10
Wisconsin	19	44
Wyoming	7	2

Province		
Alberta	6	5
British Columbia	7	15
Manitoba	3	9
Newfoundland	1	1
Nova Scotia	1	—
Ontario	1	89
Quebec	—	7
Saskatchewan	4	10

Mexico	1	—

The obvious difference between trophy and record book bruins is that the standards for record status are set by the Boone and Crockett and Pope and Young Clubs. Those standards are not flexible as they are for personal trophies. And that's the way it has to be to have a uniform, reliable system. Anyone who collects a black bear with a skull large enough for listing in either record book has certainly downed an exceptional representative of one of the most interesting big game species in North America. The animal itself deserves the status that record book listing gives it for having attained its exceptional size.

CHAPTER
19

When to Hunt

Bears stand alone as major big game species that can be hunted during both spring and fall seasons, with black bears the most numerous and widespread. However, only states and provinces with the highest black bear populations have hunts during both times of year. Spring bear hunts are common across Canada, with the exception of one province, in Alaska and in many Western states. Fall hunts only are the rule in the Midwest, South and Eastern U.S.

Bear hunting can be excellent during either time of year, provided a hunt is properly timed in accordance with the weather, which has a direct effect on bear activity. This is sometimes difficult to do, but becomes easier once the general activity patterns of bruins are known. In the spring, for example, most bears don't leave dens in states and provinces that have spring seasons, and become active, until sometime in April or May, although there can be local variations. Big males are usually the first to leave dens, some of them probably vacating winter quarters during April, with younger, smaller animals joining them later. By late May into June, breeding activity begins and males become very active in their search for breeding females.

An early spring will speed up bear emergence from dens and a late one, or a cold snap, will slow it down by as much as two weeks. So the later in the season a spring bear hunt is planned, the more bears will be out of dens and the better a hunter's chances of seeing the animals will be. One spring I had a hunt scheduled with Wayne Bosowicz in northern Ontario for mid-May. The hunt was cancelled, however, because there was still a foot or more of snow on the ground at the time and bear activity was minimal.

In Colorado, Jim Jarvis says his best hunting is always during June, the last month of the season. Most of his baiting is done at around 9,000 feet above

One of the best times to hunt black bears in spring or fall is during a light rain or drizzle with no wind. A poncho or two-piece rain suit will help the hunter stay dry.

sea level. He said that for every drop of 1,000 feet in elevation, bear activity generally picks up a week earlier. Good hunting would be expected to begin sometime during May at lower elevations then.

Hunters interested in big bears probably have just as good a chance of encountering them late in the season and perhaps the odds are even better then than earlier. There are two other factors that can play a role in planning a spring hunt though. One is the quality of hides and the other is emergence of biting insects.

Bear hides are at their best soon after animals leave dens, hairs having grown long and thick to protect against the cold during winter months. As the weather warms, heavy winter coats are shed. The animals sometimes accelerate the process by rubbing against trees and other objects, creating patches of short hair on an otherwise long coat. I've seen a few scruffy looking black bears on spring hunts, but the vast majority of mature bruins have respectable hides throughout spring seasons. Hunters who are concerned about the quality of bear hides can plan a hunt accordingly or be prepared to pass up bears with rubbed pelts, if hunting late in the season.

Unfortunately, biting insects begin emerging about the time black bear hunting gets good during spring seasons. Mosquitoes and black flies can be annoying to downright disruptive pests, but they are generally tolerable when hunters come prepared for them with headnets, gloves, and plenty of insect repellent. Mosquitoes aren't usually as much of a problem in Western mountains as they are in much of Canada and Alaska.

In Colorado during the last week of June, for instance, mosquitoes were worse than normal, according to Jarvis, and I got by without using a headnet and bug juice. Hunters who hope to avoid biting insects altogether should plan spring bear hunts during May, with the first two weeks of the month usually the safest, or late April, if there's any sign of bear activity then.

There's no truth to an old myth that black bears are not fit to eat during the spring. They may scavenge some carcasses, but most of their diet is composed of grass and other vegetation. If anything, they can be better eating then than in the fall because there is less fat, making the meat leaner. Some people contend that bear meat collected during the fall isn't good to eat either. This can be chalked up to ignorance or improper handling of carcasses.

Mosquitoes and other insect pests aren't usually a problem during fall bear hunts, although some may be present early in the season on days when temperatures are warm to hot. Black bear hides are normally in good shape by September, but hairs aren't as long then as they will be in October and November. Bear activity is generally at a peak during early fall as the animals finish layering their bodies with fat in preparation for denning, and tapers off during late fall until animals enter dens. Black bears in the Northern U.S. and Canada are most active in September and October, and some continue feeding into November. In Southern states, bruins may remain active through December and into January.

The timing of denning sometimes depends on the availability of food. When food is scarce, bears may den early rather than expend energy to obtain little nourishment. Denning may also be delayed to enable the animals to take advantage of abundant sources of food such as acorns or beech nuts available late in the year. In years when food supplies have been abundant much of the summer and fall, enabling bears to build up sufficient fat reserves earlier than normal, they may retire to dens early, too. Males usually remain active longer than females.

More specific information on when black bears enter dens during the fall in different parts of North America and when they leave them during the spring, which will prove helpful to hunters in timing hunts, is included in the first chapter of this book.

Unlike fall deer hunting in some areas, fall black bear hunting isn't always best the first week of the season, unless, of course, the season only lasts for a week or less. Opening week is usually good, but better hunting is sometimes possible later on. Fall black bear hunts start during early September in a number of states and provinces, for example. The weather then can be cool, hot, or rainy.

Cool conditions are great for bear hunting. Hot weather and heavy rain aren't. I've seen as many opening weeks with unfavorable weather conditions as favorable. Unfavorable weather reduces bear activity along with a hunter's chances of seeing the animals. Poor weather can strike at any time, but I often find conditions during the last week of September and the first two weeks of October more favorable than early September. There are other advantages of hunting then, too.

Temperatures are generally consistently cooler, resulting in optimum bear activity, and when a bruin is bagged, butchering the carcass isn't usually necessary immediately to salvage it. There are also fewer other bear hunters to contend with. This can be doubly good news in areas where baiting is legal. Once other hunters discontinue baiting, bears that were feeding at those bait sites start roaming in search of a new food supply and may end up visiting baits still being maintained. As a result, late-season baits that may have had only one bruin on them earlier, now have two or three, and the chances of scoring go up as well. Even where baiting isn't legal, there is normally a "fall shuffle" of bruins seeking out supplies of natural food.

Weather conditions that are both good and bad for black bear hunting are generally the same during fall and spring, regardless of which hunting technique is used. Heavy rain, strong wind and sudden changes in temperatures, whether up or down, are all bad news. It's been my experience that black bears just don't move much during downpours and bear hunters will be better off staying put. If there is an extended period of heavy rain, try to hunt when it lets up because bears should be active then.

Black bears may move when it's windy, but the chances of seeing them are reduced. Wind direction frequently changes from one minute to the next as the velocity increases. Bears frequently smell hunters who are stand hunting under these conditions, unless hunters are far enough from baits, natural foods, or trails that it is impossible for the animals to wind them. Hearing hounds is next to impossible when it's windy, too, and the sound of a predator call would also be drowned out. When tracking a bear in the snow though, wind may work in the tracker's favor by covering up the sound of his approach, although a bear may still smell its pursuer and disappear before a shot is possible.

Stand hunters may do more harm than good if hunting close to where they expect to see a bear when it's windy. A bear that winds men may not return for days. If the animal does return the following day, it will be more cautious than before or simply approach after dark.

Hot and cold spells frequently reduce bear activity. Cold snaps during early spring and late fall may put a temporary halt to bear movements until the weather changes. A normal cooling trend that occurs from early to late fall can increase bear activity. The same is true for normal warming trends during spring months. Temperatures that are uncomfortably warm for humans may also be uncomfortable for heavy-coated black bears, and their movements will often be restricted to the coolest hours under these conditions.

Stable weather conditions with normal temperatures for that particular time of year and a light breeze to none at all are great for black bear hunting. The only circumstances that are better, and which I rate as the absolute best for bagging a bruin, at least from a stand, are when there is a light rain or drizzle and the wind is calm. Black bears are more active than normal under these conditions, according to my experience, even the older, larger animals.

To illustrate what I mean consider the success of a father and son, Carl Klemencic Sr. and Jr., who hunted with me a number of years ago. It was the third week of bear season when they arrived and there was a steady drizzle falling. Temperatures were in the 50s and there was no wind. Conditions were ideal. I placed the two at baits several miles apart late in the afternoon, knowing there was a good boar visiting both sites.

The location where the boy was positioned hadn't been hunted previously, but the bait his father watched had been hunted on five different days during the first week of the season. A sow and cub had been seen there, and another bear that was approaching as shooting light faded was spooked as the hunter left. I had seen tracks of a decent boar at that location, but he never showed himself during shooting hours up until that time.

That changed at least an hour before the end of shooting time on that drizzly day. The boar gave the father a shot at 25 yards and he dropped it with a .30-30. The bruin later weighed 200 pounds dressed.

At about the same time the older hunter scored, his son saw an even bigger bear. Since it was the boy's first bear hunt, I stayed with him. He was sitting with his back against a tree facing the bait and the direction I expected a bear to come from. I was seated directly behind him. The bait was situated in a small opening in a thick cedar swamp.

We heard the bear before we saw it. The animal was approaching at a fast walk or a trot, branches and limbs cracking and popping under his weight. Instead of coming from the heart of the swamp, however, he came along the edge bordering a stand of hardwoods behind us. At first it looked as though

Chris Schimik with a black bear bagged in the rain. He wore chest waders to help keep him dry.

the bruin was going to pass us on our left and continue on to the bait, which would give the boy a good shot.

When the bear was even with me though, it turned abruptly, coming directly at me. The animal was close at that point, and I wanted to be ready in case he ended up in my lap, so I started to raise my .30-06. The boar saw the movement and stopped no more than 30 feet away.

It would have been a simple matter for me to nail that bear, but it was the boy's hunt. I knew he could see the animal, but it would have been awkward for him to turn and shoot. The movement required to make the shot would certainly spook the bear before he could get a shot off.

After pausing briefly, the bruin walked off, starting to circle us. We heard him breaking brush minutes later, but he never showed himself again. If the boy had been where I was, he would have connected like his father did. I estimated that bear's weight at over 300 pounds in the round, and it probably would still have topped 300, or been darn close to it, once dressed. Later that week the boy connected on a sow that was about half the size of the boar we saw in the rain.

The rain was probably not the only factor that resulted in such success for the father and son on their first day of hunting, but I'm convinced it was a deciding factor. I've seen it happen too many other times. Another hunter who has hunted black bears with me connected on boars in the rain two years in a row.

It was the second week of the season before Chris Schimik started hunting the first year. He was watching a bait that had been hunted the previous week. Several small bears had been sighted, but not the adult I was sure was in the area. He hunted a couple of days without seeing anything, then it started raining on the third day. It rained on and off, but never hard, and there was no wind.

We got wet in the morning without seeing our quarry, so changed into dry clothes and returned in the evening. About 45 minutes after we got in position a nice boar stepped out by the bait and Chris dropped it with a single shot from his .308. That bruin dressed out between 180 and 200 pounds.

The following year, Chris hunted the first week of the season. He drew a blank on opening day. It was raining hard the morning of the second day, so we didn't hunt, but it tapered off to light rain or drizzle by afternoon, so we took up stands for the remainder of the day.

Chris didn't have long to wait before a bear appeared. However, it grabbed a mouthful of food and disappeared before he could take a shot. Twenty minutes later a larger bruin stepped into view and Chris claimed an average-size boar.

The first day of my bear hunt in Colorado last spring was cloudy with intermittent rain and no wind, excellent conditions. I was on a bait that Jim knew was being used by a blonde bear. He said to expect activity from 8 p.m. on. Activity on that bait was far better than expected and I think the weather was responsible.

A red-coated bruin showed first at 7 p.m., an hour earlier than activity was normally noted. From that point on I saw bears on and off until it was too dark to see. I saw at least three different bears and possibly a fourth. There were at least two different blonde bears.

Why is bear hunting in the rain so good? I don't know for sure, but I've got some theories that I think make sense.

I suspect part of the reason bear hunting during a rainy, windless day can be so productive is the animals know from experience that they are less likely to encounter hunters under those conditions. Let's face it, hunting in the rain certainly isn't as pleasant or comfortable as on clear, dry days. As a result, there are fewer hunters afield. I won't pretend to understand a black bear's powers of reasoning, but I suspect that over a period of years, older bears become aware of this pattern and adjust their movements accordingly.

Black bears might also be more comfortable moving during periods of light rain, especially when the weather is warm, because the water keeps them cool when temperatures sometimes reach the 70s or 80s, making them warm. Their heavy coats shed water, so getting wet doesn't concern them.

Water-soaked ground makes walking quieter for bears, too, for those that wish to make little noise at any rate, and maybe this helps make them feel more at ease. Barometric pressure might have something to do with bear movement as well, but I haven't checked that while bear hunting under various weather conditions.

Whatever the reason or reasons, I know that black bears are active, as a rule, on rainy, windless days, if it's not raining hard. One advantage to hunters under these conditions is their scent is usually confined to their immediate area. Rainfall tends to keep scent close to the ground. This is a big aid to hunters because the black bear's nose is one of its most important lines of defense against detection by hunters. Many bears approaching feeding sites smell waiting hunters and disappear without hunters realizing it. This is less likely to happen during a light rain.

If there were a reason for not hunting black bears in the rain, it would be that the chances of losing a bear are increased because rain might wash out the blood trail of an animal that has been hit. However, this consideration is of little concern, provided hunters pick their shots properly, which is the key to clean kills regardless of hunting conditions.

Black bears can be on the move during any hour of the day, especially during the spring, but also in the fall when bruins are actively feeding. Stand hunters should spend more time afield during morning hours than many now do. While hunting with hounds in Ontario during late May and June we've frequently struck hot scent between 11 a.m. and 1 p.m. I've also seen bears on bait at virtually every hour of the day during fall months.

The best time to hunt black bears is any time during spring or fall when you can and there's a season open. To increase the chances of seeing bears though, it helps to time a hunt to coincide with when most of the animals are out of dens, the weather conditions are right and you can spend as many hours as possible in the field each day.

CHAPTER
20
The Future

The future looks pretty good for black bears in North America at this point, at least in areas where healthy populations exist and the animals and their habitat are being looked after to ensure continuing supplies. Over the past 10 to 15 or 20 years there has been an upward trend of black bear numbers in the lower 48 states. The same may be true in Canada and Alaska, but there has never been a scarcity of black bears in those areas as in parts of the lower 48.

Over that period of time, healthy bear populations have been re-established in Arkansas and Louisiana through transplants and the animals have come back on their own through increased protection in states such as Pennsylvania. Bear numbers are climbing slowly in other states such as New Jersey, Connecticut, Kentucky, and Maryland. There's potential for more of the same as wildlife managers and people in general learn more about the animals, and the critters begin to be more accepted for what they actually are rather than what people think they are.

Enough knowledge about black bears and their habitat requirements is already available to enable wildlife managers to increase bear numbers further where they already exist and reintroduce them to areas where they are absent. Before these measures can be justified though, there has to be greater public acceptance of black bears. Such efforts will be largely wasted if local residents fear the animals and don't want them around.

Black bears are more adaptable than most people realize or give them credit for. They not only survive and flourish in some of the most rugged and remote real estate in North America, black bears also feel right at home on the outskirts of cities and towns, plus within subdivisions, as long as there are suitable blocks of habitat for them. The presence or absence of suitable black

Small black bear that could be either a cub or yearling. It was photographed during July. Despite its small size, I think the bruin is a yearling female.

bear habitat determines where the animals will be and in what numbers, more than any other factor. As the habitat goes, so go the bears. That's why it is important that available habitat be maintained and managed in areas where black bear numbers are low, if the animals are to be maintained.

Even where black bear numbers are now healthy, the vigor of existing populations can only be kept that way as long as their habitat remains. The shrinkage or loss of bear habitat to development usually results in the loss of bears and the population shrinks. The importance of habitat on the welfare of black bears was a common theme in letters I received from biologists across North America responding to a questionnaire about bear numbers in their respective states or provinces.

Al LeCount in Arizona wrote, "Habitat loss is the biggest threat to bear populations and if habitat is not saved, we can forget about having bears to hunt."

Cathy Carter, Associate Curator of Mammalogy at the Mississippi Museum of Natural History wrote, "The last reported breeding population was in Issaquena County in 1976, when five bears, including two cubs, were present in a 4,300-acre wooded tract surrounded by agricultural land. This tract has since been cleared and converted to agricultural usage.

"The black bear is officially listed as a threatened species in the state and receives protection under the Non-game and Endangered Species Act of 1974. However, this law has no provisions for habitat management or preservation."

Reggie Thackston from Oklahoma wrote, "Bear populations in Oklahoma are limited by poaching and lack of suitable habitat. Habitat limitations have become even more critical during the past ten years due to industrial forest management practices. Rugged and remote areas of mature oak-pine forest, once capable of supporting bear populations, have been opened up with logging roads and converted extensively into even-aged pine plantations."

Thackston's comments illustrate that the composition of the habitat, meaning the types of trees present, is as important as the size of habitat when it comes to supporting black bears. Eugene Widder in Alabama made similar statements.

"Alabama does have a black bear population, although it is relatively small when compared to more northern states such as Michigan. This is mainly due to the lack of favorable habitat types. Alabama's forestry practices have created extensive pure pine stands with a scarcity of mature hardwood and mixed pine-hardwood types."

So even though the future outlook for black bears in North America is generally good, there are some trouble spots where habitat quality and size is and has been declining. If unchecked, the situation will worsen as will the status of black bears in these areas. It's not a matter of these bears being intolerant of development. As mentioned earlier, the animals are adaptable to some human encroachment, such as housing developments, and, in fact, may be more healthy and productive in association with humans than those in wilderness settings. Information from Pennsylvania bears this out.

However, problems result when large-scale habitat changes are made, especially where environmentally critical and sensitive habitat such as swamps and bogs are involved. These areas are important to black bears as well as many other forms of wildlife, plus they have an impact on flood control and cleaning water supplies.

We know that black bears can adapt to people, but can people adapt to bears? In areas where they can't, the bears will suffer.

As Gary Alt said, "It isn't what the bears do that gets them in trouble so much as what people think that they might do. People are afraid of bears, basically. It's one of the biggest problems we have. That's cost the bear a lot over the years.

"If we can do any justice to the bears, it would be to try and convince the people not to fear bears, but to respect them as you would any large mammals."

Indifference toward black bears among hunters and non-hunters is almost as much of a problem as the dangerous bear syndrome. These people don't care if bear habitat is destroyed, how many are shot, if the animals are shot out of season or even if there is a hunting season for black bears. Bear poaching thrives because of this indifference. Some people who care about the welfare of the animals don't realize the extent of poaching and those who do know about it don't care. Increased law enforcement efforts are underway in California as well as other states in the northwest U.S., and Wisconsin, in an effort to reduce the poaching of black bears. Tips from citizens about illegal activity they see or hear about would help officers put a tighter squeeze on individuals responsible for these activities.

Rolf Johnson in Washington reported that a husband and wife were recently arrested in the Aberdeen area for selling bear parts illegally. The taking of over 200 black bears was involved in this case, which is an example of the numbers of animals being poached. Poaching is having a significant impact on black bear populations in a number of states, and will continue to do so until everyone works together to control it.

At the present time, the recreational potential of black bear populations through hunting is tremendously underutilized in most of Canada and Alaska. Most provinces have appropriate hunting seasons established, but not many hunters take advantage of them, although this is beginning to change. Ontario is probably the most popular province for black bear hunting, and there are still plenty of animals to go around, as well as areas that go unhunted.

One province that is behind the times when it comes to hunting black

A large male black bear weighing over 400 pounds.

bears is Nova Scotia. Current regulations only permit the hunting of black bears during deer season, which opens during late October or early November. Most bears are denned by then, providing little hunting opportunity. The province certainly has enough bears, estimated at 3,000, to hold a September or early October hunt when the animals are active. Bears can be snared there starting September 15. Even if locals don't want to take advantage of an earlier bear season, I guarantee hunters from the U.S. will. The economy of the province would benefit as a result. Maybe not by a lot at first, but it would eventually catch on.

In effect, the black bear resource is being wasted in Nova Scotia. However, I predict that in the near future an early fall bear season, and perhaps a spring season, will be established there along with a separate bear license. Bears can now be shot under a deer license.

Even in some of the lower 48 states, hunting opportunities for black bears are not being fully realized. My home state of Michigan is a prime example. There is only a fall season in the Upper Peninsula, where most of the state's bears live. Plenty of hunting pressure results during this season and there is no need to expand it. However, there is potential for a spring hunt. Every spring, a number of black bears, many of them big males, are shot by home-owners as the animals wander through their yards, rummage through garbage, or become nuisances. The carcasses from many of these animals are discarded and wasted.

A spring hunt, perhaps conducted under a permit basis, could be timed for a period when males are most active, so they would make up the bulk of the harvest. Their removal wouldn't hurt the population and may eliminate some animals that would have become problems anyway. Such a season would certainly increase recreational opportunities without hurting the resource. Whether such a season is ever established there or in any other states where the potential exists, will depend on the support from hunters and wildlife biologists.

Hunting is the best means of managing or controlling their populations. "It's not a question of whether to hunt them," Gary Alt said, "but how."

Controversies among hunters over how black bears should be hunted loom as potential problems in some states for the future. How these differences of opinion are settled will have more impact on bear hunters than the animals themselves, but will ultimately affect black bears somehow. In states where both hunting with hounds and baiting are legal, the two factions are sometimes at odds, which is unfortunate. Disagreements of this type ultimately hurt all hunters. All bear hunters are hunters regardless of the methods used, as long as they are legal, and more can be accomplished by working together than as separate entities.

Some Wisconsin bear hunters know what can happen if everyone doesn't work together. Back in 1973 a bill was introduced in the state legislature to outlaw the use of bait for bear hunting. Houndmen supported the bill, but those who preferred to stand hunt obviously didn't. Eventually, an amendment was tacked onto the bill to outlaw all bear hunting in Wisconsin, and the legislation was passed by both bodies of state government. Fortunately, for all bear hunters in the state, the governor vetoed the bill. However, the end result was that both baiters and dog hunters ended up with less than what they originally had before the controversy started.

Hunters who prefer one method over another are always poor judges of what should or should not be permitted or what is right and wrong because they have a vested interest. Final determinations of what hunting methods are legal for black bears and when they should be employed should be left up to wildlife biologists because their chief concern and responsibility is the resource. Input from all hunters should be sought and play a role in the decision-making process, of course, but the ultimate decision rests with managers, and hunters should be able to live with those decisions until they come up with facts that might change a manager's mind.

As big game animals, black bears are challenging and exciting to hunt and should be hunted where their populations warrant, to both control their numbers and to promote the wisest use of the resource.

It may take years for attitudes toward black bears and black bear hunting to change for the better in some parts of North America, but I'm confident it will happen. I'm looking forward to when it does, along with other fans of one of the continent's most interesting and misunderstood species of big game.

State Listings

Alabama

Wildlife biologist Eugene Widder from Alabama said there are roughly 200 black bears in the state, with the largest population in northern Mobile and southern Washington counties. The population appears to be stable to increasing slightly, according to Widder. Bears are also found in small portions of Baldwin, Monroe, and Clarke counties, with additional sightings made in Escambia, Covington, Crenshaw, Greene, Pickens, Tuscaloosa, Saint Clair, Cherokee, Cleburne, and Jackson counties. For additional information contact the Department of Conservation and Natural Resources, Division of Fish and Game, 64 N. Union St., Montgomery, AL 36130 (205-832-6357).

Alaska

There is no population estimate available for black bears in Alaska, but their numbers are listed as stable to abundant in many of the management units where they are found. Dates for hunting seasons vary among management units and so do bag limits. Season dates for some units were and are September 1, 1984 through June 30, 1985. There is no closed season for black bears in other units. Unit 4 is closed to black bear hunting through the spring of 1985. Bag limits vary from one to three, depending on the area hunted, so be sure to check a current copy of Alaska's hunting regulations carefully before planning a hunt.

Cubs and sows with cubs are protected in all units. Bear hunters who use bait or hounds must obtain a permit from the Department of Fish and Game. All black bears bagged by hunters must be sealed by a representative of the Department. The recorded black bear harvests in Alaska during 1982 and '83 were 1,011 and 1,148. In 1983 there were 687 bruins sealed during the spring and 461 in the fall. For more information contact the Department of Fish and Game, Box 3-2000, Juneau, AK 99802 (907-465-4190).

Arizona

Bear biologist Al LeCount estimates there are between 2,000 and 3,000 black bears in Arizona on non-Indian lands, with the population stable. The number of bruins on Indian lands is presently unknown. Most of the bear hunting is done during the fall in this state, with a limited spring hunt.

The fall season in 1984 began on August 31 in all management units where bear hunting was permitted, but closed in some units on September 13 and remained open until December 9 in others. A spring hunt during April 12-28, 1985 is set for units 31 and most of 35A. Fifty permits are available for 31 and only 3 for 35A. Any black bear is legal during fall hunts and sows with cubs are protected during spring seasons.

The use of bait for hunting black bears was only possible in units 1 and 27 from August 31 - September 13 during 1984. Only biodegradable matter can be used for bait, which must be put in a single metal container not exceeding 10 gallons in volume. A permit is required to bait bears and permit numbers must be on bait containers. Baiting is not permitted prior to August 15. Dogs can be used to hunt bears in Arizona during fall hunts only.

All bears bagged by hunters must be registered. The bear harvest has been between 250 and 300 over the past six years, with kills of 268 and 274 during 1982 and '83. The number of bear hunters has been declining due to increased license fees and restrictions on baiting. There were 6,183 bear tags issued during 1983 compared to 8,494 in 1981 and 8,985 during 1978.

Game violations can be reported 24 hours a day by calling 1-800-352-0700. For additional information contact Game and Fish Department, 2222 West Greenway Rd., Phoneix, AZ 85023 (602-942-3000).

Arkansas

There are an estimated 1,200 to 1,500 black bears in Arkansas. Their numbers were thought to be as low as 40 to 50 in 1950. Between 1959 and 1967 an effort to restock parts of the state with bruins was carried out in cooperation with Minnesota and Manitoba. A total of 254 animals were released in the Ozark and Ouachita national forests.

Limited fall hunting seasons have been held in Arkansas since 1980, with no dogs or baiting permitted. There were 19 bears harvested during a 7-day hunt in 1982 and 31 bagged during a 4-day hunt in 1983. Dates for the 1984 season were November 3-6. Any bear is legal during Arkansas seasons and bagged bears must be reported. There were 5,242 permits issued for the 1983 hunt, with nonresident hunters limited to 50. For more information write or call the Game and Fish Commission, No. 2 Natural Resources Dr., Little Rock, AR 72205 (501-223-6346).

California

There are an estimated 7,000 to 11,500 black bears in California, with populations suffering in a few areas due to poaching. As a result, hunting season dates and lengths may be adjusted to help the animals recover. Archery bear season was from August 18 through September 9, 1984 and the regular season was from November 3 through December 23, 1984 in designated counties.

Most bear hunting is done with dogs in this state; however, hounds can't be used during the bow and arrow bear season. Bear dogs can be trained during July and August, plus October and November. It is illegal to bait black bears. Cubs and sows with cubs are protected. Hunters must report bear hunting success and save the lower jaw from bruins that are bagged, for inspection.

The bear kill during 1982 and '83 was 783 and 601. Highest kills both years were in Siskiyou, Shasta and Trinity counties. There were 11,332 bear tags sold during 1983, down 56.2 percent from the 25,859 tags issued in 1982.

To report poaching and other violations call 1-800-952-5400. For more information on black bears in California write the Department of Fish and Game, 1416 Ninth St., Sacramento, CA 95814 or call 916-324-0769.

Colorado

Colorado has an estimated 15,000 black bears, although this figure will probably be modified in the future as a result of a 10-year bear research program that began in 1979. Bruins are being studied on Black Mesa, which is in parts of management units 53, 54, and 65. The study area is closed to bear hunting. Bruins tagged or collared for the project sometimes wander out of the study area and hunters who see bears wearing collars or colored ear tags are asked not to shoot them. Anyone seeing marked bears are asked to report sightings to Division of Wildlife offices in Montrose or Grand Junction.

Both spring and fall hunting seasons are held in Colorado. The spring season began April 1 during 1984 and closed June 17 in some units and June 30 in others. Black bears are also legal during archery and muzzleloader deer and elk seasons in the fall. Hounds can be used during the spring hunt, but not fall. Bears can be hunted over bait both times of year. Bait can't be put out until 15 days prior to season openings. Refer to a current copy of big game hunting seasons and regulations for more information on baiting.

Evidence of sex must be left on carcasses of bagged bears, and they must be sealed within five days by Division of Wildlife personnel. Gun hunters must wear a minimum of 500 square inches of fluorescent orange. Hunters born after January 1, 1949 must have a hunter safety certificate or card to obtain a bear license in Colorado.

The recorded black bear harvest for 1982 and '83 was 848 and 733. There were an additional 14 bears taken by federal and state trappers during '82 and 13 during '83. There were 12,525 bear licenses sold during 1982 and 12,666 during '83. Approximately 300 bruins were bagged during the 1984 spring season.

To report bear hunting violations call 1-800-332-4155 outside Denver and 295-0164 in Denver. For more information contact the Division of Wildlife, Department of Natural Resources, 6060 Broadway, Denver, CO 80216 (303-297-1192).

Connecticut

Connecticut's black bear population is low, according to Wildlife Biologist Dale May with the Department of Environmental Protection, and is concentrated in the northwestern corner of the state in the Berkshire foothills. May said the animals may be increasing, and are totally protected. For more information or to report bear sightings write or call the Department of Environmental Protection, 165 Capitol Ave., Hartford, CT 06106 (203-566-4683).

Delaware

This small state does not have any black bears and they are thought to have been absent since colonial times.

Florida

Researchers are presently trying to determine how many black bears inhabit this state. Populations of the animals are known to exist in Apalachicola, Osceola and Ocala national forests in the northern part of the state and in southern swamps.

Black bears were legal game during deer season (November 10, 1984-January 6, 1985) in only two counties—Baker and Columbia. They are protected in the rest of the state. There were 50 bears bagged in the Osceola National Forest during the 1982-'83 season. Bears were also legal in the Apalachicola National Forest during 1982 and '83 when there were 12 and 16 bruins reported taken by hunters.

For more information contact the Game and Freshwater Fish Commission, 620 South Meridian St., Tallahassee, FL 32302 (904-488-1960).

Georgia

There are an estimated 1,300 black bears in Georgia, with three distinct populations, according to Dave Carlock. He said there are about 600 animals roaming mountains in the northern part of the state, 200 in the Piedmont and upper coastal plains, plus 500 in Okefenokee Swamp to the south.

Limited, two or three-day hunts have been held in certain counties during various years. Check current listings of seasons for future hunts. Dogs have been permitted for bear hunting during some seasons that have been held.

Sows with cubs have been protected. For more information contact the Department of Natural Resources, Game and Fish Division, 270 Washington St. S.W., Atlanta, GA 30334 (404-656-3530).

Idaho

Idaho's black bears number between 20,000 and 25,000, according to Wildlife Research Supervisor John Beecham with the Bureau of Wildlife. Populations in remote backcountry areas are thought to be stable, but declining in some areas with easy access.

An estimated 1,000 to 1,200 bruins are bagged in this state by approximately 20,000 hunters annually. Both baiting and hunting with hounds are legal, although there are limitations on each method in certain management units and at specified times of year. Two black bears could be taken in certain management units during 1984, with the purchase of an extra tag.

Fall seasons opened September 1 in 1984 with some units closing to hunting during November and others in December. There was an archery-only bear season in units 48 and 49 from September 1-28 last fall, with no dogs allowed. Spring seasons for 1985 begin April 1, with some units closing at the end of May and others remaining open until the end of June. Pursuit-only seasons for dogs were July 1-15 and July 16-August 15 in specified units during 1984. A pursuit season has been set for June 15-30, 1985 in eight units.

Sows with cubs are protected and the skulls of bagged bears must be presented at Fish and Game offices for removal of a tooth so the animals can be aged. Bear hunters should review a copy of Idaho Big Game Regulations to get an accurate picture of which units are open when. Call 1-800-632-5999 to report violations. For additional information write the Department of Fish and Game, 600 South Walnut, Box 25, Boise, ID 83707 or call 208-334-3700.

Illinois

No free-roaming black bears are to be found in Illinois, according to Forrest Loomis with the Department of Conservation. To report information about the animals or sightings contact the Department at Lincoln Tower Plaza, 524 S. Second St., Springfield, IL 62706 (217-782-6384).

Indiana

Black bears were gone from Indiana by the late 1800s, with the last report of the animals in the state recorded about 1888, according to Department of Natural Resources, Division of Fish and Wildlife, 607 State Office Bldg., Indianapolis, IN 46204 (317-232-4080).

Iowa

Black bears are rare in Iowa, but some have turned up in various locations during recent years. The animals have a tendency to follow protected river valleys, moving into the state from Minnesota and possibly Wisconsin. Conservation Commission, Wallace State Office Bldg., Des Moines, IA 50319 (515-281-5918).

Kansas

Kansas does not have a resident population of black bears, although an occasional bruin wanders into the southeastern part of the state from Missouri or Arkansas and from Colorado to the west. A bear was captured alive in Morton County in 1983 and released in Colorado. Another animal showed up in Douglas County during June of 1966. Fish and Game Commission, Rt. 2, Box 54A, Pratt, KS 67124 (316-672-5911).

Kentucky

John MacGregor with the Kentucky Department of Fish and Wildlife Resources said there appears to be a small resident population of black bears in the Cumberland Mountains of southeast counties where the state borders Virginia. Sows with cubs have been seen in Letcher and Bell counties in 1983 and '84. Bears have also been sighted in Harlan County and the southwest corner of Pike County. Contact the Department of Fish and Wildlife Resources, #1 Game Farm Rd., Frankfort, KY 40601 (502-564-4336).

Louisiana

There isn't much known about black bears in Louisiana at the present time, except their habitat is shrinking, according to Lewis Brunett. In addition, bears are known to take nutria and muskrats from traps in coastal marshes. The state's bear population was estimated at 350 in 1977. There were 161 bruins transplanted to Louisiana from Minnesota over a four-year period starting in 1964. Thirty-five of those animals are known to have been killed. Some of them wandered into Mississippi and Texas from release sites.

Limited hunting seasons have been held in designated areas since 1974. The season was October 15-23, 1984. There has been little participation in bear seasons, according to Brunett, because there is limited public access to locations where the animals can be hunted. Most of the land is leased by hunting clubs. The number of bears bagged annually has varied between 0 and 2.

For more information contact the Department of Wildlife and Fisheries, P.O. Box 15570, Baton Rouge, LA 70895 (504-568-5855).

Maine

There are far more black bears in Maine than biologists realized until recently. The state's bear population estimate was updated during the fall of 1984 to 18,000 plus, almost double the previous estimate of 10,000. Increased information about the state's bruins was gathered through intensive research over the past several years.

Bears are so abundant in some parts of the state that nuisance complaints are increasing and biologists recommend reducing the population in these areas. To do this, they would like to see an annual harvest of 2,000 to 2,500 animals. This is a substantial increase over the 1,221 bruins bagged in 1982 and 1,412 taken by hunters in 1983. The season may have to be lengthened from the September 1 through November 30 dates that have been in effect for the past three years to accomplish this goal.

The highest bear harvest on record in Maine was 1,630 in 1979 when the season was May 1 through late November. The last spring season in Maine was in 1981, having been eliminated after that due to concern that too many black bears were being harvested in the state.

Both baiting and hunting with hounds are permitted, as is trapping, with a bag limit of one bear of any size and sex a year. One bear hunting method that is prohibited in Maine is driving the animals. All bears bagged by hunters must be registered at check stations. To report bear hunting violations call 1-800-253-7887. More information can be obtained from the Department of Inland Fisheries and Wildlife, 284 State St., State House Station 41, Augusta, ME 04333 (207-289-2871).

Maryland

Black bears are increasing in Maryland, according to Gary Taylor. They were listed as an endangered species in 1972. By 1979 bear sightings were up dramatically in the western part of the state and their status was changed to a nongame species. Taylor said Garrett County has the most bruins, but they are also present in Allegany, Washington and Frederick Counties. For more information contact the Forest, Park and Wildlife Service, Tawes State Office Bldg., Annapolis, MD 21401 (301-269-3195).

Massachusetts

An estimated 525 black bears live in Massachusetts according to Wildlife Biologist James Cardoza, with the bulk of the population located west of the Connecticut River. A split, two-week fall season has been held from the last Monday in September through the following Saturday and from the third Monday in November to the following Saturday, for the past several years. Hounds can be used during the first week of the season only. No baiting is allowed. Bear dogs can be trained prior to the opening of hunting season. Only Berkshire, Franklin, Hempden, Hampshire, and Worcester counties are open to hunting.

There were 823 and 774 bear permits sold in Massachusetts during 1982 and '83 with resulting harvests of 13 and 10 bears. For additional information contact the Division of Fisheries and Wildlife, Leverett Saltonstall Bldg., Government Center, 100 Cambridge St., Boston, MA 02202 (617-727-3151).

Michigan

Michigan claims a black bear population numbering between 5,000 and 6,000 animals. The bulk of the state's population of bruins live in the Upper Peninsula where every county is open to bear hunting from September 10 through October 31 with gun or bow and then again during the November 15-30 gun deer season, but bears are only legal then to hunters possessing bear licenses.

There are also 16 counties in the northern Lower Peninsula that are open to bear hunting with gun and bow during a 10-day to two-week season in September. The dates were September 10-19 in 1984. Those same counties reopen to a bow-only hunt, usually during the first 10 days of October. Dogs are not permitted for bear hunting in the Lower Peninsula during the October bow season or in the Upper Peninsula during November. Otherwise, hunting with hounds is permitted, as is hunting over bait.

Dog hunters must obtain a free permit from a Department of Natural Resources office, and are limited to a pack size of six for chasing bears. Hounds can be trained on bears from July 16 until September 9. Dog handlers cannot possess guns or bows during the training season.

Bowhunters can hunt from elevated stands, but gun hunters cannot. Gun hunters must wear a cap, vest or coat of hunter orange material. Bowhunters are exempt from this rule. All bears bagged in the state must be registered at a DNR office within seven days. Only the head or head and hide have to be presented for registration. Cubs are protected. To report bear hunting violations call 1-800-292-7800.

The estimated bear harvest in 1982 was 1,506 with 1,253 tagged in the U.P. In 1983, an estimated 1,049 bears were bagged in the state, with about 850 of those taken in upper Michigan. For more information contact the Department of Natural Resources, P.O. Box 30028, Lansing, MI 48909 (517-373-1263).

Minnesota

Black bear hunting in Minnesota is by permit only. Permit applications are usually available in March and have to be submitted by mid-April. This state went to a permit system in 1982 when there was concern that too many bears were being bagged when licenses were unlimited. The harvest was 1,660 during the fall of 1981.

The kill dropped to 392 the following year when hunter numbers were limited. The number of permits issued and the resulting harvest have increased since then. There were 3,550 bear hunting permits issued during 1983 and 3,880 during 1984. Hunters registered 1,038 black bears in Minnesota in 1983.

All bears bagged in the state must be registered within 48 hours. Cubs are protected. Hounds can't be used for bear hunting in Minnesota, but baiting with biodegradable materials is legal. Hunters must send descriptions of bait sites to the DNR and post name and address at baits. Baiting is not permitted before August 17. Both gun and bowhunters can hunt from tree stands.

Bear permits are issued for five zones in the northern part of the state. The best hunting has been in the east-central (950 permits) and the north-central (1,050 permits) zones, with the most permits available for 1984. West-central (770 permits) and northwest (600) zones were rated second best and the northeast zone had the fewest permits available at 510. Season dates were September 1 through October 14 in 1984.

Minnesota's bear population is estimated between 8,000 and 10,000 animals. For further information write or call the Department of Natural Resources, Division of Fish and Wildlife, Box 7, Centennial Office Bldg., 658 Cedar St., St. Paul, MN 55155 (612-296-6157).

Mississippi

Fewer than 25 black bears roam this state's woodlands, according to current estimates, and the animals are protected. Sightings have come from the Delta National Forest in Sharkey County and the Bienville National Forest in Scott County, plus counties in the southeastern part of the state—Stone, Perry, Neshoba, Marion, Lamar, Jackson, George, and Jefferson Davis. Three of the bear reports include animals killed by cars and two were killed by poachers.

Game and Fish Commission, P.O. Box 451, Jackson, MS 39205 (601-961-5300).

Missouri

There are a few black bears in Missouri, where they are protected. However, 20 of the animals have been shot over the past 30 years in this state for various reasons. Bruins have been sighted in 39 of the state's counties, primarily in the south. Some bears move into Missouri from Arkansas, although reports of reproduction of black bears in the state have been verified. Wildlife Research Biologist Dave Hamilton said he doesn't think Missouri will ever support a bear population large enough to allow hunting and there are no plans to transplant any of the animals. Department of Conservation, P.O. Box 180, Jefferson City, MO 65102 (314-751-4115).

Montana

A population estimate isn't available for black bears in Montana, but they are common in the western portion of the state with their numbers stable to increasing. Spring, summer, and fall hunting seasons are held, with no bait or dogs permitted.

Seasons for most numbered districts that start with 1 or 2 were April 15-May 31 and September 8-November 25 in 1984. Black bears were legal in most districts starting with 3 or 4 from April 15-November 25 in 1984. Most districts beginning with 5 were open to bear hunting from April 15-May 31 and October 21-November 25 in 1984. There were a number of exceptions to season dates for districts in each category, so refer to a current copy of Montana Bear Hunting Regulations for the most accurate information on season dates in specific districts. Some districts, such as 284, were only open to archery hunting during 1984, and all 300-series districts, except 324, were open to bowhunters only from September 8-October 14 in 1984.

The bag limit on black bears in Montana is one per year. Cubs and sows with cubs are protected. Evidence of sex must be left on the carcass or hide of black bears. Skulls from bagged bears should be presented to any Fish, Wildlife and Parks employee for removal of a premolar tooth to age the animal. The reported black bear harvest in the state for 1983 was 1,814, with 1,025 bagged during spring and summer months and 789 during the fall. The black bear kill for 1982 was 1,277—546 in the spring and 731 during the fall hunt. All gun hunters must wear no less than 400 square inches of visible orange material above the waist. To obtain current black bear information contact the Department of Fish, Wildlife and Parks, 1420 E. 6th Ave., Helena, MT 59601 (406-444-2535).

Nebraska

The only black bears in Nebraska are in zoos, according to Bill Baxter with the Game and Parks Commission. He said the animals were probably gone from the state by the turn of the century. Game and Parks Commission, P.O. Box 30370, Lincoln, NE 68503 (402-464-0641).

Nevada

There might be 100 black bears in the Carson Mountain Range of Nevada, according to Wildlife Biologist Mike Hess, and occasional sightings of bears are made in mountains near the Idaho border. The animals are protected in this state due to their low numbers. Department of Wildlife, P.O. Box 10678, Reno, NV 89520 (702-784-6214).

New Hampshire

Black bear hunting seasons in this state start September 1 and extend to late November. Dogs and bait can be used to hunt bruins, although hounds are prohibited once firearm deer season opens during early November. The training of bear dogs is possible from April 1 through August, but bears can't be run off bait after August 1. Any bear is legal and hunters who connect must have the carcass sealed by the Fish and Game Department within 12 hours.

Over the past five years hunters have harvested an average of 218 bears annually. The kill for 1982 and '83 was 179 and 251. For additional information contact the Fish and Game Department, 34 Bridge St., Concord, NH 03301 (603-271-3421).

New Jersey

An estimated 100-120 black bears are in New Jersey, according to Patricia McConnell, Leader of the Black Bear Program for the state's Division of Fish,

Game and Wildlife. She wrote that the bear population there reached a low point of about a dozen animals in the late 1960s and early 1970s. By the late 1970s, bears started moving into the state from Pennsylvania, increasing the population to the present level. There may now be enough females to maintain the number of bruins in the state without additional movement of animals from Pennsylvania. Most bears are in the northwestern part of the state, primarily in Sussex and Passaic counties, but sightings have also been made in Hunterdon, Morris, Somerset, and Warren counties. There is no bear season in New Jersey. Department of Environmental Protection, Division of Fish, Game and Wildlife, CN 400, Trenton, NJ 08625 (609-292-2965).

New Mexico

Hunters who are interested in bagging a black bear in New Mexico must now purchase a bear license. Until 1984 bear tags were issued with any big game license. The change was instituted so the Department of Game and Fish can determine how many bear hunters there are in the state.

Black bear populations are thought to be stable in New Mexico, according to Big Game Project Leader Bruce Morrison. Hunters tagged 227 and 252 bruins during spring and fall hunts in 1983 and 1982. Fall hunts are generally from August 1 through mid-December. The spring season for 1985 will be May 1-June 30. Cubs and sows with cubs are protected. All bears bagged in the state must be registered with the Department of Game and Fish within five days.

Hunting with hounds is permitted, but baiting is not. A training season for dogs starts June 1. A toll-free phone number to report game law violators is 1-800-432-4263. For additional information contact the Department of Game and Fish, State Capitol, Santa Fe, NM 87503 (505-827-7882).

New York

New York has an estimated 4,100 black bears, according to John O'Pezio, and they are separated into three district populations. He said there are approximately 3,600 in the Adirondacks, 400 in the Catskills and 100 in the Allegany zone. O'Pezio said 550 bears were bagged by hunters in this state during 1983: 468 in the Adirondacks, 65 in the Catskills, and 17 in the Allegany region. The average bear harvest in the Adirondacks over the past five years has been 600, but O'Pezio said up to 800 animals could be taken from that region annually without hurting the population.

The 1984 hunting seasons in the northern zone were September 15-October 11 and October 20-December 2 for firearms, September 27-October 19 for bow and arrow, and October 13-19 for muzzleloaders. In the Allegany region bears were legal to gun hunters from November 19-December 11, for bow-hunters from October 15-November 18 and December 12-16. The bow bear season in the Catskills was October 15-November 18 and November 24-December 11 for gun hunters.

Bagged bears must be presented at check stations. Limited hunting with hounds is possible in the Adirondacks under permit. Bear hunting over bait is not legal. For more information contact the Department of Environmental Conservation, Fish and Wildlife Division, 50 Wolf Rd., Albany, NY 12233 (518-457-5400).

North Carolina

A rough approximation of the number of black bears in North Carolina is 2,000 to 2,500, according to John Collins. About 200 to 300 of those are in Great Smokey Mountains National Park. Between 1967 and 1977, private groups released about 100 bears in the western part of the state that were obtained from other states.

Bear hunting seasons for 1984 were October 15–November 17 and December 10–January 1 in the west and November 10–January 1 in the east. Ten counties in the northeast part of the state are closed to bear hunting. Hounds are legal for bear hunting. Baiting is legal only on private property, not on public land, and efforts are underway to outlaw all baiting for black bears in the state.

There were 314 bears bagged in North Carolina during 1982 and 306 during 1983. For more information write or call the Wildlife Resources Commission, 512 N. Salisbury St., Raleigh, NC 27611 (919-733-3391).

North Dakota

There is no resident population of black bears in North Dakota. Bruins occasionally cross the border from either Minnesota or Canada. Game and Fish Department, 2121 Lovett Ave., Bismarck, ND 58505 (701-224-2180).

Ohio

The last report of a resident population of black bears in Ohio was in 1957, according to Patrick Ruble with the Ohio Department of Natural Resources. An estimated 15 bruins lived in two counties—Adams and Scioto—in the southern part of the state then. That small population has long since disappeared. In recent years, Ruble said an occasional black bear wanders into the state. Some have been reported swimming across the Ohio River from West Virginia. Department of Natural Resources, Division of Wildlife, Fountain Square, Columbus, OH 43224 (614-265-6789).

Oklahoma

The Ouachita National Forest in southeast Oklahoma's Leflore County is the black bear's last stronghold in this state, although neighboring counties of McCurtain, Pushmataha, Latimer, Adair, and Cherokee also contain bears. The population has increased over the past 20 years, according to Reggie Thackston with the state Department of Wildlife Conservation, but their numbers are still low—approximately 30.

Some bears move into Oklahoma from Arkansas via the Ouachita Mountains. Black bears are protected in the state and are limited by poaching, plus the lack of suitable habitat. Due to the lack of suitable habitat in Oklahoma, problem animals are captured and released in remote areas of Arkansas. For more information contact the Department of Wildlife Conservation, 1801 N. Lincoln, P.O. Box 53465, Oklahoma City, OK 73105 (405-521-3851).

Oregon

An estimated 20,000 to 25,000 black bears are found in Oregon, according to Staff Biologist Rod Ingram with the Department of Fish and Wildlife. Fall hunting seasons are held from late August through November. Dates for 1984 were August 25-November 30. Both baiting and hunting with hounds are legal. A pursuit-only season for dog hunters was July 14-August 19 in 1984.

Ingram said that 20,775 bear hunters harvested 1,420 bruins during the 1983 season. The bag limit is one bear a year, with cubs and sows with cubs protected. Hound hunters account for 56 percent of the harvest, although only 10 percent of the state's hunters hunt in this fashion. A pursuit permit costing $5 is required to participate in the no-harvest season.

A toll-free number to report game law violations is 1-800-452-7888. Ingram feels the bear population is slowly increasing in the state. For additional information write the Department of Fish and Wildlife, 506 S.W. Mill St., P.O. Box 3503, Portland, OR 97208 or call 503-229-5551.

Pennsylvania

This state has an estimated 6,300 black bears, with the population increasing in some areas. Two-day hunting seasons have been held the past three years, with 100,000 permits available. Dates were November 19 and 20 for 1984, with an option to extend the season to four days if poor weather resulted in a low kill.

There were only 500 bears harvested during 1982 due to rain and fog during the short hunt. Conditions were more favorable during the 1983 season, resulting in a harvest of 1,529 bears, the minimum needed to keep the state's bear population stable. Plans are underway to divide the state into management units for bear hunting, with permit quotas established for each unit. Under such a system, the bear season may be lengthened to a week in Pennsylvania.

All bruins bagged by hunters must be registered. Any bear is legal. No baiting or hunting with hounds is permitted. Drives are the most popular bear hunting technique in the state. For more information write or call the Game Commission, P.O. Box 1567, Harrisburg, PA 17105 (717-787-3633).

Rhode Island

The last authentic record of a black bear in this state was in 1734, according to John Cronan, Chief of the Department of Environmental Management's Division of Fish and Wildlife. He said they were probably gone from the state by 1800. Department of Environmental Management, Division of Fish and Wildlife, Government Center, Tower Hill Rd., Wakefield, RI 02879 (401-789-3094).

South Carolina

No population estimate is available for black bears in this state. A small group of animals lives along the coast and is protected. Most of the state's bears live in mountainous areas where there is a limited hunting season.

There are usually two bear hunts held in designated management units. The first is for stillhunters and the dates for this hunt were October 15-20 in 1984. A party dog hunt was held October 22-27. There was one bear bagged by houndmen during 1984 and two during 1983. Baiting for bears is prohibited. For more information contact the Wildlife Resources Department, P.O. Box 167, 1000 Assembly St., Columbia, SC 29202 (803-758-0001).

South Dakota

A sighting of three black bears in the Black Hills of South Dakota was reported around 1970, but the sighting was never confirmed. The animals could have moved in from Wyoming or Montana or escaped from a zoo, according to a spokesman for the Department of Game, Fish and Parks. Bear Country USA is a wildlife exhibit at Rapid City that contains black bears. Department of Game, Fish and Parks, Anderson Bldg., Pierre, SD 57501 (605-773-3485).

Tennessee

An estimated 750 to 800 black bears live in this state, with 300 of them in Great Smokey Mountains National Park. The population is considered stable and short hunting seasons are held during the fall that vary from eight to 13 days. An average of 23 bears are taken per year by hunters. Additional animals are shot by poachers, which is a serious problem in this state as well as neighboring states. Hounds are legal for bear hunting, but bait isn't. All bruins bagged by hunters must be reported. For additional information contact Wildlife Resources Agency, P.O. Box 40747, Nashville, TN 37204 (615-360-0621).

Texas

Black bears received total protection in Texas by 1983. There were four reports of bears in the state in that year that were considered valid, two in Brewster County and one each in Smith and Zapata counties. One of the sightings in Brewster County involved two animals. The bear in Zapata County was electrocuted when it climbed a power pole. That animal is thought to have crossed into Texas from Mexico. There has also been movement of bears from Louisiana and Arkansas into Texas.

From 1965 through 1971 there were numerous sightings of black bears in southeastern Texas counties and 11 of the animals were killed. There were 161 bruins transplanted to Louisiana during that period and the animals seen in Texas are thought to have been from the releases.

Since 1977, other confirmed reports of bears have come from the following counties: ValVerde, Angelina, Reagan, Frio, Kendall, Morris, Maverick, and Culberson. Bears seen in ValVerde, Reagan, and Frio counties were killed and all proved to be migrant males weighing between 225 and 300 pounds. The animal seen in Morris County during September of 1980 was from Arkansas. The 300-350 pound female was captured and returned to Arkansas.

To report bear sightings contact the Parks and Wildlife Department, 4200 Smith School Rd., Austin, TX 78744 (512-479-4800).

Utah

An estimated 1,000 to 2,000 black bears live in Utah and they are distributed throughout mountain habitat in the state. Their population is stable to increasing. Both spring and fall hunting seasons are held, and dates for last fall were September 1-October 15. Hunt dates for spring of 1985 are April 16-June 15. All bears bagged must be registered. Only bowhunters can hunt bruins over bait. Hounds can be used to hunt bears here, too. Pursuit permits are available to chase bears during closed seasons.

There were 229 bear hunting permits issued in Utah during 1982, resulting in the harvest of 38 animals. The bear harvest was 30 for 1983. To report bear hunting violations call 1-800-662-3337. For more information contact Division of Wildlife Resources, 1596 West North Temple, Salt Lake City, UT 84116 (801-533-9333).

Vermont

Vermont has a fall bear season and the dates for 1984 were September 1-November 18. Black bear harvests have averaged 239 animals over the past 10 years, according to John Hall, Chief of Information and Education for the Department of Fish and Game. The 1983 and '82 harvests were 246 and 333. Hall said there are an estimated 2,300 black bears in the state.

Hunting with hounds is legal under a bear-dog permit. No more than six dogs can be used on a bear chase. A dog training season starts June 1 in Vermont. Bears cannot be hunted over bait in this state. For additional information contact the Department of Fish and Game, Montpelier, VT 05602 (802-828-3371).

Virginia

There are an estimated 1,200 to 1,400 black bears in Virginia, according to Dennis Martin, with most of the animals in the north. He said Shenandoah National Park has the highest concentrations of bears at a density of one per square mile.

Fall hunting seasons are held in the state. The bow season was October 13 through November 10 in 1984. Southwestern counties were open to gun hunters from November 1-January 5 and November 26-January 5 in northwestern counties.

Bait can't be used for bear hunting, but hounds can be at specified times in designated areas. Cubs are protected. Bagged bears must be presented at check stations. Hunters harvested 334 bears during 1982 and 365 during 1983. In 1982 bowhunters accounted for 13 percent of the kill, deer hunters 42 percent and dog hunters 45 percent. For more information contact the Commission of Game and Inland Fisheries, 4010 W. Broad St., Box 11104, Richmond, VA 23230 (804-257-1000).

Washington

There are 20,000-plus black bears in Washington, according to Rolf Johnson, Big Game Program Manager for the state's Department of Game. He said the population bottomed out around 1980 at 20,000 and appears to have increased slightly since then. In the 1950s there were an estimated 46,000 black bears in the state.

Annual bear harvests have averaged around 2,000 during recent years, according to Johnson, with the bulk of the kill—1,900—occurring during fall seasons and approximately 100 bagged on spring hunts. Most of the bruins are taken in the state's Region 1 in northeastern Washington, with Region 4 (Puget Sound area) ranking second. Next highest harvests, in declining order, come from Region 6 (Olympic Peninsula), Region 5 (St. Helen's and Williapa Hills), and Region 2 (Okanogan area).

Only specific units are open to bear hunting during spring seasons, May 1 to June 30, to control damage to conifer trees in the western part of the state. Bear hunters can shoot as many bears as they have tags for during the spring, but the bag limit is one in the fall, which was August 1 through October 31 in 1984. Both hunting with hounds and baiting are legal. Bear hunters must purchase a hunting license and bear tag, and if hunting with dogs, a hound stamp. There is a pursuit-only season for dog hunters in northwestern Washington.

The number of bear hunters in the state has declined in accordance with the reduction in bear numbers, resulting in reduced hunting opportunities and increased tag fees. There were 12,000 bear tags sold in Washington during 1983 compared to about 24,000 in the early 1970s. For more information contact the Department of Game, 600 Capitol Way, Olympia, WA 98504 (206-753-5700).

West Virginia

Although the number of black bears in West Virginia isn't known, the population trend is upward. A record kill of 129 animals was established during 1983, according to Joe Rieffenberger, and he predicts that record will not stand for more than three or four years. Annual bear harvests are expected to remain over 100 in the future. The highest kill until 1983 was 97 in 1978.

Hunters are required to report bagged bears. Hounds can be used for bear hunting, but baiting is prohibited. For additional information write or call Department of Natural Resources, 1800 Washington St. East, Charleston, WV 25305 (304-348-2754).

Wisconsin

A conservative estimate of the number of bruins in Wisconsin made by Wildlife Research Biologist Bruce Kohn is 4,000 to 4,400, with the bulk of the animals living north of Highway 29. Highest harvests have come from Sawyer, Douglas, Lincoln, Bayfield, Price, Ashland, and Iron counties. Bear hunters registered 934 bears in Wisconsin during 1983 and 1,433 during '82. Wildlife biologists would like to lower the annual harvest to about 800 animals.

Season dates for 1984 were September 15-30 for firearms and September 15-November 11 for bow and arrow. Cubs are protected. Bear hunting with hounds is only permitted in northern Wisconsin counties (refer to hunting regulation booklets for boundary line), while baiting is permitted throughout bear range. Materials used for bait must be confined to a hole in the ground no more than two feet square and are limited to fruits, vegetables, grains, pastry, or liquid scent. Meat and honey cannot be used to bait bears in Wisconsin.

Hound hunters must obtain a permit from the DNR, and can use no more than six dogs to chase a bear. A training season for bear dogs was July 10 through August 20 in 1984.

Both gun and bowhunters can hunt from tree stands. All bears bagged in the state must be registered within 24 hours. The toll-free hotline to report game violations is 1-800-362-3020. For more information contact the Department of Natural Resources, Bureau of Wildlife Management, Box 7921, Madison, WI 53707 (608-266-1877).

Wyoming

There were an estimated 2,275 black bears in Wyoming during the winter of 1982-'83. Both spring and fall seasons are held. Spring seasons began May 1 during 1984 and closed either June 15 or June 30, depending on management units. Area 25 was open to bear hunting from May 1-November 15. There was more variation among fall hunts, with most areas opening September 1 or October 1. Check a current copy of Wyoming's Black Bear Hunting Regulations before planning a fall bear hunt there.

Sows with cubs are protected during all bear hunting seasons in Wyoming. Bait can be used to hunt black bears, but hounds are prohibited. The skull and hide from bagged bruins must be presented at a Game and Fish Department office within 10 days. There were 348 black bears bagged in the state during fiscal year 1983 and 236 during FY1982. There were approximately 1,800 bear licenses sold both years.

All gun hunters must wear one or more item blaze orange in color including a hat, vest, coat or sweater. To report poaching and other hunting violations call 1-800-442-4331. For more information write or call the Game and Fish Department, Cheyenne, WY 82002 (307-777-7735).

Provincial Listings

Alberta

Alberta has an estimated 50,000 to 60,000 black bears and an annual total harvest of 4,000 to 5,000, according to Director of Wildlife R. R. Andrews. He said efforts are underway to encourage the harvest of 6,000 to 7,000 of the animals. To help accomplish this goal, baiting may be legalized. Hounds cannot be used to hunt black bears in this province.

Both spring and fall seasons are held for black bears in Alberta. Dates for the 1984 fall hunt were September 1-December 3. Spring hunts generally begin in early April and close on June 5. Bag limits have been two bears a year with the bagging of both during one season possible. For more information contact Fish and Wildlife Division, Main Floor, North Tower, Petroleum Plaza, 9945-108 St., Edmonton, Alberta T5K 2C9 (403-427-8580).

British Columbia

There are an estimated 35,000 to 90,000 black bears in this province, with spring and fall seasons, except in region 1 where only a fall hunt was held during 1984. Two black bears a year can be taken throughout most of the province, but as many as five a year can be taken in parts of regions 3 and 7. There is no closed season in portions of regions 3 and 5. Spring and fall seasons vary from region to region and within management units in the same region, so check a current copy of "British Columbia Hunting Regulations Synopsis" prior to planning a hunt here.

Black bears cannot be hunted over bait in B.C. Hounds are permitted. Bear dogs can be trained during closed seasons. Estimated black bear harvests during 1982 and '83 are 1,208 and 1,280. One of the objectives of black bear management in the province is to achieve an annual harvest of 4,000 bruins. For more information contact Fish and Wildlife Branch, Ministry of Environment, Parliament Bldg., Victoria, B.C. V8V 1X5 (604-387-1628).

Manitoba

Manitoba has approximately 50,000 black bears, according to Wildlife Program Coordinator Ron Larche, and the population appears to be increasing. He said highest densities occur in the Riding, Duck, and Porcupine mountains, plus the Interlake and Southeastern regions.

Bear seasons are established during spring and fall months, with bag limits of two animals for residents and one for nonresidents. Spring hunts began April 1 during 1985 and ended on May 31 or sometime in June, depending on which management unit was involved. The 1984 fall season was August 27-November 17. Units 34B, 35, 35A, and 37 are reserved for bowhunting only during the spring. Some units are also reserved for bowhunters during the fall.

Sows with cubs are protected. Bears can be hunted over bait, but hunting bruins with hounds is prohibited. Black bears can also be trapped in Manitoba. Larche said there were 3,445 resident bear licenses sold and 342 nonresident tags during the fall of 1982 and spring of 1983. The estimated bear harvest for that period is 795. Trappers take an additional 200 to 300 bruins annually and approximately 300 are destroyed every year to control nuisance animals.

Beginning April 1, 1985 bear hunters will be required to wear a blaze orange hat and an additional 100 square inches of orange above the waist. For more information contact the Wildlife Branch, Department of Natural Resources, Box 24, 1495 St. James St., Winnipeg, Manitoba R3H 0W9 (204-775-0221).

New Brunswick

There is no estimate of the black bear population in this province, but Big Game Biologist Arnold Boer states the animals are numerous throughout the province, with the exception of the southeastern portion. He added that they seem to be on the increase in New Brunswick.

Hunters harvested 515 bruins during the 1983 spring season and 286 during the fall hunt, for a total harvest of 801. This compares to a kill of 655 bruins during 1982. There were 2,860 bear licenses sold during 1983 and 1,596 during 1982.

The 1985 spring season will be April 15-June 29. A two-week bow bear season was held for the first time last fall from September 10-22. Gun season opened October 1, 1984 and ended sometime during November, depending on the region. The bag limit is two bears per season.

Hunters must register bear kills and must be 18 to obtain a bear license. Nonresident hunters must employ a guide. Gun hunters must wear orange clothing. No hounds can be used for bear hunting in New Brunswick. They can be hunted over bait. For more information write or call Department of Natural Resources, Fish and Wildlife Branch, P.O. Box 6000, Fredericton, New Brunswick E3B 5H1 (506-453-2433).

Newfoundland

Bear biologist Shane Mahoney estimates that there are roughly 4,000 black bears on the large island, which is the most developed portion of the province. There is no accurate information about bear numbers on the mainland, but another biologist guessed there might be about 5,000.

Both spring and fall hunting and trapping seasons are set for black bears in this province, although there are differences between the island and mainland. Mahoney said spring seasons on the island have been May 1-June 30 and fall hunts begin during early September, extending to the end of November. Bear licenses must be purchased for a specific management unit, and hunting is limited to the unit the license is issued for. The bag limit is two a year, one each season. There were approximately 1,900 bear licenses sold on the island in 1983, resulting in the harvest of 80 to 90 bruins, according to Mahoney. He said he expected the harvest to be around 150 for 1984 due to increasing interest in bear hunting.

Seasons for the mainland during 1984 were April 4-June 30 and August 25-November 24. Bear licenses were valid anywhere on the mainland, according to Mike Parsons, with a bag limit of two animals. An estimated 200 to 300 black bears are taken on the mainland annually. Bear hunters can use bait in Newfoundland, but not dogs. For more information contact the Department of Culture, Recreation and Youth, Wildlife Division, Bldg. 810, Pleasantville, St. John's, Newfoundland A1C 5T7 (709-737-2815).

Northwest Territories

The number of black bears in this province is unknown, but the population appears to be stable, according to Wildlife Biologist Ray Case. He said these bears are found in areas with trees throughout the province. Hunting season dates for residents during 1984-'85 were August 15-June 30. However, nonresidents can only hunt black bears during the fall, August 15 through October 31, and are limited to zone E/1 in the southwest portion of the province. Nonresidents must hire an outfitter to hunt big game.

Black bear hunting with hounds is prohibited. The bag limit is one adult animal not accompanied by a cub. Case said there were approximately 250 black bears taken by hunters during the 1982-'83 season. For more information contact the Department of Renewable Resources, Box 2668, Yellowknife, Northwest Territories X1A 2L9 (403-920-8043).

Nova Scotia

The black bear is being ignored as a game animal in this province. They are only legal during deer season, which was October 26-December 1 during

1984. Most bears are in dens by that time. The purchase of a big game license entitles hunters to take one deer and any number of bears. There is no bag limit on them in the province.

It is legal to catch bears with foot snares in Nova Scotia from September 15-December 15. A free permit is required to snare bears.

The results of a recent study of black bears in the province indicates there are approximately 3,000 of them, according to Wildlife Resources Manager Art Patton. The 1982 and '83 bear harvests by hunters in Nova Scotia were 163 and 135. There were 255 and 260 bruins killed in foot snares during those same years. It is legal to bait black bears in this province. For more information write or call the Department of Lands and Forests, P.O. Box 698, Halifax, Nova Scotia B3J 2T9 (902-424-4297).

Prince Edward Island

Black bears were native to this island province, but have long since disappeared. It is thought they were gone by the early 1900s.

Ontario

Ontario's black bear population is estimated at 75,000, according to Charlie Ross. He said there are about 5,000 bears harvested annually in the province and 14,700 licenses sold. Both spring and fall seasons are held. The spring season is traditionally April 15 - June 15 and the fall hunt September 1-November 30.

Bear hunters can hunt over bait and with hounds. On an experimental basis, nonresident bear hunters trying their luck in the western part of the province were required to hunt with a guide or stay at an established resort during 1984. The same thing may be in effect on a wider scale for 1985. More changes in Ontario bear hunting regulations have been discussed or proposed, but nothing has been approved at this point. Changes may be added to the books during 1985 or '86. For more information write or call Ministry of Natural Resources, Outdoor Recreation, Wildlife Branch, Parliament Bldg., Toronto, Ontario M7A 1W3 (416-965-4251).

Quebec

Status of the black bear population in Quebec is unknown at this time, according to Helene Jolicoeur. However, she said research was begun in 1983 in an effort to gather information about the province's black bears. The animals are considered abundant south of the 50th parallel and they've even been observed beyond the tree line on the Ungava Peninsula.

Black bears can be trapped in Quebec in addition to being hunted during spring and fall seasons. Dates for the 1985 spring season were May 1-July 4. Fall hunts for 1985 were August 25-September 30 in zones 23 and 24, September 14-October 14 in zone 19, and September 21-November 10 in all other zones except 20 and 22. Bears can be trapped from May 1-June 15 during the spring and October 1-November 15 or 30, depending on zones, in the fall.

Hunters can take one bear per season and there is no limit for trappers. Hides of bruins taken by trappers must be sealed and hunters must register kills within 48 hours.

Bear hunters can use bait and hounds in Quebec. The season for dog hunters is expected to be shortened by two weeks in the future, according to Jolicoeur. She added that nonresidents who want to hunt with dogs will also have to use outfitter services in the future.

The black bear harvest during 1983 in Quebec was 2,346, according to Jolicoeur. She said hunters claimed 1,747 of those, 784 during the spring and 963 in the fall. Trappers accounted for 426 bruins during 1983 and 173 died of other causes. Hunter and trapper harvests for 1982 were 1,436 and 289. There are approximately 40,000 bear hunters in the province. For additional information write or call the Department of Tourism, Fish and Game, 150 St. Cyrille E., Quebec City, Quebec G1R 4Y1 (418-643-2464).

Saskatchewan

This province lists its black bear population at 30,000, but their numbers are increasing and expanding their range beyond forest habitat into fringe and agricultural areas, according to Big Game Biologist Ross Melinchuk. He said efforts are underway to increase the harvest of these bears in the province due to their abundance and rising conflicts with farmers and other landowners. Black bears have also been implicated as contributing to the decline of moose populations in northeast Saskatchewan.

Melinchuk said that in those areas where black bears are considered serious moose predators, two free bear tags are available with every big game license to encourage the harvest of bears. South of the Commercial Forest, the biologist said black bears have been removed from the protected list and may be shot at any time of the year without a license.

Spring and fall hunting seasons are established for black bears in most of the province. Season dates were April 16-June 16 and August 28-October 20 in 1984. Bear hunting with hounds is prohibited, but baiting is legal. Black bears can also be trapped. The bag limit for hunters is two bears, with a separate license required for each animal. Unused spring licenses are also valid in the fall.

There were an estimated 1,071 black bears harvested by hunters in the province during 1983 and 1,121 during 1982, according to Melinchuk. He said the number of bear licenses sold during those years were 4,375 and 4,437. Trappers accounted for 312 bears during 1982 and 200 to 300 in 1983. For additional information contact Parks and Renewable Resources, 3211 Albert St., Regina, Saskatchewan S4S 5W6 or Tourism Saskatchewan, 2103 -11th Ave., Regina S4P 3V7 (306-565-2300).

Yukon

There are an estimated 7,000 to 15,000 black bears in the Yukon, according to Grant MacHutchon. He said they are numerous throughout forested areas, particularly along major river valleys. Concern over bear predation on moose has led to the establishment of subzones where the goal is to reduce bear populations.

Year-round hunting is permitted in bear reduction areas. Hunters can shoot three black bears a year, provided at least one of the animals is taken from a bear reduction subzone. Black bears can also be trapped in the province. Season dates in the southern Yukon outside special reduction areas were April 15 to June 15 and August 1 to October 31 in '84. In north and central portions of the province, hunt dates were May 1 to June 15 and August 1 to October 31.

Successful hunters must present the skulls from animals they bag to conservation officers or wildlife technicians. Bait can't be used for bear hunting in the province. An average of 125 black bears a year are taken by sport hunters. Twice as many animals are killed annually in damage control actions. Department of Renewable Resources, Wildlife Branch, Box 2703, Whitehorse, Yukon Y1A 2C6 (403-667-5221).

Black Bear Hunter Organizations

There are several state bear hunter organizations plus an international organization composed primarily of bear biologists, although membership is open to anyone. Black bear hunter organizations are usually composed of dog hunters, but membership is often open to all bear hunters. Michigan, New Hampshire, Virginia, West Virginia, and Wisconsin have bear hunting groups.

Dues in the Michigan group are $5 a year. To join or obtain information write to Secretary Keith Huff, Gibbs Rd., Johannesburg, MI 49751. Dues are $3 a year for the Virginia Bear Hunters Assoc. Contact President Cecil Boggs, Rt. 3, Box 81, Waynesboro, VA 22980 (703-943-2990). Homer Fielder, 221 Klaus, Beckley, WV (304-252-3315) is President of West Virginia's organization and dues are $5.

President of the New Hampshire Bear Hunters Assoc. is Harrie Ashley, Dr. Braley Rd., East Freetown, MA 02717 (617-763-2883). Dues are $10 a year for the Wisconsin Bear Hunters Assoc. To join write Secretary/Treasurer Michael Lentz, N2368 Wegner Rd., Merrill, WI 54452. The President is Dale Decker, Rt. 5, Box 179A, Marshfield, WI 54449 (715-676-3997).

Regular membership in the International Association for Bear Research and Management is $7, but student memberships are available for $5. Dues can be sent to Secretary/Treasurer Brian Horejsi, Box 3129, Station B, Calgary, Alberta T2M 4L7. The IBA sends quarterly newsletters to members. At least some of the other bear hunting organizations have newsletters, too.

Bibliography

Adams, Chuck. *Bowhunter's Digest.* DBI Books. Northfield, IL. Undated.

Alt, Gary L. "14½ Miles of Bear Tracks." *Pennsylvania Game News.* June 1978. ps. 24-29.

_____. "Pennsylvania's Cub Law Controversy." *Pennsylvania Game News.* 51(6): 23-27.

_____. "Home Range and Movements of Pennsylvania Black Bears." *Pennsylvania Game News.* November 1980. ps. 10-15.

_____. "Rate of Growth and Size of Pennsylvania Black Bears." *Pennsylvania Game News.* December 1980. ps. 7-17.

_____. "Bear Hibernation Subject of Ecological and Medical Research." *Pennsylvania Game News.* May 1981. ps. 15-16.

_____. "Reproductive Biology of Pennsylvania Black Bears." *Pennsylvania Game News.* February 1982. ps. 9-15.

_____. "Reuse of Black Bear Dens in Northeastern Pennsylvania." *Journal of Wildlife Management.* 48(1):(1984).

Borden, Brad. "Albino Bear." *Bowhunter.* November 1984. ps. 128-129.

Cramond, Mike. *Killer Bears.* Book Division of Times Mirror Magazines, Inc. New York. 1981.

East, Ben. *Bears.* Crown Publishers, Inc. New York. 1977.

Editorial Committee Pope and Young Club. *Bowhunting Big Game Records of North America, Second Edition.* Pope and Young Club. 1981.

Editorial Committee Boone and Crockett Club. *The Black Bear in Modern North America.* Boone and Crockett Club and Amwell Press. Clinton, NJ. 1979.

Erickson, A.W. "The Age of Self-Sufficiency in the Black Bear." *Journal of Wildlife Management*. 23 (4): 401-405. 1959.

Flowers, Ralph. *The Education of a Bear Hunter*. Winchester Press. New York. 1975.

Ford, Barbara. *Black Bear, The Spirit of the Wilderness*. Houghton Mifflin Co. Boston. 1981.

Good, Bob. "Handgun Hunting—The State of the Art." *All-American Deer Hunter's Guide*. Winchester Press. Piscataway, NJ. 1984.

Hunter Services Division of the National Rifle Association (Eds). *NRA Hunter's Planning Guide and Directory*. National Rifle Association. Washington, D.C. 1983.

Lindzey, Frederick; Danvir, Rick; and Chapman, Gale. *The Black Bear in Utah*. Utah State University. Logan, UT. 1983.

Martinka, Clifford J. and McArthur, Katherine L. (Eds.). *Bears—Their Biology and Management, Papers of the Fourth International Conference on Bear Research and Management*. The Bear Biology Assoc. 1980.

Matunas, Edward A. *Deer Hunters Guide to Guns, Ammo and Equipment*. Outdoor Life Books. New York. 1983.

Meslow, E. Charles (Ed.). *Bears—Their Biology and Management, A Selection of Papers From the Fifth International Conference on Bear Research and Management*. The International Assoc. of Bear Research and Management. 1983.

McGuire, Bob. *Black Bears*. Bowhunting Productions. Bloutville, TN. 1983.

Nesbitt, William H. and Wright, Philip L. *Records of North American Big Game, Eighth Edition*. Boone and Crockett Club. Alexandria, VA. 1981.

Poelker, Richard J. and Hartwell, Harry D. *Black Bear of Washington*. Biological Bulletin No. 14. Washington State Game Dept. 1973.

Rue, Leonard Lee. *Furbearing Animals of North America*. Crown Publishers, Inc. New York. 1981.

Sauer, Peggy R. "Relationship of Growth Characteristics to Sex and Age for Black Bears From the Adirondack Region of New York." *New York Fish and Game Journal*. July 1975. 22(2): 81-113.

Schwartz, Charles C.; Franzman, Albert W.; and Johnson, David C. *Black Bear Predation on Moose*. Alaska Department of Fish and Game. Juneau. 1983.

Shelly, Howard. "World's Rarest Trophy?" *Outdoor Life*. July, 1965. ps. 36-39, 138, 140, 141, 147.

Smith, Todd. "1984-1985 Hunting Seasons." *Petersen's Hunting, 1985 Annual*. Los Angeles. 1984.

Tracy, D.M.; Dean, F.C.; Anderson, C.M.; Jordan, T.M. *Black Bear Bibliography*. University of Alaska and National Park Service. Fairbanks, AK. 1982.

Zumbo, Jim. "Blueprint for Bear." *Outdoor Life*. May 1982. ps. 76, 112-116.

INDEX